GOOD FISHING CLOSE TO NEW YORK CITY

THE GOOD FISHING IN NEW YORK SERIES

GOOD FISHING CLOSE TO NEW YORK CITY

A GUIDE TO THE GREAT CLOSE-TO-HOME ANGLING OF THE METROPOLITAN REGION

JIM CAPOSSELA

NORTHEAST SPORTSMAN'S PRESS
TARRYTOWN, NEW YORK

Parts of certain chapters contributed by Ted Keatley,
John Fritz and Rich Giessuebel

Library of Congress Cataloging in Publication Data

Capossela, Jim.
     Good fishing close to New York City.

     (The Good fishing in New York series)
     1. Fishing – New York Region (N.Y.) – Guide-books.
I. Title.   II. Series.
SH529.C37   1985   799.1'09747   85-60313
ISBN 0-942990-06-4
ISBN 0-942990-07-2 (pbk.)

Principal Photography: Per Brandin
Design: Deborah Davis
Composition: The Type House
Printing & Binding: BookCrafters

Northeast Sportsman's Press
Post Office Box 188
Tarrytown, NY 10591

Printed in the United States Of America
10-9-8-7-6-5-4-3-2

TABLE OF CONTENTS

Acknowledgements viii

List of Figures ix

Introduction x

Important Notes On The Text xi

Basic Information For The Beginner xii

PART I: The Riches Of The Croton Watershed
Chapter 1   Stalking Lunker Browns 2
Chapter 2   Bassing: Good To Excellent 12
Chapter 3   Notes On The Specific Reservoirs 17
Chapter 4   An Ice Fishing Party 35
Chapter 5   Three Streams In Praise Of Fly Fishing 42
Chapter 6   The Other Connecting Rivers 53

PART II: More Good Fishing In Westchester And Putnam
Chapter 7   A Quartet Of Interesting Brooks 72
Chapter 8   Parks: Fun For The Whole Family 79
Chapter 9   Just For Kids: Finding And Fishing Ponds ... 87

PART III: The Untapped Hudson . . . And Across The River
Chapter 10 Tips, Techniques And Timing For Stripers ... 98
Chapter 11 Summer: Blueclaws And Salty Panfish 103
                By The Pailful
Chapter 12 More Estuarine Surprises 107
Chapter 13 The Pretty Palisades 113
Chapter 14 Other Waters In Rockland 120
                And Lower Orange

PART IV: Fertile & Fishy Western Long Island Sound
Chapter 15 Bunkers, Blood And Bluefish 128
                . . . And More
Chapter 16 Bouncing For Tasty Flounder 136
                . . . And Other Easy Cellar Dwellers

Chapter 17   Detailed Access Guide For The   143
              Shore Fisherman

PART V: Island Cornucopia
  Chapter 18   Trout Streams – Out Here?   156
  Chapter 19   Ponds: No Salt But A Lot Of Spice   166
  Chapter 20   Oceanside: A World Of Good Fishing   179
               In Surf And Bay
  Chapter 21   Lunch Break Lunkers: Around The   198
               Five Boroughs
  Chapter 22   The Pleasant Peconics . . . And North   209
               Shore Highlights
  Chapter 23   Montauk!   222

Reference Section
  Synopsis Of The Croton Watershed With Permit Info   234
  Important Statistics Of The Watershed Reservoirs   235
  Complete Freshwater Stocking Reports   236
  Main Saltwater Ports   239
  Other Resources   240
  Other Titles Available   243

ACKNOWLEDGEMENTS

The following is by no means a complete list of all the people who helped me with this book.

First, many thanks to Per and Danielle Brandin, who provided absolutely essential moral support and constructive criticism all along the way. Per also provided the bulk of the nice photos in this book.

Special thanks too, to Deborah Davis, who not only did a great design job, but in general mothered me for the last six months of the project. On production, I am also grateful to Peggy Cardillo and Ruth Caban of The Type House, Inc of Mt. Kisco.

At the New Paltz office of DEC, Ron Pierce gave a great amount of his time cheerfully. Mike Gann was also very helpful, as was Wayne Elliot. At the Stony Brook Office of DEC, Charlie Guthrie cheerfully aided me in many ways, and Frank Panek and Chet Zawacki also assisted.

Other people who helped in significant ways were Nick Lyons, Vin Russo, Bill Schweizer, Bob Boyle, Chris Letts, Kathleen Ziegler, Jack Stewart, Jim Booth, Bill Rutherford, Gary Grunseich, Paul Graniello, Tim Sullivan, Jon Davis and Don Kauth.

Of course I can't forget writers Ted Keatley, John Fritz and Rich Giessuebel whom I called on when I realized I just could not cover New York's copious amount of salt water all by myself. Ted wrote the bulk of Chapters 15 and 16 and helped in other ways, too. John wrote most of the north shore material in Ch. 22, while Rich provided most of Ch. 21 and kicked in some great photos.

LIST OF FIGURES

1-a   Timing Chart For Reservoir Browns 4
1-b   Shallow Drift Rig 5
1-c   Deep Drift Rig 6
2-a   West Branch Reservoir 14
3-a   Lake Glenida 20
3-b   Lake Gilead 23
3-c   East Branch Reservoir 26
4-a   Fish Of The Croton Watershed 39
5-a   Amawalk Outlet 43
5-b   Trout Flies For Local Waters 47
5-c   West Branch Croton River 48
5-d   East Branch Croton River 51
6-a   Lower East Branch Croton River 60
6-b   Cross River Inlet 63
8-a   Map Of Westchester's County Parks 81
8-b   Parks With Fishing In Westchester/Putnam 83
9-a   Topo Maps For Finding Ponds 90
9-b   Pond Fishing Checklist 91
10-a   Fish Finder Rig 100
12-a   Angling Guide To The Hudson 109
13-a   Fishing In Bear Mt./Harriman Parks 114
15-a   Mackerel Tree 134
16-a   Flounder Spreader 137
16-b   No-hardware Flounder Rig 138
17-a   Long Island Sound Access Map 146
17-b   Inshore Timetable 148
17-c   Livelining Bunker 153
18-a   Beat Buide To The Connetquot 157
19-a   List Of Long Island Ponds & Streams 168
19-b   Long Island Freshwater Locator 169
19-c   Fort Pond 177
20-a   South Shore Access – East 182
20-b   South Shore Access – West 188
20-c   Single Hook Fluke Rig 190
20-d   Best-Bet Saltwater Calendar 195
21-a   Gateway And The New York Bight 201
21-b   High-Low Rig 206
21-c   Five Borough Pond List 208
22-a   North Shore Access – West 212
22-b   North Shore Access – East 216
22-c   Rigging For Blackfish 218
23-a   Guide To Montauk Point 225
23-b   Fishing In Long Island State Parks 229
23-c   Offshore Timetable 232

INTRODUCTION

Good fishing close to home! There's just something nice about that thought. And it isn't only because of the sobering effect of gas prices, or the convenience of being able to fit in a few hours sport after work. It's really almost intangible: The matchless satisfaction of finding good fishing just minutes from the house. No exotic trips to even the fishiest, faraway places can provide that same kind of satisfaction.

Well, if you like to fish, and you live anywhere in the New York metropolitan area, you have more than just *good* fishing in your backyard. You have some *great* fishing. In fact, some of the best variety and quality of fishing anywhere in the country.

Twenty-pound brown trout almost literally within sight of the World Trade Center? Fifty-pound Striped Bass just yards from Playland's Dragon Coaster? Six-pound Largemouths just five minutes from the Croton Harmon railroad station? Read on, and you'll find that this is just the tip of the piscatorial iceberg.

The collective good luck of the New York area angler began many eons ago. Perhaps the last ice age had the most to do with it. It left us Long Island, along with Western Long Island Sound and the amazing south shore. The saltwater angling opportunities here are extraordinary. It also left us the rich Hudson River estuary, a sport fisherman's paradise and one that is still amazingly underfished.

Then of course there is the stellar fresh water fishing. The last ice sheet also left behind the Croton River Watershed. This river system, with its 14 reservoirs and connecting streams, is now providing superb trout, bass and panfishing. And yet all this is just part of the happy picture.

This book is the one and only comprehensive guide to fishing in our area. It suggests literally hundreds of places to fish within only an hour or two of New York City.

It was designed to give you the information you want – where-to, when-to, and in many cases how-to.

It was designed to help you catch more and bigger fish.

And most importantly, it was designed to get you home in time for dinner!

IMPORTANT NOTES ON THE TEXT

No book can be all things to all people. Simply, there is only so much that can be fit in. This book's coverage is accurately described on the back cover. The freshwater coverage is quite detailed, indeed, with much how-to included. The salt-water material is of a survey nature, mainly where and when, with special emphasis on shore fishing. Shore access has gotten to be such a problem that we wanted to give it the space it deserves. Thus if you can't afford to own a boat, this book will show you that you still can take advantage of New York's superb salt-water fishing. Some information for the nearshore boater (especially bay and sound) is also included, but offshore fishing is not touched on.

There are reasons for what we included and what we didn't. For example, fresh-water is given more space because fresh-water bodies are much more stable . . . easier to tie down. They often remain relatively the same for years, even decades. Salt-water fishing on the other hand, can change from year to year, week to week and even tide to tide. For that reason, there are no "fish maps" that would have quickly become obsolete. Traditional hotspots, even very specific ones, are mentioned by the dozen all through the text. But for up-to-the-minute "where-to" reports we refer you to the several editions of *The Fisherman* magazine and to outdoor columns in area newspapers. The material in this book is of a more enduring nature.

This book is not an atlas. Too many so-called outdoor "guide books" are nothing more than listings accompanied by endless directions and maps. We hope you'll agree that this book is much more than that. Not that we've ignored directions – there are many, many maps herein that show you exactly how to get to these fine fishing grounds. But even when a fishing location is not specifically pinpointed by a map, it can easily be found by following the directions given in the text along with an ordinary road map.

We stay away from confusing abbreviations in this book, but there is one that is used frequently: DEC. This is short for New York State's Department of Environmental Conservation.

All in all, this book was designed to help as many people as possible find good *affordable* fishing close to home. That theme and that aim will be maintained in all the other books of the *Good Fishing In New York* series.

BASIC INFORMATION FOR
THE BEGINNER

First, no license at all is required to sport fish in New York marine waters. A valid New York State fishing license *is* required to fish fresh water, but only if you're 16 or older. Young anglers under 16 may fish for free (as may persons 70 years of age or older and certain handicapped individuals). The license year runs from October 1st to the following September 30th. Licenses are sold by a great many of the area bait & tackle shops and also by many village, town and city clerks. These clerks are generally located in the municipal building of the particular community.

Many out-of-staters come to New York to fish. Freshwater licenses are available to non-residents, though they cost a little more.

What can you fish for? There are at least three dozen inshore saltwater fish and freshwater fish available in metropolitan area waters, and these are of course named throughout the text. For further biological data on these fish the reader is referred to *MacClane's Standard Fishing Encyclopedia* or to any of the several guidebooks available.

When do you fish? There is some good fishing in every single month of the year. Again, the when-to of metro area angling is discussed throughout the text. When-to is also summarized in several tables . . . see List Of Figures a few pages back.

What kind of tackle do you use? This is chiefly a where and when guide book, but a good deal of how-to information is included. Freshwater how-to data is quite detailed in places, right down to the best flies, lures and rigs to use. There are also charts and diagrams of many of the best salt-water rigs and lures. More detailed advice concerning any species can easily be obtained in the bait & tackle shop nearest to where you plan to fish. Of course there are also many good books on how to fish.

Although salt-water shore fishing is covered in detail, boatless fishermen are not anchored to land. There are dozens of open "party" or "head" boats as well as private charter boats available. These are almost all concentrated in the several main ports, which are described in the reference section. Finally, you can rent small outboards in salt-water and small rowboats in fresh-water at many, many locations in the metropolitan region. A number of these are pointed out in the text.

PART I

THE RICHES
OF THE
CROTON
WATERSHED

(See "Synopsis" in the reference section.)

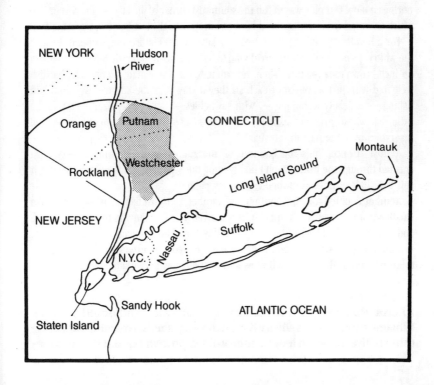

1.
STALKING LUNKER BROWNS

The northeaster rolled out of the Berkshires like the first Woodcock storm of November. 55 degrees. Huge, menacing clouds. Yet here it was Independence Day — July the fourth. Lousy weather for picnics, but excellent for big browns!

Jimmy Booth called at 10:30 a.m. and excitedly said that a couple of guys fishing Cross River had just weighed in three monsters at Bob's tackle. Two eight pounders and a ten. Or was it an eleven and two nines? Anyway, close to 30 pounds of regal brown trout, vermilion dots as big as eyeballs. I told him I'd meet him in a half hour.

We unchained our boat from the big dead locust, and shoved off into a stiff northeast blow. Our plan was to fish the southwest corner of the lake — the corner into which the wind was blowing. We'd have to hurry, though. The front was passing fast.

For a hundred yards or so, we trolled a silver U-20 Flatfish that skipped through the whitecaps momentarily before diving to its usual six-foot depth. Smack! At once, a 15-inch brown took the lure. Then, returning to our game plan, we put over baitfish weighted with just a split shot each so they'd stay near the surface. We were drift fishing — a deadly technique — with sawbellies — an equally deadly bait, and a little fish whose presence explains the explosion of big browns in the watershed reservoirs over the past dozen years.

Almost at once, Jim's rod bounced off the gunnel, and a slashing, silvery form crashed through the froth. When I finally hung the 3-pound beauty on our stringer, it spit two, half-swallowed sawbellies into my palm.

Another doubled rod! And another and another. Four lost fish, a lost *big* fish, and a smaller trout landed. Then, quickly, it was over. The fast-moving front had passed, and summer pushed back out across the valley. It had been a magical kind of day, one in a hundred, but we'd missed the best part. It ended as a bittersweet experience — the usual sup of the angler, tall tales and outright lies notwithstanding.

ALOSA PSEUDOHARENGUS, sawbelly, alewife, landlocked herring: Whatever you call this silvery little baitfish, it spells dynamite! Averaging three to five inches in length, this prolific, protein-packed fish provides

superb forage for Brown Trout. One reason is that it prefers more or
less the same temperatures as the brown. Another is that it multiplies
quickly, and likes the clean waters where salmonids thrive. And still
another reason is that it provides a direct link between the plankton
that it feeds on, and the brown trout that feed on it. Since there are
thus relatively few trophic levels in the food chain – energy is lost at
each level – trout growth rates are dramatically accelerated where
the two fish are found together. Besides the New York City watershed
reservoirs, sawbellies have also worked their magic in many other
lakes across the country, especially in recent years.

How and when did they get into these Westchester and Putnam
lakes? A story has it that way back in 1888, they were mistakenly
stocked in the pond that later became Kensico Reservoir. The stockers
thought they were planting Lake Whitefish. However, because of a lack
of adequate spawning streams, browns did not appear in any numbers
in Kensico until a concerted brown trout stocking program was begun
in fairly recent times. Some think sawbellies have also lived in Croton
Reservoir since its impoundment. But this is not a good Brown Trout
lake for reasons we'll discuss in Ch. 3. As far as the other reservoirs go,
one theory is that sawbellies entered them from the Catskill reservoirs,
where they are abundant, via aqueducts. A more likely theory is that
ambitious anglers simply planted them or that they were introduced
through the careless emptying of bait buckets. My best guess is that
they first "appeared" in Cross River and Titicus around the mid-1960's,
then spread or were introduced to the other lakes. Some fishermen
claim that there are now well-established sawbelly populations in all
14 reservoirs, though I'm not sure about a few. What's significant is
that they are plentiful where it counts: In all the lakes actually managed
for browns. These are Kensico, Cross River, Titicus, Croton Falls and
West Branch. Annual stockings in these lakes run from about 2000
browns (Croton Falls) to as many as 10,000 (Cross River). See the
stocking reports in the reference section.

Sawbellies are also abundant in a secondary trout producer, Muscoot
Reservoir. However, trout habitat and production are limited in this
relatively shallow impoundment. Good-sized browns, as well as
sawbellies, also live in East Branch, Amawalk, and some of the others.
But not in numbers enough to draw anglers away from the big five.

The most popular methods for catching browns in our reservoirs
are drifting, shallow trolling, deep trolling, night fishing, casting lures
from shore, and bait fishing from shore. (Ice fishing is covered
separately in Ch. 4) Fig. 1-a provides some rough guidelines for

matching methods to time of year. Remember that eight of these
reservoirs – including all the top trout lakes – are open to fishing
year-round. See the watershed chart in the reference section.

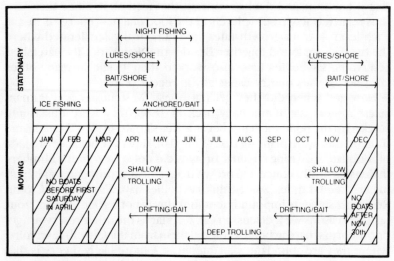

Figure 1-a. Timing Chart For Reservoir Browns

DRIFTING

This isn't necessarily the best way to create fireworks in July, but is was
a good choice on that Cross River day I described. In fact, next time
you have a summer storm accompanied by wind, rain and falling
temperatures, get your tail out on one of these trout lakes. There's no
better time to catch that trout of a lifetime.

Nasty weather/best fishing is a formula that's worked for me for
years. Summer storms seem most productive, possibly because of the
contrast they provide. For one thing, most gamefish hate direct sun-
light, so cloudy days are better anyway. Wind and thus wave action may
concentrate planktonic masses both nearer the top and toward one
shore or one corner of a reservoir; this can bring about a subsequent
concentration of sawbellies. Where will the big browns be? Often,
right underneath. Further, wind action and rain refract light rays and
create a highly disturbed surface environment where gamefish may
feel safer to feed freely.

Medium action spinning rods of 6½ to 7½ feet are effective. Some
people like the ones with long grips so the rod can be tucked under

the arm to fight a big fish. A medium-sized spinning reel and six pound test mono will round out your outfit. Consider giving yourself the advantage of heavier line for all night fishing and in murky water conditions. (Note: More and more I am getting the impression that very light line is critically important for catching big browns. See "Big Brown Secrets of a Master.")

A good hook size for a medium sawbelly or shiner is an unsnelled #4 Sproat. Go a size bigger or smaller depending on the size of the bait. When fish are near the top, as in early spring or late fall (or during storms!), you can use only a split shot or so, and simply let out enough line to get the bait away from the boat. Unfortunately, though, this method has two drawbacks. First, you are unable to set the depth accurately, and second you just can't fish very shallow because the bait will be right next to the boat. To combat these problems I devised a simple drift rig using an ordinary bobber and a rubber band (fig. 1-b). Employing this rig, my line can be set at any desired shallow depth and trailed out away from the boat's potentially disturbing wake. Also give this terminal rig a try on lake trout (Gilead, Glenida, Kensico) in early spring when they're near the top.

After about mid-May, the reservoirs stratify and a thermometer becomes tremendously useful for finding the trout's preferred temper-

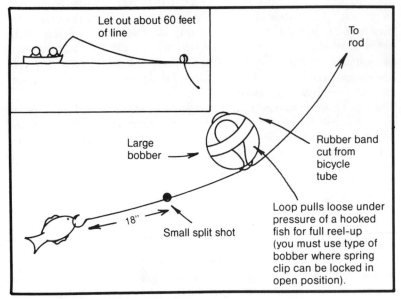

Let out about 60 feet of line

To rod

Large bobber

Rubber band cut from bicycle tube

18"

Small split shot

Loop pulls loose under pressure of a hooked fish for full reel-up (you must use type of bobber where spring clip can be locked in open position).

Figure 1-b. Shallow Drift Rig

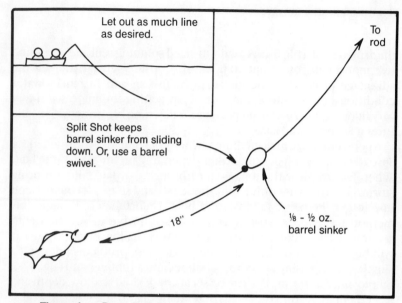

Figure 1-c. Deep Drift Rig

ature zone or "thermocline." This may commonly be between 15 and 35 feet, and to drift at these depths you'll have to add some weight (fig. 1-c). To prevent twisting, start with a barrel swivel – preferably a ball bearing model – about two feet above the bait. *Above* the swivel, slip on a barrel (egg) sinker of ¼ to ½-ounce depending on depth desired and wind and current conditions. Currents near inlets and outlets can be quite strong. For all types of drift fishing, *hook the bait fish through the mouth,* not fore or aft of the dorsal fin. It will swim much more naturally behind a moving boat.

A device trademarked under the name of Strike Guard is almost a must for drift fishing, as well as for many other types of fishing. This ingenious invention allows you to set the rod down with the bail open. It grips the line itself, but releases it under the pressure of a striking fish.

When a trout takes, the rod will bounce and you'll know it. Let him run for 10 or 20 seconds, set the hook hard and make sure nothing's tangled in the net. Then hold your breath: It could be a 20-pounder!

SHALLOW TROLLING
Here's a good, simple method that will often precipitate bent rods in spring, fall, early morning or on windy, stormy days. Since you're aiming for fish near the top, weighted line and heavy trolling rods are unnecessary. Just use the type of outfit recommended for drift fishing

(the pole could be a little heavier and shorter). We almost always tie on a U-20 Flatfish lure for this kind of work. Patterns that have brought success include red top/white bottom, all white, and all silver. Some sharp reservoir men modify their Flatfishes by removing all those small treble hooks and replacing them with two bigger ones. It makes sense for those big, tough-mouthed browns.

The Flatfish is good for at least two reasons. First, because of the way it swims it sets up a steady throbbing of the rod tip, letting you know that the rig is untangled and working fine. And second, it returns to the surface if you pause in your rowing. This type of lure is called a "floater-diver." Just remember this point: The more placid the lake surface, the more distance you want between the boat and lure.

DEEP TROLLING

In summer, and on bright days, the fish are usually too deep to reach by most methods. You can try very early in the morning, which is positively the best time. Or you can drift or anchor with bait, setting your sawbelly down as far as you want. But the consistently best summertime method may be deep trolling.

A 5½ to 6½-foot casting rod is the best for this technique. For a reel, try picking a trolling model with a high, narrow arbor. Line? Mono will belly and stretch, and limit your depth. That leaves lead-core line, wire line, or downriggers.

Downriggers are now coming down in price and are definitely here to stay. They get you to a very precise depth, and some even have thermistors that tell you, topside, what temperature you're running at. And most importantly, they release the main line with the pressure of a strike, enabling you to fight your fish on light spin tackle.

Between the other two, wire line will run deeper but it takes some getting used to and is not seen too much any more. I prefer lead-core, and I've been happily using the same Cortland "Ker-Plunk" line for years. The big advantage over wire or mono is that lead-core lines are color coded. Let out one color (30 feet) and if nothing happens, let out another color, and so on. Since without downriggers you can never tell exactly what depth you're at while trolling, due to variable line angles, color coded lines are extremely helpful. If you do nail a trout, just let out the same number of colors and continue fishing. It's the next best thing to a downrigger for deep work.

NIGHT FISHING

Bring warm clothes! A catalytic heater and a Thermos bottle of hot tea or soup will also help. This can be a long, cold ordeal, especially in spring when it works best. You'll also need two anchors and ropes, a pail of sawbellies, one or two lanterns of the type made by Coleman, and special hooks to suspend the lantern(s) over the water. These S-shaped hooks generally fit into the oarlocks; you can also devise your own.

In a nutshell, the aim is to anchor in fairly deep water, and suspend the lanterns over the side. The light will usually attract a school of sawbellies, which in turn will attract the browns. Then you fish just below the school of flashing, darting sawbellies in hopes that a brown drawn up will see your bait first. Try different depths, 10 to 30 feet or even a little more as summer approaches. To keep the bait down, you'll need anything from a large split shot to a ½-ounce barrel sinker. Some anglers do well using only a split shot and an open bail so the sawbelly can swim where he pleases. This will cause more tangled lines, though.

Try to get as much angle into your anchor ropes as possible. This will lessen the problem of hooked fish running around the ropes and snapping off. Perfectionists drop two anchors and secure them to buoys, *then* tie the boat to the buoys with horizontal ropes 50 or more feet in length.

If you couldn't buy sawbellies before heading out, bring an extra pole rigged up with one or two small treble hooks. Schooling sawbellies can be snagged quite easily.

PER BRANDIN

Night is when big browns are most active. The very best hours are between 3:00 a.m. and dawn.

CASTING LURES FROM SHORE
March 17th! Corned beef and cabbage, boiled potato, green beer, the unicorn song. It's a great day for the Irish.

It's a great day for local fishermen, too.

St. Paddy's has long been the unofficial opening of the flounder season in local waters. But there's another direction you can head, and I don't mean to Kelly's Bar or Irish Eyes. It's Titicus Reservoir, or Cross River or any of the other brown trout lakes. Just bring a 7-foot spinning pole, some 3-inch spoons and something green for good luck.

The name of the game is to fish *slowly.* The water will be very cold, and the trout's metabolism will be down. It's doubtful that a large brown, at this time of year, will exert precious energy to chase a fast moving lure.

To chuck out those big wobbling spoons, often into the teeth of an early spring gale, a lot of reservoir men have gone to medium action saltwater rods. These range in length from about seven to eight feet. In researching this book, and talking to dozens of other fishermen, I continually came across this admonition: *Use light line.* As to lures, some brand names that have proven themselves as good sawbelly simulators are the Krocodile, Sidewinder, Phoebe, and Hopkins. Most of the time it doesn't pay to cast wooden or plastic plugs because you just can't get any distance with these big, air-resistant creations.

When browns are near shore, mainly just before and after ice-out, a windy day can be excellent, even if the sun is shining. A steady chop can churn up the littoral zone where browns may be cruising, and the murkiness can mask the artificiality of your lure. It can also concentrate baitfish. Therefore, the advice here is to fish *into* the wind. The best wind during cold water periods is a south wind, because it will "push" warmed surface water towards the north shore. Just a few degrees can help excite the trout's metabolism.

BAIT FISHING FROM SHORE
Bait fishing from shore is most productive from ice-out to about April 20th, and then again from early November to ice up . . . even right through the winter when there is little or no ice (an occasional happening). Fishing at night is usually best. But at the fringes of winter, trout are liable to bite even during the day, though feeding periods at all times in cold weather seem to be short. As with all the other methods described, you simply have to put in your time to score.

Rig up your sawbelly or shiner with a #4 hook, then add a ⅛ or ¼-ounce barrel sinker. A split-shot about two feet above the bait will prevent the barrel sinker from sliding down to the hook. Cast out

PER BRANDIN

BIG BROWN SECRETS OF A MASTER

Bait dealer Jack Dykstra, of Wanaque, New Jersey, has caught more than *fifty* browns of over 10 pounds on the New York City watershed reservoirs. But the culmination of this enviable career had to be the 20-lb. 7-oz. brute pictured above. Although this fish was taken at Canonsville — a NYC reservoir in the Catskills — verified browns of over 20 pounds *have* been taken from the Westchester-Putnam reservoirs as well. And Jack's special tactics would apply down here too.

Jack does not venture forth with just any old "rod & reel." His $350 outfit is highly refined. First, he insists that light monofilament line is crucial for success. But he was unable to find any spin reels with drags smooth enough to allow the use of 4-6 lb. test line. Thus he uses a precision Fin-Nor fly reel and a long, sensitive graphite rod.

Like all big brown specialists I know, Jack insists that water temperature is by far the most important factor. He thus uses a $100-plus Waller electronic thermometer. In fact, he and his buddies often take *two* thermometers and check one for accuracy against the other!

Although browns prefer a temperature of roughly 58-60°, Jack asserts that there is much more to the science of temperature fishing than that. Browns cannot tolerate very warm water. You can safely eliminate any water over about 78°. But they can easily tolerate water as cold as water gets, which is of course 32°F. They may, in fact, be in cold water even if 58 degree water is somewhere available to them. This has to do largely with a fish's need to adjust slowly to temperature changes.

Dykstra stresses that anglers should fish "the breaks," the stratum where the greatest *change* in water temperature occurs. This stratum is called the Metalimnion (the Thermocline is found within the Metalimnion). Keep in mind that in early spring or late fall, the lake may vary only a few degrees, say from 40 to 43 degrees. But if you can find the exact level where it changes, say from 40-42 degrees (a relatively enormous change) you may hit the lottery. Even if an unusually warm wind comes along, creating 58 degree temperatures at, say, 10 feet, the fish still have to move up slowly.

gently so as not to lose the bait, then prop your rod up on a forked stick. Then loop your line around a little stick set in the opening of an empty can. When a fish takes, the can will be pulled over onto the rocks, creating a clamor that will rouse you out of dreamland. It's the most exciting alarm clock in the world!

AUTHOR PHOTO

2.
BASSING: GOOD TO EXCELLENT

The days you *really* want to show somebody something are the days you get skunked. But not always.

Lake Gilead shimmers like a Swiss tarn, there atop a hill just south of Carmel. Per Brandin and I had come to the lake to try and get some pictures for a *Field & Stream* article some years back. I'd told him about Gilead's interesting mix, and he had brought along enough rolls of film to jinx any fishing trip. We shoved the boat off at about 4:00 p.m. and headed for the north end of the lake and some thick, shoreline brushpiles I knew of.

The first blowdown was a real honey, its mossy branches projecting over and into about 15 feet of water. I knotted on a Texas-rigged rubber worm, and aimed it to fall just short of the branches.

The cast went astray — that is, right on target — and at once I was into a slam-banging largemouth. Somehow I kept the 4-pounder out of the brush, and somehow Per got the picture, and somehow for once I didn't get skunked trying to show somebody something. As a matter of fact, the day didn't end there.

At about 6:30 I piloted the rowboat towards Godfrey's Dock and dropped anchor at precisely 28 feet. Corn out, worms down, bails open we leaned back into the discomfort of the 12-foot jonboat. It wasn't long before coils of line began shooting out, and minutes after that Per had a 3-pound rainbow thumping at his feet. We also landed some platter-size bluegills that day, as well as two portly yellows.

Some salesmen take their clients out for scotch and soda. I would take mine to Lake Gilead.

BASS FISHING ON the Croton Watershed is good to excellent. By that I mean that it's excellent if you stop the car at Croton, Amawalk or Muscoot. Even anglers not familiar with one of these reservoirs can expect to get into some bass after a few trips afloat. Not far behind in bassiness (if at all) are Cross River, Titicus, and Kensico . . . but all the others are good too, even Gilead, better known for its rainbows. For certain, largemouths are better distributed and generally more abundant than smallmouths. But a fisherman who really knows a *specific* reservoir can lug home a good stringer of bass. The fish are there, but there's just no substitute for learning the whims and fancies of a particular body of water.

Here, now, are some general guidelines for chasing old bucketmouth and old brownsides on these lakes. More advice, specific to each reservoir, can be found in Ch. 3 and in the reference section.

TWO STORY FISHERIES

Many would doubt that warm water bass could thrive in waters cold enough to support trout. Well in the Croton Watershed they're not exactly roomates. But they frequently share the same "building" (lake). Some of these relatively deep, cold impoundments are what biologists call two-story fisheries, containing both cold-water and warm-water species. To roust out the bass, you first must find his apartment.

Broadly speaking, the bass carves his niche both nearer shore and in generally shallower water. The upper ends of the reservoirs – nearest the inlets – are shallower and thus offer more good habitat for largemouth. Farther down the lakes, though, there is still plenty of good largemouth water. Downlake, look especially for the more gently sloping shorelines (some drop off precipitously), lakeside brushpiles, and overhanging foliage. Look for smallmouths a little deeper, around the steeper shores, and especially around rocks, islands, points and prominent sandbars.

SPECIFIC CONDITIONS AND STRUCTURES TO LOOK FOR

Most of the time, the black bass is a bottom dweller, but not any old bottom will do. "90% of the fish are in 10% of the water" goes an old expression, and it's sure true on these reservoirs. A good book on structure fishing and a depth finder will help. So will the following tips.

Since these reservoirs are continually tapped for drinking water, any prolonged drought can cause serious drawdowns – up to 50% or even more. This condition can occasionally bring on great bass fishing.

In the late 1970's, for example, Amawalk was way down, and the fishing was excellent right through the summer doldrums. In 1980, East Branch was nearly gulched, yet when it started filling again in 1981, anglers reported unusually good action. Although the biological effects of drawdowns are complex, and not completely understood, anglers should keep an eye out for them.

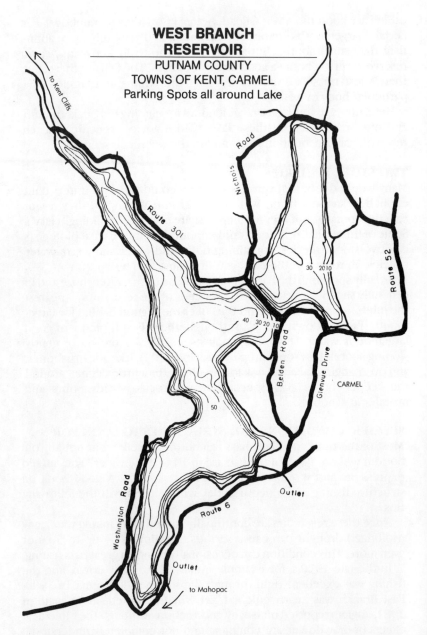

WEST BRANCH RESERVOIR
PUTNAM COUNTY
TOWNS OF KENT, CARMEL
Parking Spots all around Lake

Figure 2-a.   COMPLIMENTS NYS DEPARTMENT ENVIRONMENTAL CONSERVATION

Many of these reservoirs are fed by pipes carrying water from other parts of the watershed system. *Where legal*, fishing can often be productive around such pipes – especially in winter or summer when the incoming water will provide a sharp contrast in temperature (more moderate).

Any inlet where a tributary feeds a reservoir should arouse the interest of a fisherman. This holds for all types of fishing, not just bassing. Warmer water – or colder, depending on time of year – shallow weedy flats, moving bits of food: All these attributes make inlets potential honeyholes.

You don't need sonar or maps to find weedlines. However some weedlines in these reservoirs will be far more productive than others. What you *don't want* is a broad band of weeds that tapers slowly from very dense to very sparse. This almost always signifies a monotonous, even-sloped bottom. What you *do want* is a band of very dense weeds that just ends. This often marks a drop-off of some sort, and the edge of such a weedline can be excellent.

Old road beds are known travel routes for bass; scarcely a reservoir in this system is lacking in these ancient thorofares. Old road beds are difficult to find, even with a depth finder, so the best advice is to locate them during drawdowns. The maps distributed by Angler's Aid (see the reference section) are a big help in pinpointing old roads and

PER BRANDIN

other bass-holding structures.

Walls and foundations are among the best bass structures on the watershed reservoirs. Most of these lakes were once farmlands, and the engineers of yesteryear built very good walls, indeed. Now submerged, many of these walls – and occasional foundations – still stand, providing perfect cover for both largemouth and smallmouth bass.

Fig. 2-a shows the location and contours of West Branch Reservoir. Other reservoirs are shown in the following chapter. Contour maps of most of these watershed reservoirs are available free from the New Paltz office of DEC.

AUTHOR PHOTO

3.
NOTES ON THE SPECIFIC RESERVOIRS

In the valley of the upper West Branch, darkness was settling in along with a late September drizzle. As I donned my rainsuit, I listened to the silence. The mist deadened all sounds save one. It was the electrifying "ker-splash!" of a piece of slate being dropped into the water. I thought: September 23rd; water level up; rain, and a faint roll of thunder up the valley. I smiled to myself. Angels don't really bowl. Or drop slate on reservoirs.

The droplets grew heavier as I walked the short path down to where Boyds Corners Outlet meets West Branch Reservoir. A man fishing there acknowledged me with a nod, as he turned his collar to an ever steadying rain. In the funnel of the inlet, gaudy boils and splashes were coming off at about two per minute. These were pre-spawning browns, mostly three to eight pounds — not easy to catch, but catchable, at certain times. Everything told me this was one of those times.

There was ten minutes of light left, and the man should have stuck it out that much longer. But the rain got to him. I stepped right into his boot marks, tied on a #2 gold Mepps, and cast it just below the last riffle. My almost instant yell brought the man — who hadn't even reached his car yet — back down to the lake.

There, twinkling on the sand, was a fabulously-colored brown of 23½ inches. The man winced, and I truly sympathized with him. But I was tactful enough not to give him the advice I'll now give you: You don't quit fishing when it rains, you *start* fishing.

WEST BRANCH, STILL called "Reservoir D" by some old timers, is one of the five primary brown trout lakes. Is it as good as the others? Well, there is so much "fabricating" about which big brown was caught in which reservoir that it's hard to tell. West Branch has some pluses and some minuses. I always thought that its maximum depth of only about 55 feet would be a greatly limiting factor. Not so, say state biologists. West Branch exhibits a "thick enough" stratum of water (thermocline) where the oxygen-temperature mix is suitable. This is the primary criterion. Still, I would place West Branch at least a bit behind the other four in the production of big browns.

On the plus side, West Branch has a good feeder stream in the form of Boyds Corners outlet. There is also Horse Pound Brook where some spawning might be possible. Thus, like Croton Falls Reservoir, West Branch is strengthened by a strong contingent of naturally spawned fish . . . fish that will usually live longer and grow bigger than stocked browns. In fact, a biologist on these lakes estimates that perhaps an average of 50% of the browns in these two reservoirs are natural fish (the figure is higher in Croton Falls). This is in contrast to Cross River and Titicus, where 10% or less of the browns present were spawned naturally, and Kensico, where there is virtually no reproduction. Hence the much higher stocking quotas in these latter three reservoirs.

Two springs ago, a large body of white perch moved up into the inlet area where Boyds Corners outlet enters. They seemed to stay for weeks. I believe these panfish were attracted by the unusually high water that year. In any event, like most of the other watershed lakes, whites are there if you can locate the school.

The largemouth bass population appears to be quite healthy in West Branch, and there is plenty of good shoreline as well as submerged structure. The entire inlet area is good, and I also like the back arm where Horse Pound Brook runs in. This secluded area, by the way, is trafficked by big browns because I have seen them rolling in October.

One state expert told me flatly, "both largemouth and smallmouth bass are present in *all* the reservoirs and in a fine size distribution." That may be, but I have neither caught nor seen caught any smallies from West Branch (or from Glenida or Gilead for that matter). They may be present, but if so I can say with some certainty that they're no where near as plentiful as in Cross River, Croton, or some of the others.

CROSS RIVER

Many of Cross River's angling patterns are representative of a lot of the other watershed reservoirs. Bass fishing, for example, is by far at its best in the "off season." Both bucketmouths and bronzebacks in large sizes are easy to catch in May and early June, then again in October and November. Of course in the spring, you must throw all bass back. But if you're interested in fast action, the traditional bass months of June through September are not the time to be out.

Also like many of the other reservoirs, the trout fishing seems to be best nearest the dam. It is illegal to fish within 1000 feet of the Cross River dam, but even at that distance there are effects that can create good fishing. I believe that the "pull" of an outflow creates strong subsurface currents where suspended browns find good feeding conditions. Big, predatory browns which suspend may also favor a lake's deepest water – virtually always near a reservoir's dam – since they can quickly escape to the depths in the event of danger. Another Cross River truism that holds water elsewhere is this: Largemouths are found in largemouth water, and smallmouths in smallmouth water. It's an accurate stereotype. Both species are present in fine numbers here, but you must look for them in their separate niches. For smallies, try around rocky outcroppings, around all the rocky islands, and along the steeper shorelines where there are rocks, sandbars or drop-offs. For largemouths, look for weed beds in shallow water (see Ch. 2), places where high water has innundated the shoreline brush, and weedy shoals or high spots where there is shallow water in the middle of the lake. In hot weather or on bright days, look for both species over submerged walls or other structure in deeper water *closely adjacent* to the primary habitat.

GLENIDA
Arm-long lakers, ten pound rainbows, five pound largemouths, abundant pickerel, extraordinarily fat yellows, calico bass, even occasional Lake Whitefish: This is the superb mix in that reservoir-by-the-town, Lake Glenida (also spelled Gleneida). Like Gilead, it is deep and spring-fed, and while it is less secluded, the angling opportunities are more diverse.

One day my friend Jim Booth was anchored out on Glenida. He asked a man rowing by if he'd had any luck.

"Took one rainbow, three or four pounds" the man yelled back without any apparent emotion.

"Anything else?" Jimmy pressed.

"Got a laker about 17 pounds" the man said flatly.

"O.K." Jimmy said, getting the joke. "Have a nice day."

The man took a few more strokes on the oars when something – perhaps Glenida's overall reputation – prompted Jimmy to yell again.

"Seriously – what'd you really catch?"

"I told you" the man said, somewhat irritated now. "I got a laker about 17 pounds."

He sure as heck had! And there was an article about it in the paper the next day. Two ten-pound rainbows were also reported taken that year.

Glenida is a lake that is changing. An extensive survey done by DEC here in the summer of 1983 revealed some interesting facts.

Most noteworthy was that sawbellies were found to be present for the first time since surveys began. This appears to be having some good effects and some bad effects. On the plus side, growth rates for the

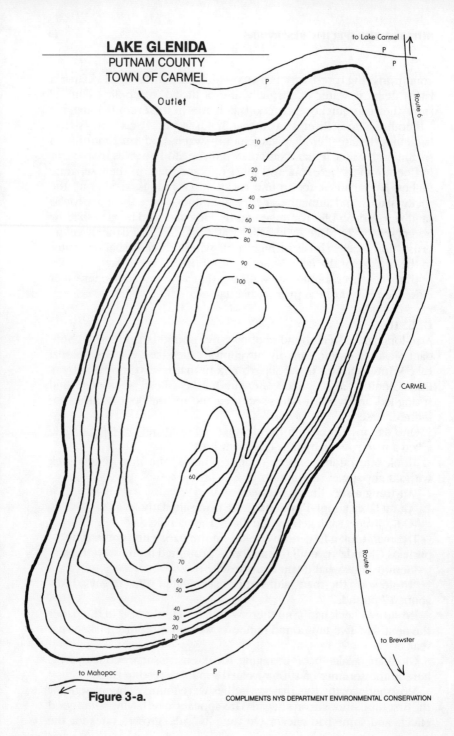

LAKE GLENIDA
PUTNAM COUNTY
TOWN OF CARMEL

Outlet

to Lake Carmel

P

P

Route 6

10

20

30

40

50

60

70

80

90

100

CARMEL

60

70

60

50

40

30

20

10

Route 6

to Brewster

to Mahopac

P

P

Figure 3-a.

COMPLIMENTS NYS DEPARTMENT ENVIRONMENTAL CONSERVATION

natural self-sustaining Lake Trout are improving. However, most of the Lake Trout – well-known as primarily a bottom species – were taken in mid-water net sets over the deepest portions of the lake (right where the sawbellies were taken!) Anglers with depth finders should keep this in mind. On the minus side, no holdover rainbow trout were captured. Like Gilead, the 'bows here used to grow fat and fast on a rich diet of plankton (chiefly Daphnia) and scud, a freshwater shrimp. Now, though, it appears that the sawbellies are competing with the rainbows for plankton. And unlike the Lake Trout, which *did* have sawbellies in their stomachs, the rainbows do not appear to be switching over to baitfish (i.e. the sawbellies) as they grow older.

Thus came the recommendation by DEC to split the annual rainbow quota between 'bows and browns. However just before press time, the brown trout plan was scrapped, and instead DEC will be trying a Finger Lakes strain of rainbow that will presumably feed on the sawbellies more effectively.

Although Glenida is deep, bottoming out at about 110 feet, there is a shallow band around the lake that is very productive for warm-water species. There are fine largemouths in moderate numbers, and equally fine pickerel. I have seen expert angler Jack Stewart murder the pickerel through the ice down at the south end of the lake, though I haven't yet decoded his technique. Glenida also sports some of the biggest yellow perch in the region. They're plentiful and even big enough to filet. Unlike Gilead, there are also Calico Bass (crappies) here.

GILEAD

This, the smallest of the watershed reservoirs, is a twin sister to Glenida. The same changes happening in Glenida appear to be occurring in Gilead. Both lakes, just a few years ago, boasted superb put-grow-take fisheries for rainbows. The fish did not reproduce, but they did grow fast and their pink flesh (shrimp diet) was unbelievably delicious. Now, it appears that rainbow holdover has diminished greatly. For the same reasons discussed under Glenida, management may swing over to brown trout here sometime in the near future, but not before that different strain of rainbow is tried.

Gilead is also weedier and – in the opinion of some – less clear than it was some years back. It used to be possible to see a shiny object more than twenty feet down. Now, visibility is not that good. In addition, Gilead now has a band of thick weeds around it for the first time. Some anglers think this has brought on a resurgence of pickerel and, in fact, I know of a few huge 6- pound plus pickerel nailed here in the past few seasons. Bass fishing also seems to be improving (no smallmouths, only largemouths).

Also, as discussed under Glenida, the growth rate for Gilead's small number of lakers seems to be improving. This is a wild population – certainly not huge, but fishable.

Like the other few dozen Gilead regulars, I used to have the rainbow formula down pat. We used to anchor in about 23-30 feet of water, chum with corn, and bait our hooks with nightwalkers or a combination of worm and corn. Best action was between 7 and 10 pm, and it was quite predictable. Now, I am hesitant to recommend that formula to you. Some anglers report that it no longer works, and that daytime casting with lures is more productive. Clearly, it's a whole new ballgame at Gilead, and it may take a while for things to shake out. Nonetheless, the lakers are still there, and the warm-water fishing may be on the upswing. While you're enjoying these opportunities you can start learning the new trout patterns that may pertain.

Ice-out usually comes around mid-March, and from that point up to late April, small numbers of the cold-water-loving Lake Trout are taken from shore by casters (also at Glenida). In April, you can legally launch your boat, and shallow drift or surface troll for lakers. In early spring it's Lake Capossela or Lake (insert your name) since only a few hearty souls will be in evidence. The shore casters, by the way, seem to favor large wobbling spoons.

Come May, you still might pluck a Lake Trout without going too deep, and late May *used to be* when the first rainbows were taken.

In the clear waters of Gilead, bass always seemed to stay quite deep. Weighted rubber worms in clear green or purple, or lead head jigs were good lures. With the increased weediness, shoreline fishing may improve. If you anchor with live bait you are liable to latch onto anything.

Recently, vandalism of a small dam on Gilead lowered the lake several feet. I understand this will be repaired eventually.

AMAWALK

When I was only five or six years old, I remember driving up to Amawalk with my father and old family friend John Morabito. It was the first watershed lake I fished, and to a young boy, even the hapless "red-eyed" rock bass seemed magical. That's almost thirty years ago now, and while "progress" has certainly altered the face of once-sleepy Westchester, Amawalk is still a fine bass lake. There is no question that there are more brown trout here than before, and in fact, the reservoir

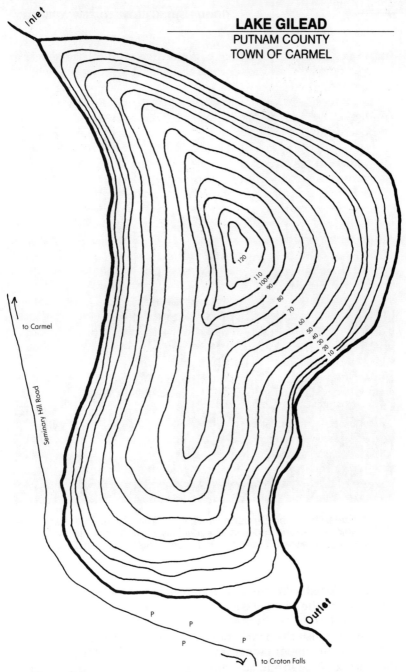

LAKE GILEAD
PUTNAM COUNTY
TOWN OF CARMEL

Inlet

to Carmel

Seminary Hill Road

120
110
100
90
80
70
60
50
40
30
20
10

Outlet

P P
P P

to Croton Falls

Figure 3-b.

AUTHOR PHOTO

A scale-stretching 5-pound smallmouth from Cross River Reservoir. Try around rocks, and especially around rocky islands, and use crawfish if you can get them. Angler is John Cronin of Ossining.

was just opened to year-round trout fishing not too long ago. Again, you can thank the sawbellies for the increase in browns. The lake is not stocked with trout, by the way, and the browns in the lake are thought to be stocked fish that have strayed down from the inlet area.

The best largemouth water is up at the north end of the lake. Here there are some large mid-lake shoals, submerged roads and walls, and shoreline weeds. Jim Weaver, of North Tarrytown, has done very well on Amawalk and he has taught me a few things about the lake. For one thing, he thinks the fishing here is best by day rather than at night. I don't know why it is so, but my own experience tends to substantiate this theory. By working rubber worms over structure you can sometimes score even at high noon, though early morning is the very best time in summer.

When the water is up, it is very important to cast your lures as far back into the shoreline weeds as possible. Bigmouths often hang well back in there, and if your cast is even inches short, you may not tempt your target out. When you are fishing a band of weeds that grow out a ways from shore, cast your lure to the very edge of the weeds. A floating, silver Rapala is absolutely tops for this kind of largemouth fishing. We've tried colors other than silver but they don't seem to work nearly as well.

There is some excellent smallmouth water at the other end of the lake, near the dam. Bronzebacks lurk here along the rockier and much steeper shoreline.

Amawalk is also a very good pickerel lake. Because of this, and because of a fine head of crappies and perch, Amawalk is a popular destination for the ice fisherman. The tip-up and jig pole set can expect faster action here than on most of the other reservoirs. But as I've mentioned elsewhere in this book, ice fishing is overall quite slow, especially after the ice has gotten thick. Successful ice fishing requires knowledge and fortitude.

EAST BRANCH (SODOM)

Sodom remains pretty much a mysterious lake to me. The best I can say is that Artie Venier and I had some good luck ice fishing here some years back. However, in recent years the action seemed to tail off. (It may be my imagination, but it seems to me that ice fishing is not as good now in these reservoirs – especially for brown trout – as it was in the 70's when the lakes were first opened to winter-time trout fishing.)

At one time or another, I have taken Smallmouth Bass, Largemouth Bass, pickerel, yellow and white perch, bluegills, crappies and even bullheads here. Once, while ice fishing, I was even surprised by a 13-inch brown which I dutifully returned. Though it is not managed for trout, some have to be present because Sodom is fed by a large stream that does contain trout. In spring, this stream creates a fine current, and the long thin funnel of the inlet would be a good starting point for all species. Recently, low water revealed that there is some super rock structure in this part of the lake.

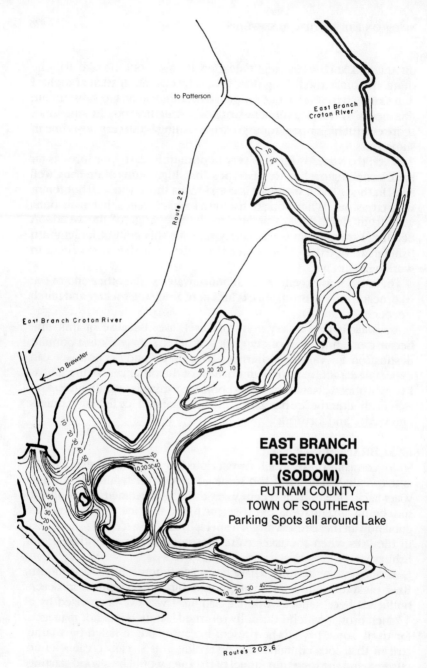

to Patterson

East Branch
Croton River

Route 22

East Branch Croton River

to Brewster

40 30 20 10

10
20

**EAST BRANCH
RESERVOIR
(SODOM)**
PUTNAM COUNTY
TOWN OF SOUTHEAST
Parking Spots all around Lake

10
20
30
40
45

50
10 20 30 40

60
50
40
30
20
10

10

10 20 30 40

Routes 202,6

Figure 3-c.   COMPLIMENTS NYS DEPARTMENT ENVIRONMENTAL CONSERVATION

CROTON FALLS

This reservoir is often called "Hemlock," though technically Hemlock is a place name referring to a particular section of the lake. To me, this is one of the more interesting of the area impoundments.

Like so many of these reservoirs, a number of species have been experimented with over the years. Back in the '50s, for example, Landlocked Salmon were stocked here, and though some good-sized specimens turned up, this fish never took a toe-hold. At that time, the lake had a good supply of smelt, the ideal forage fish for landlocks. There was even a small but dedicated group of smelt fishermen. These guys mainly ice fished, concentrating in Stebbins Cove in late winter, but some also dip-netted in the tribs during the spring spawning run. The smelt appear to be gone now, though, and authorities who constantly fish the lake report that they haven't seen a smelt in seven or eight years. Some say it was the sawbellies that pushed the smelt out.

In terms of quantity, Croton Falls may not be the top brown trout producer, but it has yielded some of the biggest fish over the past half-dozen years. A lot of people drift fish with sawbellies, but some of the most successful anglers troll with color-coded lead core lines and "flutter spoons." Relatively new to this region, this type of spoon is very thin and thus provides more of what the name promises. However you pursue the browns, though (see Ch. 1), know that Hemlock is notorious for "turning off" for weeks at a time. As always, the people who score are the ones who put in their time.

There appears to be a parallel with bass: Not as many fish as some of the other reservoirs, but some exceptionally big ones. For largemouth, try inside the cove behind the Stebbins causeway or in the extreme northeast arm where few anglers venture. The dean of Croton Falls, Jack Stewart, reports that there are also some jumbo smallmouths. Look to the rockier areas, as just north and south (west bank) of the Stoneleigh Causeway.

Hemlock does not appear to have a lot of pickerel, though there may be some in the back coves. There are nice white perch here, but schools of this fish seem to appear and disappear. Then of course there is the usual roster of bluegills, yellow perch, catfish and eels. I've even heard of a bowfin or two wrestled out of the depths of Croton Falls.

MUSCOOT

If you're a commuter, you can get off the train at Golden's Bridge, walk a few feet, chuck out a big Daredevle, and possibly tie into a Barracuda-like fish with writhing power, steakknife teeth and 20 pounds or better of weight. Nestled right along the Harlem Railroad line is swampy Muscoot Reservoir, and nestled among its murky waters is that hybrid powerhouse, the Tiger Muskellunge or "Norlunge." Weedy, shallow and rife with baitfish, Muscoot was deemed to be just right for Norlunge, and 7200 fingerlings were stocked here in 1980. Local bait shops recorded bigger and bigger specimens each subsequent year, and in 1984, a fish of 16¾ pounds was conquered by angler Charles Tyra. Unfortunately, New York City has not approved continued stockings, which are necessary since this hybrid fish does not propogate. At this time, it does not appear that approval is forthcoming.

As you might deduce from the above description, Muscoot is also "just right" for Largemouth Bass and Pickerel. The entire lake should be considered prime bass water, with the most acreage of optimal habitat being north or Wood's Bridge. South of Wood's Bridge, the water appears to be better for smallmouth, as well as brown trout which occur naturally here – they are not stocked. Doubtless, many of these browns, which seem to average 2-5 pounds, drift or migrate down from Muscoot's many trout-holding tributaries. Still, the main attraction here is Largemouth Bass, and the many shallow, winding coves north of Wood's Bridge comprise choice bigmouth water.

Bring a selection of weedless lures when you fish Muscoot. Also, learn where the bottom structure is. There is a lot of it. Old bridge abutments, old foundations, labrynthine stream channels, stone walls, little islands: Muscoot has it all. As this lake is frequently drawn way down, such fish-holding structures are relatively easy to locate, especially in early fall.

Muscoot also sports a great population of panfish: Whites, yellows, crappies and bluegills. The many tips for finding and catching panfish scattered throughout this section will apply to Muscoot. For crappies, in particular, always try around the bridges. Muscoot has a bunch of them.

A sad note on Muscoot is the development that is encroaching upon it. (If only the city owned a *larger* protective strip around each reservoir.) Both Pepsico and IBM are now building large complexes near the lake in Somers, and it is hard to tell what impact this will have. Certainly, Muscoot is the reservoir that will be suffering the most aesthetically in the coming years.

CROTON

For its size, Croton is definitely underfished and also amazingly unspoiled and remote-looking considering its southerly position in the watershed chain. Of seven watershed reservoirs checked recently for angler use, Croton finished 6th. Only West Branch was more lightly used.

Most anglers wonder about trout possibilities in this, the largest of the Croton Watershed reservoirs. Undoubtedly there are a few monster browns (perhaps even rainbows or lakers) lurking in this deep impoundment. And though it is not stocked with trout, some specimens must migrate down from feeder streams. However it is not and will not be managed for trout because it is not biologically suited to salmonids. That is because it exhibits an adverse oxygen-temperature profile as determined by recent comprehensive testing on the part of the DEC.

Many anglers know of two large stockings of trout here: 20,000 Brown Trout yearlings in 1971, and 4300 Lake Trout in 1972. These were surplus fish that were originally earmarked for other waters. Virtually no returns of these fish were reported or secured in subsequent netting. Croton is not a trout lake.

Following that 1980 survey, biologist Mike Gann of the DEC recommended the introduction of a pelagic, predatory fish: The Striped Bass. Landlocked stripers in Croton, Gann believes, would help control the unmanageable sawbelly population and present an exciting new sportfishing possibility. The recommendation must be approved by New York City, but as of late 1984 that approval does not seem likely.

PER BRANDIN

Both Croton and Muscoot are crossed by a number of bridges. Many species — especially smallmouth bass and crappies — congregate around these bridge abutments.

The black bass fishing here is excellent, among the best in the system. There are both largemouths and smallmouths, as well as some pickerel. Smallmouth addicts cast around the bridge abutments and the rockier shorelines. The rocky, shoaly Hunter Brook section is rightfully regarded as one of the best smallmouth areas. Largemouth and pickerel live side by side in the shallower, weedier sections of the lake. The entire upper third of the lake, above Pine's Bridge, is good largemouth country, but you simply have to find the structure. The bottom here is relatively smooth, and you could spend days fishing totally fishless water. The southerly back arm bordered by Rt. 134 is a good cove for bigmouths.

Tight-lipped locals know of an excellent, hearty bait for bass: The Banded Killifish ("killie") which can be easily trapped in the nearby Hudson River. The A-Number-1 bait for smallmouths is crawfish.

The panfishing opportunities in Croton are superb. All the local species are present. Croton has one of the best populations of White Perch, and these fish can be located by trolling different depths; a string of three spinners followed by a worm is a popular rig. Some anglers tie a balloon with a long string to the first fish caught under the presumption that the fish will return to the school. I tried this dirty trick with Striped Bass on the Hudson but to no avail.

We've also enjoyed good crappie action on Croton. Again, around the bridge abutments can be excellent. Yellow perch and sunnies live in Croton, too, but in smallish sizes. Other fish present include suckers, carp, eel, White Catfish (in good sizes) both Brown and Yellow Bullhead and of course tons of sawbellies.

Few people really know how to track down the panfish schools in Croton and elsewhere around the circuit. It would be a major challenge, one with especially nice rewards for the ice fisherman.

TITICUS

All of the main brown trout reservoirs, of which Titicus is one, seem to go through a cycle: Sawbellies "appear," the browns get bigger and more numerous, then they get even bigger but less numerous, then the lake tapers off somewhat. Titicus and Cross River were probably the first brown trout lakes where sawbellies became firmly established, and in the mid to late '70s these lakes appeared to peak out. In the past few years, though, Titicus and Cross River have not produced browns as well as Croton Falls (where sawbellies appeared later) or some of the others. Whether there is anything to this, and whether Titicus will "re-cycle" are subject to question.

Unlike Cross River, Smallmouth do not seem to be important in

AUTHOR PHOTO

Gil Bell, one of the best of the local reservoir fishermen, with two nice browns from Titicus.

Titicus. That may be because Titicus has less rock and other favorable habitat for smallies. The largemouth fishing is very good, though, and the fish run large with many over 6 pounds taken. Pickerel are not widely dispersed in either Cross River or Titicus, but they are present. Stick to weedy water 15 feet and less, which pretty much means the back coves and the more easterly portions of the lake.

Along with Croton, we've hit the best schools of white perch in Titicus. They are very much here today and gone tomorrow, though. Yellow perch are also in there in average sizes, but the crappies that are abundant in Cross River have never showed up on one of my hooks.

KENSICO
To learn more about Kensico, I talked to Bill Rutherford of Valhalla, who has fished the reservoir all his life. One of the best anglers in the area, Bill filled me in on some interesting facets of this, the most southerly of the local Watershed reservoirs.

Lake Trout are still present in Kensico, but since they are not regularly stocked now, the trout present are primarily natural fish. Since the stockings stopped a number of years ago, fish are much fewer and where it use to take an expert four hours to troll up a fish, it now may take four days. Like most lake trout specialists, Rutherford still uses wire line and trolls right near bottom most of the time. To find the correct depth, he uses a thermometer to seek out the 48-50 degree water lakers prefer. He also uses a depth finder to make sure he is over the right depth. All this is not as easy as it sounds, for many reasons. For one thing, strict attention must be paid to the rod tip to make sure the rig is "ticking" along bottom. Bill feels sure that lakers relate to bottom rocks and rocky structure, and here is where there is just no substitute for learning a lake well.

Sawbellies have been present in Kensico for decades, perhaps since its very impoundment as discussed in Ch. 1. Lake trout will briefly leave their preferred temperature zone on bottom to chase sawbellies, and thus they may be found at almost any depth. But Rutherford thinks they quickly return to their "holding lie" on bottom. In this 150-foot deep lake, Bill has taken lakers up to 90 feet down, and his largest is 19½ pounds. At least a few fish of 20 pounds or better have been boated down through the years.

Browns and rainbows are stocked in Kensico in moderate numbers (see the reference section). As there is no large tributary, these fish will not reproduce, but they do grow quite large. Rainbows and browns are much more pelagic, roaming various depths off bottom in search of alewives and other food. They prefer warmer waters, and 58-60 degrees is often mentioned as ideal for these species. Since they're not generally as deep as lakers, the usual gear for trollers is lead-core line as opposed to wire. For all three species of trout, most experts I talked to now use a single "flutter spoon" as the terminal rig. Flutter spoon has become a generic name for a very thin and thus very flashy type of wobbling spoon. There are numerous brand names. Recommended to me by Rutherford is the 06 Miller Flutter-Lite, the 06 Elmer Hinckley, and the Williams Thinfish. Whether you use wire or lead-core, a leader of 28-30 feet is recommended. Interestingly, downriggers – which have taken over in many lakes – are still not seen too much on area reservoirs.

Kensico's bottom is not very weedy, but the many rocky areas make for some good smallmouth fishing. You have to find those rocks, though, and it really helps to have a depth sounder. Largemouths are present here, too, but to a lesser degree.

Kensico has a good population of yellow perch, and Bill has taken them up to an eye-popping 16¼ inches. He has not seen any white perch in many years, though. In the extreme northern cove, where it is shallow, some nice pickerel can be taken. In fact, over the years, some of the biggest pickerel I've heard of being caught on the watershed have come from Kensico.

This is the only watershed reservoir where ice fishing is not permitted. Right after the ice goes, though, there is often some good shore fishing for trout.

DIVERTING

As of recently, all of two boats were registered on Diverting Reservoir. Granted, the fishing here is not of glamorous proportions. But almost certainly the lake is good enough to justify a little more play than it gets.

A fine trout stream, the East Branch of the Croton (Ch. 5) empties into Diverting. But Diverting just doesn't have the characteristics to hold trout. If you take any trout here, it will probably be in the inlet area.

A recent DEC survey showed that there were black bass in good supply. Surprisingly, it was found that smallmouths outnumbered largemouths. The usual roster of panfish are also present. So if you're after strictly bass, and you want a lake all to yourself, try Diverting. As always a boat will help, but Diverting also has a good shoreline for casters when the water level is down a bit.

BOG BROOK

As the watershed chart in the reference section shows, Bog Brook is the only reservoir that has not been surveyed by DEC in recent years. Thus my information was not verifiable as it was with all the others.

The last survey was in 1953, and I have a copy of that lengthy report. It's likely that things haven't changed much. The problems Bog Brook had back then – notably in regard to the chemical foundation of the lake – are almost certain to remain in force today.

Bog Brook is part of the scorned trio, the others being Middle Branch and Diverting. As with all the other non-trout reservoirs a few specimens may be noted from time to time. But Bog Brook has very poor dissolved oxygen levels below the 30-foot depth level. This is a very limiting factor, and one that definitely precludes a trout fishery. For *all* species, you can pretty much eliminate the deeper water here during the summer.

The shoreline is essentially rocky and steep and generally unsuitable for insect food production or as a spawning area. As you will conclude, it is not a largemouth lake. Smallmouths predominate, but even this rock-loving gamefish will not reproduce as well as in many of the other reservoirs. Nonetheless, some fishermen do report pretty good action on smallies and almost total lack of angler competition has to help. I can tell you that the lake has an amazing crawfish population, and if you come here you will have no trouble collecting your own bait supply.

Way back in that 1953 survey, Bog Brook exhibited a superabundance of white perch. Whether they are still that plentiful I do not know. I've tried ice fishing here, specifically for the whites, but found the action to be very slow.

The survey referenced above also showed there were good numbers of Black Crappies, another species that I have found largely around rocks. Neither pickerel nor yellow perch – species which usually do well where the largemouth thrives – were found in anything better than meager numbers.

MIDDLE BRANCH

Still called "Tilly Foster" by some, this lake has a thin summer-time thermocline and is thus not at all suited to trout. Black bass – predominantly largemouths – are present and the competition from other anglers will be slight. Middle Branch has a very good population of White Perch, and for that reason is a worthy destination for the ice fisherman. I couldn't find anyone who fishes here regularly so more detailed information is not available for me to pass along.

4.
AN ICE FISHING PARTY

Always bring a gaff when you ice fish the watershed. I'll long regret not having one on one very cold, late January day.

The stage had been set by a new, 4-inch coating of clear black ice on Titicus Reservoir. It was a doubly exciting happenstance: First ice is the very best fishing, and with clear ice, you can see everything that happens below . . . kind of like a motion picture.

The morning had begun with a bang — or rather, a yank. After chopping four or five holes at various points over the sandbar, we began fishing with jig poles and Swedish Pimples tipped with mousie grubs. Sometime around 10:00 a.m., a chubby 14-inch brown succumbed to this offering; so did a few small yellows. Then, at about 2 O'Clock, my pole was sucked downward like a one-armed divining rod. Fortunately, there was a nearby angler who had a gaff, and he lent it to my partner Jim Booth who expertly speared the fish: A sparkling, full-bellied brown that taped out at 20½ inches.

Company is fine, and ice fishing can even be gregarious. But truly great bucks and great fish visit the hunter in the quietest moments of his aloneness. At 5:40 p.m., as shadows melted into gloom, the great brown came to call.

There's never any *real* certainty in a lost love or a lost fish. I might have sharpened the hooks better, or played him longer, or chopped a bigger hole. I certainly would have stood a better chance had I a gaff. He was a magnificent trout, at least 8 pounds, maybe 10, and we traded glances through the clear ice for most of the 10-minute struggle. I'll never forget watching that little silvery hook pop out of his mouth just as my hand touched his gill covers.

ICE FISHING opportunities on the Croton Watershed are virtually limitless. Relative to the amount of water and fish available, few ice anglers venture forth. And only a handful really know what they're doing. Maybe it's better that way. Ice fishing always has a party

Lake Glenida is a fine choice for the ice fisherman. Chain Pick-
kerel is only one of Glenida's several attractions.

atmosphere, what with people mingling on the ice, comparing catches,
sharing a Thermos bottle of coffee. In fact, it's a kind of sport that
should exclude no one: kids, wives, girlfriends, and grandparents can
and do get in on the fun.

If you insist on taking it seriously, though, here are some notes I've
made over the years, including some thoughts on how to cook on the
ice (no food will ever taste better!)

TRIES FOR TROUT

You can legally keep trout taken through the ice from eight of the reservoirs: Cross River, Titicus, Amawalk, Muscoot, Croton Falls, Gilead, Glenida, and West Branch. Trout taken elsewhere must be immediately returned. Bass cannot be kept anywhere in the watershed in winter. Without exception, we have done best, on all species, during the first week or two of safe ice. Perhaps it has something to do with light penetration and, subsequently, oxygen production. Whatever the reason, try to get out there at the gun.

Conversely, there are a few devotees who claim that last ice is also good. One reputed expert scores heavily on West Branch by fishing all night during the last ice of early March.

Overwhelmingly, our jig poles have outproduced tip-ups for browns on the area reservoirs. Sure, it's fun to race for a fluttering red flag. But more and more, tip-ups have become a boring ritual that we simply omit. With a jig pole, the lure is constantly moving (shiners sit like statues unless you keep tugging at them). This fact, combined with the mobility of jigging, adds up to better fishing.

As for terminal tackle, we like Swedish Pimple jigs in the medium sizes for browns. They're very flashy, sink fast, and are heavy enough to let you know when you've hit bottom – an important consideration since *usually* you will want to be just *off* bottom. Mousie grubs, sold by most local bait shops, are little larval worms which, when added to a jig lure, seem to improve its fish-catching ability.

When the lakes first freeze, early morning seems to be a little more fruitful than other times of the day. Things can also pop from 3:00 p.m. on, and especially around sunset. Cloudy days are better than sunny days, and warm, drizzly, foggy days are best of all.

Here now are some specific locations where we've scored over the years.

In Muscoot, try just north and south of Wood's Bridge, and try to locate sandbars southwest of the bridge. In Titicus, fish over the sandbars near the first cove on the north side of the lake. At Croton Falls, there are two places I'd recommend. One is near the dam and just off the conifers on the east side of the lake. You'll usually see other anglers here. Another spot is in the old stream channel, from the inlet downlake about ¼ mile. This latter spot is hottest when the lake is drawn down enough so the channel is in about 25 feet of water (15 to 25 feet seems to be a good, all around range for browns in winter).

At West Branch, we've had our best luck at the north end. There is normally only a narrow band of safe ice here, from where the stream

enters down to the influx chamber. It's a good spot, but exercise
caution.

At both Gilead and Glenida, ice anglers can catch Rainbow and Lake
Trout. Though the rainbows are not too tough in summer, they're
extremely difficult to nail in winter. I've witnessed only a few, and
these were caught either with shiners or nightcrawlers. Rest assured,
though, that the 'bows are there for some sharp individual who can
pick up the formula.

Lake Trout may actually be a little easier to catch in winter, but never
in any great numbers. Here are six tips for taking forktails from Gilead
and Glenida:

1. Concentrate your efforts between 25 and 50 feet of water.
2. If you use live bait, try *active* bait like small suckers or dace.
3. Use large Swedish Pimples, and try painting the treble hooks a
   phosphorescent color. (Remember: There is little light penetration in deep water.)
4. Try to get out at dawn, and on foggy, drizzly days.
5. Rather than move, keep jigging! Feeding periods are short; you
   may have to jig a hole for 7 hours to hook one laker.
6. Chum the hole with perch roe or chopped egg shells.

PICKEREL PANACEA

Chain Pickerel are present in all the reservoirs, but the quality of the
fishing varies greatly from lake to lake. Year after year, ice fishermen do
best on this toothsome torpedo at Muscoot, Amawalk, and Glenida.
Muscoot probably has the highest percentage of favorable habitat
– shallow, weedy water – as well as the biggest pickerel. There is an
even more fearsome gamefish in muddy Muscoot, first cousin to the
pickerel, but much longer, tougher, and toothier. It's the hybrid
Norlunge, a fish that can attain a weight of 30 pounds or more. This
introduced species is discussed further in Ch. 3. One last note: North
of Wood's Bridge it is quite shallow; all of this water should be
considered prime pickerel grounds.

Amawalk has a fine population of this ice fishing staple, and a fair
amount of suitable habitat. Much of the northern third of the lake is
choice pickerel territory, as are both shores for about two-thirds of the
way down the lake.

Deep lake Glenida has a fairly narrow littoral (shore) zone of good
pickerel water, but it's very productive. Try along Rt. 6 and at the very
southern tip of the lake. Kensico and West Branch also yield good
numbers of fish, and these producers are followed closely by Titicus

FISH OF THE CROTON WATERSHED RESERVOIRS

	Brown Trout	Rainbow Trout	Lake Trout	Large-mouth Bass	Small-mouth Bass	Chain Pickerel	Norlunge (Tiger Musky)
KENSICO	ES	GS	ON	GN	GN	GN	
CROTON	ON			EN	EN	GN	
MUSCOOT	ON			EN	GN	GN	X
AMAWALK	ON			EN	GN	EN	
CROSS RIVER	ES			GN	EN	UN	
TITICUS	ES			GN	GN	UN	
CROTON FALLS	ET			GN	GN	UN	
WEST BRANCH	ET			GN	UN	GN	
GILEAD	*	GS	GN	GN		GN	
GLENIDA	*	GS	GN	GN		EN	
EAST BRANCH	ON			GN	GN	ON	
MIDDLE BRANCH				GN	ON	UN	
BOG BROOK				ON	GN	ON	
DIVERTING				GN	GN	UN	

LEGEND

FIRST LETTER: Quality of Fishery
- E   Excellent angling opportunity
- G   Good opportunity (may range from fair to very good)
- O   Appears to be an occasionally occurring species
- U   Present but author unsure of quality of fishery

SECOND LETTER: Stocked or Natural
- N   Naturally reproducing, no stocking
- S   Stocked, no or virtually no reproduction
- T   Stocking supports natural reproduction

OTHER SYMBOLS USED
- X   Stocked experimentally in 1980 only. State unable to secure permission from city to continue stockings and future stockings unlikely at press time. This is a sterile hybrid that will not reproduce.
- *   Some specimens present. Origin uncertain. No plans for stocking at press time.

OTHER NOTES
- Also see complete stocking reports elsewhere in the reference section.
- Panfish: White Perch, Yellow Perch, Black Crappie, Rock Bass, Bluegill/Sunfish generally common in all reservoirs though quantity and quality will vary considerably.
- Rough Fish: Carp, Sucker, Catfish/Bullhead (two or three species), Eel all generally common
- Rare Species: Bowfin, Lake Whitefish, Brook Trout (probably only those that incidentally drift down from feeders).

Figure 4-a.

and Cross River. Croton has certain sections suitable for pickerel, though ice fishermen (including the author, who lives only four miles away) seem to shun this sprawling reservoir. It's definitely the place to go for solitude.

Wherever you go, though, remember that pickerel prefer *live bait*. That means tip-ups, medium size shiners, #4 hooks, and short, tough, mono leaders.

PILES OF PANFISH

If you're not hung up on wall trophies, but do like fast action, white perch are what you're after. It's seldom easy to find a school, but if you do, you're in for a great day on the ice.

Whites are the glamor panfish of the watershed reservoirs. They're the biggest and hardest-fighting, best eating, and they run in the biggest schools. With the exception of Gilead, white perch seem to be present all around the circuit. Bog Brook, the northermost reservoir, may be #1 for whites, though all the others are good, too.

Like browns, whites seem to like sandbars in winter. They are known to suspend in tight schools, but in the local reservoirs, we've done best by fishing just a foot or two off bottom. Once again, we prefer Swedish Pimples – but in the smaller sizes – tipped with mousie grubs or kernels of corn. Small shiners work, too. If you don't hit whites quickly, move. If you do hit them, *don't* move! Finding the school is the toughest part, but once done, you can catch 25, 50 or even more of these sweet-eating fish.

Other desirable panfish are black crappies, yellow perch, and bluegills. Cross River and Croton have proven themselves for crappies, but it's doubtful that many of the lakes lack these scrappy papermouths. You'll take yellow perch everywhere, whether you want them or not. But if you're really looking for a mess of jumbo yellows through the ice, head for Lake Glenida, or secondarily, Gilead.

Small jigs and small shiners seem to work equally well on yellows. It's hard to recommend *where* in a lake to look for them, we've caught them at so many different depths. The best advice is to walk around the ice a lot, talk to other anglers, and see where the action is good. Generally speaking, weedy bottoms are better than open bottoms, but submerged rock or other structure can also hold yellows.

Although bluegills and sunfish are unquestionably the most numerous species in these reservoirs, I don't know a single ice fisherman who chases after them. This, I think, is another illustration of the fact that ice fishing just hasn't been developed in this region as it has further north. There is a lot to be learned yet, but the potential rewards are great.

COOKING ON ICE

Fire building is not allowed on or around the city reservoirs, but it's doubtful anyone would object to the heating up of a simple meal on a propane-fueled stove. For those fishermen who like to play chef, here are some tips for cooking on ice.

Forget all about cold cuts and other sure-to-get soggy sandwiches. What you want is something *hot* to warm up the troops. Wide-mouthed vacuum bottles are fine for bringing hot soup from home. To cook on the spot, the best gear is a small, one-burner backpacking stove, or a two-burner Coleman stove. For utensils, it's tough to beat those Boy Scout type nesting cook sets. Here you have cup, fry-pan, kettle, and dish all in one. Whenever possible, bring food that can be prepared at home. Chili, tangy venison stew, franks and beans, maccaroni with cheese and meat: These are one-dish meals that can be brought along in plastic containers and simply heated up.

If you plan to make a small open fire, in places where that is legal, it's wise to take a folding camp saw to cut firewood. Your ice skimmer will do a wonderful job of grilling a hamburger! There are also mini backpack grills for cooking over an open wood fire.

In a separate plastic container, bring along some bread crumbs that have been seasoned with dried dill or tarragon and parsley. This is to coat some tasty fish filets in case you get lucky (you'll need a bit of butter or oil here, too). If you have a large group of people, it's great to have a small, folding card table to set things on. For a true ice fishing "party", you're sure to want a coffee pot and a hibachi. The smell of grilled hot dogs, venisonburgers, steaks or chops wafting across the ice might well be the most magical aroma in the world!

5.
THREE STREAMS IN PRAISE OF FLY FISHING

As we walked the dirt path up to the lower end of Amawalk Outlet, any doubts we might have still had about planet Earth being a paradise were laid to rest. It was May first, give or take a day, and the woods shone like a newborn baby. Everything was an incredible translucent green, save for a few Nodding Red Trilium and white, wild Dogwoods that speckled the forest.

Jim Weaver took position up around the first bend, while I started just below that. It was 10:00 a.m., too early for the Hendricksons, so I plotted some different mischief.

Fished as a streamer, my #10 Muddler Minnow produced nothing. Then I turned it into what I call a "One-Two-Punch Fly": one you can fish both dry and wet on the same cast. It was a tactic I had first tried with a Royal Trude out in Montana, and it was dynamite. A liberal coating of floatant kept the muddler high and dry, and a few fish took it that way. Most, though, took it "on the twitch," just as I jerked it hard to sink it at the bottom of the float.

The ten browns were vintage Amawalk, long and sleek and pretty. The eleven-inch brookie was a surprise. The best part of the day, though, was an encounter with a large, black snake that was sunning itself in the path, oblivious to us and to the whitetailed deer that snuck about in the alders.

IN WINTER, AMAWALK Outlet sleeps gently, its woods filling with snow, and the snow filling with the pockmarks of hungry, roaming whitetails. At this time, the famous "rock rollers," a contingent of local Trout Unlimited members, do stream improvement projects here. One of this region's three "quality streams," Amawalk Outlet is a place worth visiting.

If there were a set of theorums in angling, one would surely read: *The quality of the fishing experience shall improve in inverse proportion to the presence of roads.* Except for a few hundred yards, the Amawalk's three odd miles are pretty much off the road. Fig. 5-a

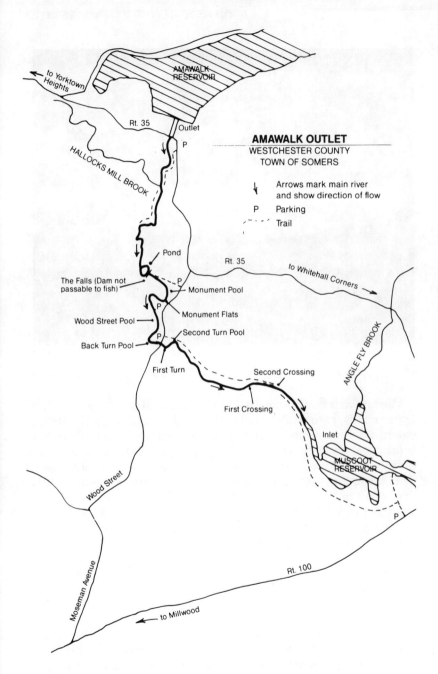

to Yorktown
Heights

AMAWALK
RESERVOIR

Rt. 35   Outlet
              P

HALLOCKS MILL BROOK

AMAWALK OUTLET
WESTCHESTER COUNTY
TOWN OF SOMERS

↓   Arrows mark main river
      and show direction of flow
P   Parking
--- Trail

Pond

Rt. 35   to Whitehall Corners

The Falls (Dam not   P
passable to fish)   Monument Pool

                      Monument Flats
Wood Street Pool   P
                              Second Turn Pool
Back Turn Pool   P

First Turn   Second Crossing

                    First Crossing

ANGLE FLY BROOK

Inlet

MUSCOOT
RESERVOIR

Wood Street

                                              P

Moseman Avenue

Rt. 100

← to Millwood

Figure 5-a.

PER BRANDIN

illustrates this, depicts access points and shows most of the better pools.

The Amawalk flows between Amawalk and Muscoot Reservoirs. The upper end is quite shallow and rocky, and here Hallock's Mill Brook enters. But downstream of Hallock's, the stream becomes somewhat brushy and swampy and while backcasting is limited the water is deeper and there is interesting variety. From just below the old broken dam, angling pal Jim Booth once extracted a 19-inch brown. This upper part of the stream is normally the only part of the river that is stocked. Currently, special regulations on the Amawalk Outlet allow the taking of three trout 10" or better on artificial lures only.

Amawalk's lower section, that water below the falls, is characterized by alternately sandy and rocky riffles, and hemlock-shaded runs. Several deep pools are for rent to any large browns looking for accomodations. Backcasting conditions are generally good, and hip boots are often all you need for wading. There are a few brookies, but mostly naturally-reproducing browns averaging 8-11 inches.

Per Brandin *guarantees* that you will hit the Amawalk's first important mayfly – the Hendrickson – if you visit the stream on April 29th (the permission he granted to quote him on that was vague). The Hendricksons are, in fact, the first important flies to hatch, and late April to early May is the time. Nymphs, emergers, duns and spinners can all work at various stages of the hatch; hook sizes should be 12-14. Blue Duns (Paraleptophlebia) are also early spring visitors, though they're less common. A tactic that has worked very well for me is mentioned in this chapter's opening vignette. The small muddler, fished as described, starts to produce as soon as the water warms enough to get the trout moving. A Gold-Ribbed Hare's Ear or a Hendrickson nymph would also be a good searching fly in spring when no naturals are coming off. One especially fine angler I know fishes Wooly Worms right on the bottom during cold water periods.

I once watched Amawalk ace Tony Jansic catch fish after fish on a bright day when I couldn't do a thing. Interrogation revealed that his secret fly was an "Amawalk Special." It is tied thusly:

Amawalk Special (Palmered Adams)
Hook: #16 Dry Fly
Hackle: One grizzly palmered over body; One grizzly and one
            dark ginger wound together up front
Tail: Dark ginger fibers
Thread: Black
Wings: None
Body: Gray Muskrat

The Adams, Henryville Special, and similar types of impressionistic patterns will also help you imitate the caddis that hatch quite prolifically from May onward. A dynamic caddis imitation that has burst on the scene recently is the Vermont Caddis. Be sure this fly is in your vest.

Ephemerella dorothea, the "sulphur" or "pale evening dun", has held up well on the Amawalk. The last week in May through two weeks of June is the peak time. The flies start coming off an hour or so before dark.

As summer wears on, smaller flies become necessary. A good selection of both creamy-colored flies and darkish flies in sizes 18-26 will help you cope with the doldrums, as will several compartments worth of ants, jassids, and small terrestrials. Remember that in summer, trout may lie in *very* shallow water, if it is well oxygenated. Ignore not the thinnest parcel of bubbly water.

In January of 1981, fuel oil tanks located near Hallocks Mill Brook were vandalized, allowing nearly 13,000 gallons of fuel oil to spill into the Amawalk Outlet. This spill had a devastating temporary effect, virtually wiping out the trout – which either died or migrated down to the lake – and the insect life. However, according to Dr. Sandy Fiance, an entomologist and Trout Unlimited member who has done much work on local streams, the Amawalk has come a long way back.

"The bugs," in his words "are all back." Prior to the spill, the trout in the lower section of the Amawalk (below the big dam) sustained themselves through natural reproduction. But since the spill, thousands of browns have been stocked in an attempt to restore the fishing. In the spring and summer of 1984, anglers found surprisingly good fishing, perhaps due to the decreased fishing pressure precipitated by the two poor previous seasons. Overall, it appears that if the Amawalk is not already fully recovered from the oil spill, it will be soon.

THE WEST BRANCH
Writing about fishing the West Branch is like watching a beauty contest: It only makes you wish you were part of the action. Hopefully, I'll finish this chapter by three so I can get up to the stream before the sulphurs start popping up.

No hatchery trucks pull up alongside this secluded brook and none need to. The brown trout here sustain themselves perfectly and there are great numbers of them. Another special regulations stream, current rules here allow the taking of five trout 9" or better.

About the best thing that can be said for their size is that they're good dipped in flour, egg and cornmeal then pan fried. Figure on two to three of these small brownies per diner, and don't be afraid to keep them. The West Branch can take the pressure.

Like the Amawalk, roads are pleasingly absent. The stream emanates from West Branch Reservoir at Rt. 6 and flows through a very shady and still unspoiled valley. Only near its terminus at Croton Falls Reservoir does another road come near it. Thus as shown in Fig. 5-c, you have two simple access options: Walk down from Route 6, or walk up from Drewville Road. There is parking at either end and logically, the farther you walk the more solitude you will find.

Startled Mallards honk, Ruffed Grouse drum, and occasional Woodcock whistle. What more could you ask for. It's a charming stream to fish.

April is a good month to catch "the skunk" on the West Branch. One, the water's cold. Two, the previously dependable early hatches (Hendricksons and Little Blue Quills) of several years ago seem to have disappeared. Why these good hatches have dried up and whether they will return are matters of conjecture. The bottom line now is this: Bring patience and nymphs in early season. Perhaps you will also have a little more luck than I have had with bucktails in this brook.

Come late May, things get interesting. Excellent numbers of sulphurs hatch from late May through June, and the browns rise freely and quite dependably to them. Extending up to nearly mid-July, the sulphur

TROUT FLIES
FOR LOCAL WATERS

Figure 5-b. Some Proven Patterns For Area Rivers.

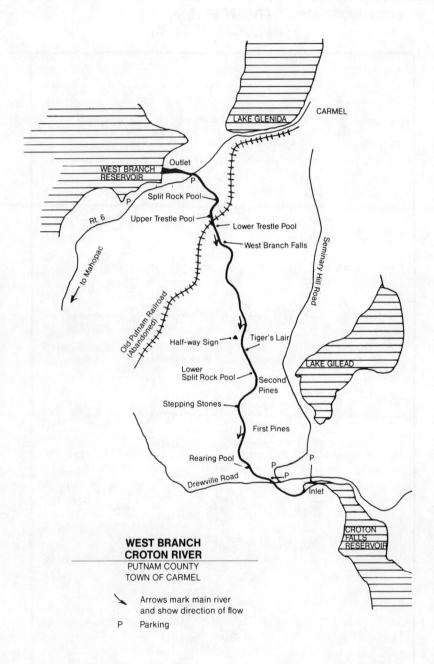

CARMEL

LAKE GLENIDA

WEST BRANCH RESERVOIR

Outlet

P

Split Rock Pool

P

Rt. 6

Upper Trestle Pool

Lower Trestle Pool

West Branch Falls

Seminary Hill Road

to Mahopac

Old Putnam Railroad (Abandoned)

Half-way Sign

Tiger's Lair

LAKE GILEAD

Lower Split Rock Pool

Second Pines

Stepping Stones

First Pines

Rearing Pool

P

P

P

Drewville Road

Inlet

CROTON FALLS RESERVOIR

WEST BRANCH CROTON RIVER

PUTNAM COUNTY
TOWN OF CARMEL

Arrows mark main river
and show direction of flow

P   Parking

Figure 5-c.

hatch is basically a 7-9 p.m. occurence. By all means bring a small light and fish those waning minutes of daylight (and into darkness) when hatching may actually intensify and trout become less cautious. Switch over to an all-white poly "loop wing" spinner for after dark work. You'll see it better and the fish will take it for a sulphur. Make the size correct, though. Flat wing poly spinners also work during this hatch, since the ovipositing adults appear right after the duns. Tie some with orange egg sacks.

A small, yellow stonefly dances over the West Branch from late May to September. Well imitated by a "Yellow Sally" tied fore and aft, size 16-18, it is a good hatch. Several species of caddis come and go during this time frame; a delta-wing caddis seems to work especially well at certain times. Study up on caddis imitations and try them all, matching size and color closely while experimenting with different silhouettes.

The foliage that overhangs a good deal of the West Branch drops a buffet of terrestrials into the water. Carry a good selection, especially in summer.

Though most browns here are small, electrofishing has revealed that some eye-popping reservoir fish ascend the West Branch in autumn. Fish of 5 pounds and better have been shocked or netted, and there are entertaining stories of much bigger fish having been landed. You do have a chance of hooking a big, early spawner in late September before the season closes, but spawning trout are notoriously tight-mouthed.

In 1978, a landmark fishing regulation was begun on the West Branch. This so-called "reverse limit" allowed the taking of five fish *under* 10 inches. It's intent was to see if culling more of the small trout could increase the average size of the browns and thus make for more interesting fishing. My studies of the Croton Watershed have shown that the trout in the entire West Branch drainage system have run very small, possibly due to the chemical foundation. Even the reservoir fish were notably long and thin before the appearance of sawbellies. In any event, the plan was discontinued at the end of 1981 after there was no appreciable increase in the size of the fish. I think the moral is clear: Enjoy the West Branch and its small trout, and accept it the way it is.

THE EAST BRANCH
Both the diversity of fly life and the diversity of water will challenge you on the East Branch of the Croton River. Often canopied by garish highway superstructures, the East Branch nonetheless flows cold, clean and inviting. Once rated among New York's "Fishiest 50" trout streams, it's a fine example of our good fishing close to home.

The "piece" of the East Branch we speak of here flows between East

Branch Reservoir and Diverting Reservoir, a length of about 2¼ miles. Fig. 5-d shows where to park and names the famous East Branch pools. This, too, is a special regulations stream where, currently, you can keep one trout of 14" or better (artificial lures only). Another section of the East Branch is discussed in Ch. 6.

You will encounter a wide spectrum of water types, including deep slow pools, shallow riffles, deep churning riffles, long silty flats and brushy backwaters. There are many angular, undercut rocks where browns of over 18 inches hide. This river has more character than either the Amawalk or the West Branch.

Although natural reproduction appears to be minimal, there are thousands of browns and rainbows stocked annually. The fish caught average a hefty 12" or so, but 14-16 inchers are far from uncommon. In looking the stream over, you're liable to muse, "There's *gotta be* a few three and four pounders in this stream." Well, you can think in even grander terms than that.

On the evening of July 28, 1983, Scarsdale angler Al Case was swishing a Grey Ghost streamer through the East Branch's famous Phoebe Hole. Earlier in the season, serious local fly fishermen had reportedly glimpsed "something big" in this area of the river. But I doubt even those reports prepared Al for the monster that came out of the shadows to inhale his fly. As Casey Stengel once observed, "you can look it up", because the brown Al caught – 10 pounds 13 ounces of him – now stands as an IGFA World Record on four pound test tippet!

Fine insights into fishing a good spring hatch on this river – the midge hatch – can be found in Ernest Schwiebert's book *Nymphs*. Midging is a subtle and demanding art, and he covers it well in his unnumbered chapter titled "Tiny Two-Winged Diptera And The Smutting Rise." Often, tiny pupal imitations fished in or just below the surface film will outperform hackled patterns. Hook sizes for these minute Diptera imitations should be 20-26. The naturals are sometimes already on the water when April 1st rolls around, but midge hatches may occur on the East Branch throughout the season.

Also in evidence when the Trout Lillies bloom are several species of Blue Winged Olives (Baetis) and also Little Blue Quills (Paraleptophlebia). The former average size 16-20, the latter size 16-18. The minnow life in the East Branch is excellent, so bucktails and streamers in a variety of sizes and patterns are well worth toting in early spring and whenever the water is up and murky. Some bucktails that have proven themselves on the East Branch are the Muddler Minnow, Marabou Muddler, Black Ghost and several of the Thunder Creek

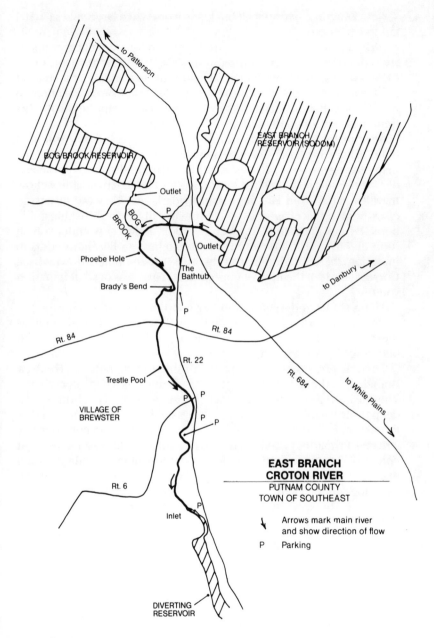

to Patterson

BOG BROOK RESERVOIR

EAST BRANCH
RESERVOIR (SODOM)

Outlet

P

BOG BROOK

Phoebe Hole

P

Outlet

The Bathtub

Brady's Bend

P

to Danbury

Rt. 84

Rt. 84

Rt. 22

Rt. 684

to White Plains

Trestle Pool

VILLAGE OF
BREWSTER

P   P

P   P

Rt. 6

Inlet

P

DIVERTING
RESERVOIR

**EAST BRANCH
CROTON RIVER**
PUTNAM COUNTY
TOWN OF SOUTHEAST

↓   Arrows mark main river
    and show direction of flow

P   Parking

Figure 5-d.

series. Sometimes, very small bucktails work when larger sizes (4-10) fail to get a nod.

Although the closely-related mayflies often lumped together under the common name Hendrickson are less abundant than on other local streams, they nonetheless are present on the East Branch or at least certain sections of it. One recent report I got from an East Branch regular was that the Hendricksons were sparse except below Brady's Bend where very good numbers were observed.

Also in May, a smallish tan caddis (16-18) starts buzzing around. I once fished this hatch for weeks on end in The Bathtub pool (see map), luring many nice trout with an Elk Hair Caddis. Towards the end of May, the sulphurs help the action along. These dependable, yellow mayflies hatch from late afternoon to dark, and they are discussed elsewhere in this chapter as well as in virtually every fly fishing guide book. By most accounts, the better caddis action gets under way in June, and to repeat: I believe it's tough to beat an Elk Hair Caddis in imitating these predominantly tannish, green-bodied downwings. Correct size is of the utmost importance, regardless of what imitation you use.

Along about mid-August, another good mayfly hatch appears, the microscopic "Tricos." Plan on being at the stream early, though, as these size 22-26 flies start emerging around 6:30 a.m. (even if the better action may be a little later).

There is one other very important thing to take note of: The East Branch, like the Amawalk and the West Branch, is a tailwater stream. This means that at least part of its flow comes off from the bottom of a deep reservoir where the water is always cold. This further means that the stream will flow considerably colder in summer than non-tailwater streams. Primarily, of course, this strengthens the fishery and lets you enjoy good trout angling even during the July-August doldrums when many other local waters are too hot. Another implication is that the hatching schedules of certain insects may be thrown off.

Fig. 5-b shows some of the flies that have proven themselves on these Westchester/Putnam waters. Many of these are discussed or mentioned in this chapter, and also in Ch. 18.

6.
THE OTHER CONNECTING RIVERS

"When love is evergreen, evergreen,
It will last, through the summer,
And winter too.

When love is evergreen, evergreen,
Like my love for you."

Roy Orbison is a true romantic, I thought, as I turned off the eight track and pulled up along Cross River Outlet. Then I thought how well the song applied to fishing and hunting. Now, again, the season was about to change . . . but I knew summer had a few good trout left in it before the first woodcock rode in on the moon.

How much Brown Trout spawning goes on in local waters is an interesting question. In some streams, like Amawalk and West Branch, there is excellent reproduction. But do the reservoir browns ritualistically run up all the feeders, even those where a successful spawn would be impossible?

The water ran dark and cool, and the first fish hit my salted minnow like a ton. In September, they always hit like that. And this 13-incher, like other equinoctal specimens, seemed a little brighter, firmer, and longer than the average mid-season fish.

I worked downstream, twitching the 2-inch long minnows through swirls and eddies where bright crimson leaves were collecting. Eleven to twelve inch browns, three of them, gathered in my creel, and were startled when I dropped a 10-inch crappie on top of them. When I got to where the stream meets lake, I took out a 4-inch Rebel to see if any largemouth had moved into the inlet for the cooler water. Just as I edged into casting position, a loud whistling "Whir-r-r!" knocked me off balance. Woodcock! Then I thought about the date. Ten more days and we'd be in Maine, in Biscuit's bird hunting camp. Kneeling in the mud, I cleaned my fish and smiled. True love really is evergreen.

ONE OF AT LEAST 15 trout-holding streams of the Croton Watershed – exclusive of the three discussed in Ch. 5 – Cross River Outlet is interesting. It's a lot like Titicus Outlet, only a little nicer. It's one of those local streams that seems to attract me in September.

Don't let its shortness fool you . . . there are often some nice trout here. First, the over and underflow from the reservoir keeps the water temperature cool nearly all the time. Second, the lower end blends into Muscoot to form a nice, long inlet area. In between, you never know what to expect. Trout, bass and crappies launch their attacks from deep, frothy pools, fallen logs and undercut banks. Right now, *something* is waiting to smash your lure.

As mentioned many times throughout this book, inlet areas of reservoirs can be explosive. A boat is the best way to fish the inlet area. Just up from the inlet proper, there is a fine section that is still slow, somewhat swampy, and brushy to the bank. Largemouths cruise freely in and out of this section, but to catch them you must approach the stream stealthily. Foot-long and longer smallmouths are found throughout the stream, and may also migrate back and forth from the lake.

As with Titicus Outlet, the upper end is off limits. Unfortunately, it appears as if the off-limits "yellow sign" area has been extended downstream. Further, I have found this stream very murky and even grossly discolored on two separate recent occasions.

Since there are now fewer pools, it is important to fish each one carefully. Here's how.

First, fish from one side of the pool, moving very slowly from top to bottom. You'll find that you get a sightly different drift at each "station." Then, cross the stream and do the same thing from the other bank. Especially when it's cold and the fish are sluggish, a minutely different drift of the bait or lure can make all the difference.

To reach Cross River Outlet, get yourself to the northern terminus of the Saw Mill River Parkway where it meets Rt. 35. Take Rt. 35 east for a mile or so and you will see parking spaces on the right before you get to the Cross River Reservoir dam.

HUNTER BROOK

If Wordsworth or any of his romantic counterparts could have visited a particular back section of Croton Reservoir, the result would surely have been "Ode On Hunter Brook." This modest-sized trib is replete with tumbling little rapids, majestic sentinel conifers, Ospreys and impressive quietude. There are even trout.

The essentially shallow nature of Hunter Brook limits its potential. An average of 600 8-inch brookies are stocked every year, and some may make it to the following spring. However, the fishing must be considered essentially put and take.

This stream, it seems to me, was put there for young boys to explore. Although it actually extends north beyond Rt. 202, the best section is from that road down to Croton Reservoir – a beautiful five miles untouched by roads but widely used by a fascinating mix of wildlife. Ultralight spinning will help you negotiate this brook, much of which gets heavily overgrown in summer. Small garden worms have worked best for me, followed closely by tiny lures. Where Hunter Brook enters the reservoir, there is a large, deep pool that should not be ignored. In summer, bass may congregate here for the cooler water, as may Calico Bass. At certain times, especially in mid-Spring, large carp bunch up at the head of the pool just below the white water. They are taken with worms, but more commonly with bow and arrow and even such nefarious means as snatch-hooking. Try under the bridge here for calicos and perch.

Best parking is by the little bridge where Hunter Brook enters Croton Reservoir. This arm of Croton, inside Hunter Brook Bridge, has a road around it. Access is off of Rt. 129.

PER BRANDIN

Many streams of the Croton Watershed are tailor made for the spin fisherman. Author took these two brookies from the East Branch Croton.

TITICUS OUTLET

It always hits the fan on a rainy day, or so it seems. It was noonish on a dreary day in mid-May when Jim Booth's '57 Chevy pulled up in front of my house. Back in those teen-age days, Jimmy and I had a fierce fishing rivalry, and I'm not sure what insult he tossed at me as he pointed to the floor of the car on the passenger side. There, laid out side by side, were five browns averaging 16 inches – all dark, streamlined, and incredibly beautiful like only stream trout can be.

"Titicus Outlet," he smirked. "They're bitin' like hell."

I called him a liar, then dashed down to the garage to get my rod and reel. In 30 minutes we were back on the stream, but the sun had come out and all we caught were a few small ones. Were his outsized brownies true resident fish? Were they "breeders" put in as part of a "sneak stock" by the conservation department (a phenomenon I've often heard about but never really witnessed. Supposedly, these sneak stocks involve breeder fish that are no longer fertile or useful). To this day, we'll never know. Titicus Outlet, while quite boring 9 days out of 10, is capable of some interesting surprises.

This is a rocky, shaded and quite shallow stream except for a few nice pools you should come to know. Technically, you're not allowed to fish just below the dam, but there are twin pools formed by a pipe and a reservoir overflow respectively. Just below this are two or three more pools, very deep and inviting even in summer. The next piece of good holding water is from the bridge down to Muscoot Reservoir. The bridge pool is nice, and there are often some chunky largemouths in this section, especially around the mouth of the stream.

Jimmy made his extraordinary catch with a Gold Mepps spinner, a lure that seems to work well. The bass at the lower end respond to a smallish Rebel twitched enticingly. Try this stream during rainstorms. In September, I've caught some handsome fish – dressed in spawning colors – that found my salted minnows to their liking.

Parking will be found at the bridge where Rt. 116 crosses the river. This is just east of Interstate Rt. 684.

CROTON FALLS OUTLET

Perhaps there was a day when Croton Falls Outlet *wasn't* running pretty and full to the bank. If so, I missed it. It's a good place to go for some interesting fishing, and especially in summer when other local streams dry up.

Water from Croton Falls Reservoir bubbles over *and* under a mammoth dam, and creates this one-mile segment of the West Branch Croton (see lower East Branch map). You can't fish from the dam down to the first bridge. The open water is thus from that bridge down to the stream's confluence with the East Branch just below the Rt. 100 bridge.

Although recent state stocking reports do not mention this stream, I always catch a few bland-looking, white-fleshed trout that are unmistakably "stockers." Happily, many of the browns in here are apparently *not* extracted, and thus grow to respectable sizes. Large, lake-run browns would also seem to be an occasional possibility, though I have no proof of it, (again, though, think rainstorms and late September). It's equally nice to know that river smallmouths (ounce for ounce, pound for pound, etc.) live in the outlet, and will gladly smash your bucktail or Mepps spinner. A few largemouths, and the usual mix of panfish round out the register.

Croton Falls Outlet must be fished slowly and deliberately. There is more to this river than meets the eye. The fish, for some reason, seem to be abnormally concentrated in a few, particular stretches, some of which do not even appear to be good holding lies. If you catch a fish, stay put, and remember that spot.

Bucktails, spinners and salted minnows are good enticements, and all work as well on the trout as on the smallmouths. Two good pools are by the upper bridge, and then about 30 yards below this bridge. The riffle that stitches these two pools together also holds fish. Some 75 yards downstream, there is a long shallow riffle that nearly always produces a few browns for me. It is very shallow, but fast. The pool below this riffle is one of the deepest in the river and should be fished thoroughly.

An especially interesting section is from the Rt. 100 bridge down to Muscoot Reservoir. It is slow and silent, completely unfished by my observations, and hard to approach from shore. Give this section a try. Float-fishing from a raft or small boat would be a good tactic.

MAIN BRANCH CROTON

This is a stream for those anglers looking for something a little bit different. Extending from New Croton ("Cornell") Dam down to the Hudson River, it can be a raging white river in spring or a nearly bone-dry gulch in summer. Between those two extremes – and even during them – the fishing can sometimes be interesting.

This, the last leg of the bountiful Croton River, gets a modest stocking of about 700 small browns and brookies, and I believe some of those browns do hold over for several years (in this area, you can figure on pretty much zero holdover of stocked brookies). Don't let the frighteningly low water levels of summer scare you away. Every so

Many anglers are surprised by the excellent fly fishing that can be found close to New York City.

often a brown that cracks the 3-pound mark is tallied here, and this is no doubt attributable to the several extremely deep pools. Apparently, the bigger fish successfully migrate to these deep pools when the water begins to drop. When it comes up again, they can be found anywhere.

If you chuck out a spinning lure hoping for trout, don't be surprised if you come up with a striped bass or even, possibly, a shad! Plentiful in the Hudson, these two salty gamesters have been witnessed in the Croton River all the way up to the dam. In addition, both Smallmouth and Largemouth Bass, as well as panfish, are present.

The area around the dam is a county park, and as long as its open, you can park in the big lot off Rt. 129 and fish your way down. A parking fee is collected at certain times. However there are also two or three small pullovers between the dam and Quaker Bridge Road where you can park for free. This entire upper section comprises some nice water.

Below Quaker Bridge Road, the Croton River drops into a progressively steeper gorge, and here too the angling can be interesting. To gain access, you will have to park wherever you can along village streets and hike down in. The lowest end of the stream becomes tidal, and here you may encounter stripers, black bass and thick schools of spawning smelt and herring in the spring. This lower end is best accessed by running up from the Croton Trestle in a small boat or canoe.

To reach the Croton River, take Rt. 129 for a few miles east of the village of Croton-on-Hudson.

STONE HILL RIVER

While visiting the Stone Hill recently, after an absence of several years, I was glad to see a DEC sign prominently displayed on Beaver Dam Road: "Public Fishing Area. For Hiking, Horseback Riding and Fishing in Season." For a span of time in previous years the stream had been closed to all but Bedford residents.

Although the Stone Hill is a fairly lengthy stream, most of the water upstream of Beaver Dam Road is posted. It's possible that there is some open water upstream and east of Rt. 121, and this would be worth checking into. The headwaters lie in Ward Pound Ridge Reservation, where fishing is allowed.

The piece we speak of here is the mile and a half between Beaver Dam Road and Muscoot Reservoir. The water is pretty and there are even some surprisingly good fly hatches in late spring and summer. Not only can browns move up from Muscoot, but nice trout also drift down from the upper section which is or at least was, privately stocked. By the way, the section of the Stone Hill *below* the Saw Mill River Parkway is very lightly fished since there is no easy parking down there.

This is another one of those streams that seems to come to life during heavy rains. At such times, worms, salted minnows and spinners work best. If you find yourself on the stream in mid-April, you can harvest a fine free meal in the form of fiddlehead ferns. Walk down from Beaver Dam Road till you get to where the stream bends sharply to the left. On the left, there is a swampy area where the tender greens grow in abundance.

Access to this stream is via Harris Rd. off the Saw Mill River Parkway.

THE LOWER EAST BRANCH

In the previous chapter, we discussed the special regulations area of the East Branch – that section between East Branch and Diverting reservoirs. That is where most of the fly fishermen congregate. Yet there is another section, one suited to both fly *and* spin fishing. It's that segment from Diverting down to Muscoot Reservoir . . . about 3 miles. I heartily recommend this segment to you, especially during or just after a heavy summer rain.

Even during the worst droughts, there are plenty of pools where the

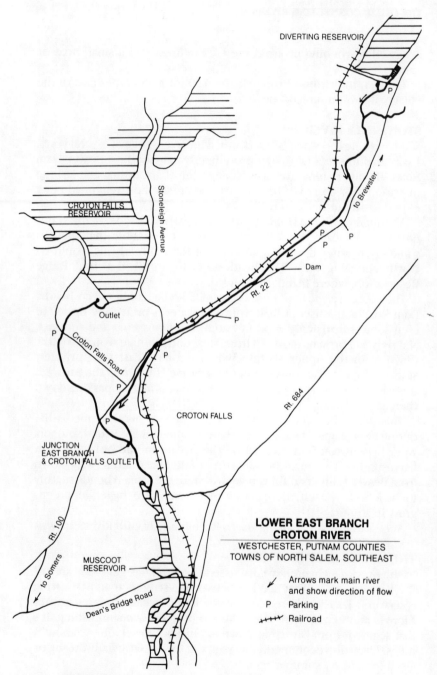

DIVERTING RESERVOIR

to Brewster

CROTON FALLS
RESERVOIR

Stoneleigh Avenue

Dam

Rt. 22

Outlet

Croton Falls Road

P

Rt. 684

CROTON FALLS

JUNCTION
EAST BRANCH
& CROTON FALLS OUTLET

Rt. 100

to Somers

MUSCOOT
RESERVOIR

Dean's Bridge Road

**LOWER EAST BRANCH
CROTON RIVER**
WESTCHESTER, PUTNAM COUNTIES
TOWNS OF NORTH SALEM, SOUTHEAST

Arrows mark main river
and show direction of flow

P   Parking

+++++   Railroad

Figure 6-a.

water remains waist-deep or deeper. This stream has holding power, as witnessed by the 3½-pound brown seduced by friend Bill Schweizer just above the railroad trestle.

This segment of the East Branch has two fairly distinct sections. Above the big dam (see fig. 6-a), the stream is relatively slow and smooth, even a bit swampy in places. Limited access keeps the crowds somewhat away. Below the dam, the stream is markedly faster and rockier. While wading here is difficult, access is not so this section gets more pressure.

In the upper section, there is a waterfall and a nice pool just below Diverting, and then a couple of more nice pools just below that. Probably the best way to get at this upper section is by parking at Diverting then wading down. To fish the east bank, park in one of the several pulloffs along Rt. 22 as marked on the map.

A few hundred yards or so below the big dam is a broad pool where water tumbles in from a broken pipe. A few years ago, I had some good fly-fishing here to a hatch of small sulphur mayflies. Don't think that fly hatches are restricted to the special regs section above Diverting. From the bridge just below that pool down to Rt. 100, the water is very fast, and slippery jagged rocks make wading difficult. This is water capable of holding some hefty fish.

From that first Rt. 100 bridge down to the stream's junction with Croton Falls Outlet the East Branch is moderately fast and nice looking, but heavily fished since it runs right next to the road. A slow, deep and quiet section that hardly anyone fishes is from the junction with Croton Falls Outlet down to Muscoot Reservoir. Using two cars, you could canoe or boat this section all the way down to the first bridge over Muscoot, and you are liable to find some very interesting fishing for trout, bass, pickerel and panfish.

CROSS RIVER (CROSS RIVER INLET)

There is an axiom in trout management that the fishholding power of a river is largely determined by the purity of its headwater drainage area. Cross River has a big advantage here: A large portion of its upper drainage is protected in perpetuity, thanks to its location within sprawling Ward Pound Ridge Reservation (Westchester's largest park).

Trout Unlimited's Croton Watershed Chapter got interested in this stream four years ago, and where there is TU there are fly hatches. Yet not only are there mayflies in fair abundance, there is also some very pretty water not very heavily fished. TU was the force behind the instigation of a "no-kill" section on this stream, as marked in fig. 6-b. TU now does stream improvement work on this river.

The variety of the water is very pleasant. Some segments are rocky and fast, others slower and brushy. Browns are stocked, but there is definitely some natural reproduction of browns, too (perhaps quite a bit). There are a lot of brookies and apparently these are all natives since none are stocked. The insect population is varied, and mayflies seem to predominate. The presence of mayflies is a sure indicator of good water quality, and it's a happy twist in this age of caddisflies, terrestrials and other bugs that seem better able to adapt to pollution. Good hatches here include Hendrickson, Grey Fox, and sulphurs. Isonychia, Stenonema and even pure-water loving Epeorus nymphs have been collected in the faster runs, so there may be even more different hatches than most fishermen yet know about.

A notably limiting factor at Cross River is high water temperatures in summer – even though springs do enter to provide life-supporting refuge for the trout. Thus, it may be that this stream is best fished early in the season. That is the way we have found it the past few years. Perhaps because of the warmer water, the hatches do seem to arrive a little ahead of schedule.

The very lower end of the river is a good place for bait fishing. Large browns can be and have been taken. In the upper section, trout of up to about 14" are creeled, but most are smaller. The fish, though, display some incredibly beautiful coloration. Above Kimberly Bridge the water is quite small, and this is brook trout country. Rumor has it that, hiding in the swampy headwaters, are native brookies that no angler ever sees due to virtual inaccessibility. Float tubes, anyone?

Note: This is sometimes called the Waccabuc River though, properly, the Waccabuc is a tributary to the Cross River. It is mentioned toward the end of this chapter.

KISCO RIVER
Perhaps you'll have more luck on this pretty-looking brook than I've had. It's a fair-sized stream and is, in fact, Croton Reservoir's largest tributary. Since Croton is not a trout lake, any fish in the stream are true stream fish, either stocked or wild.

Stocking reports from a few years back indicated that this brook did receive fish. However the 1983 report, reproduced in full in the reference section, no longer lists the Kisco River. Why this is I do not know.

This stream essentially begins at Howlands Lake, east of Mt. Kisco and just south of Rt. 172. It starts to look like a bonafide trout stream about where it passes under Rt. 17 right near downtown Mt. Kisco.

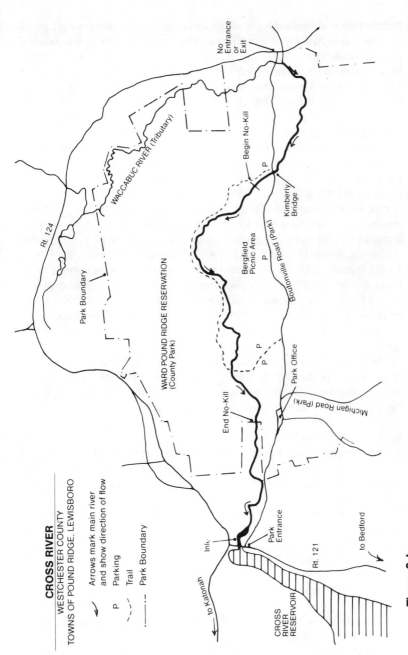

CROSS RIVER
WESTCHESTER COUNTY
TOWNS OF POUND RIDGE, LEWISBORO

↘ Arrows mark river main river
and show direction of flow

P   Parking

– / – Trail

– · – Park Boundary

Figure 6-b.

Below this it drops into a swamp and is joined by three other small brooks. I got curious about this stream early this spring, and started tracking down its headwaters. It is fed by Chappaqua Brook, a swampy little feeder that parallels the Saw Mill River Parkway from just north of Pleasantville to a point about one mile north of Reader's Digest Road. Here, Chappaqua joins the Kisco River and just above and below this junction is some very deep water. It's likely that very, very few people explore this area. It is just west of the Harlem Railroad tracks, and also just west of Oakwood Cemetary. If you cannot find parking in or around the cemetary, park where you can in Mt. Kisco and walk the tracks down. Alternatively, you can park on the little pulloff where the railroad tracks pass the Reader's Digest and walk up.

Just downstream of the above-named junction, the Kisco River passes under the Saw Mill River Parkway. The stream grows quickly here, and starts to weave in and out of residential areas. Probably the nicest section is that one mile segment just above Croton Reservoir. There is parking by the inlet, and also on side streets that shoot off of Pines Bridge Road. You can also park on Croton Avenue just north of Rt. 133. I've taken browns and brookies of up to about 12" in this lower section, and I have heard of slightly bigger ones brought to net. I should also say that I have been skunked here more times than I've scored.

The Kisco River drains a very highly developed area, and there is more new construction all the time. Give it a try anyway. There may be some native brookies in that headwater area, and downstream there have to be a few nice browns.

SMALL BROOKS
Adventure can be poking about for lions deep in the forests of Kenya. It can also be poking about for trout, in solitude, on some of the smaller streams of the Croton Watershed. Sometimes the best things happen on a small scale.

These small, intimate brooks are scattered about the drainage system, and the following list is by no means all-inclusive. First, though, are some random tips on fishing small brooks.
1. Trout become unbelievably spooky in small waters where they know they are vulnerable. A careful approach at all times is recommended.
2. Little brooks are best fished on rainy days. Resident fish lose much of their caution, and larger, migratory fish from the main river or reservoir often appear like magic.
3. Very small water can hold some *very* large fish. Locate a big fish, then try for him at night or during heavy rains.

PER BRANDIN

4. There are usually not only *bigger* fish, but also *more* fish in a small brook than you realize.
5. Examine all bridges that span small streams. Often, bridge pools are among the few places where deep water can be found.
6. After you approach the banks of a small stream, wait as long as you can before presenting your lure. This gives spooked fish a chance to settle down.
7. Undercut banks can become very important holding lies on small streams.
8. Though bait is the overall best bet, some lures will work. Where casting is difficult or impossible, use lures that can be held to twist and dodge in the current (The Super Duper and Daredevle are two).

I make no promises for the following waters. Most are very small, but some do hold trout on a year-round basis. During high water periods, these little brooks may hold bigger fish that migrate up from a reservoir or larger stream.

TITICUS INLET (TITICUS RIVER). This is a small stream of interesting water variety. Feeding Titicus Reservoir, it flows from its headwaters in Connecticut through the farm and horse country of North Salem.

From the Reservoir up to the junction of Rts. 116 and 121, Titicus Inlet is alternately swampy and rocky. There is more than ample water for trout to holdover from year to year. Above this junction, where the stream is smaller, there are a few amazingly deep pools and the stream widens into a pond in one or two places. Watch for posted signs.

HORSE POUND BROOK. On a first-time visit to this secluded little stream recently, I saw fish (native brookies I believe) darting for cover, Woodcock chalk on the wet October leaves, and a Great Blue Heron winging out ahead of me. Nestled way back in the woods, and known to few fishermen, this small brook is worth a visit.

The stream is reminiscent of a Maine flowage: Slow, smooth and alder choked. Unfortunately it's quite shallow. There are no roads anywhere near it. The hidden back arm of West Branch Reservoir, into which it runs, is also inviting, and would be an excellent spot for shore fishermen seeking a little off-the-beaten-path solitude. Gain access from Nichol's Road near Carmel.

THE UPPER MIDDLE BRANCH. Here we are speaking about that stream segment above Middle Branch Reservoir. Like the West Branch, the headwaters of the Middle Branch are semi-swampy, fairly slow, and fun to explore if you like that kind of thing. Even above the Kent Highway garage, just off Rt. 311, the little Middle Branch maintains adequate flows (ultralight spinning with bait would be recommended).

PER BRANDIN

Fly rodding for bluegills and other panfish is highly overlooked in this region — both in the streams and the reservoirs.

Just below this, it flows into Lake Carmel. The bottom section, below Fair Street, is much more vertical and rocky, but here the stream leaves the road for a stretch. This always makes for more pleasant fishing.

BOYD'S CORNERS OUTLET. Most of what was once Boyds Corners Reservoir is now a stream. Some years ago, this reservoir was drained and now only a little pond remains. If the reservoir is not eventually refilled, it is possible that this section will become viable trout water again. In any event, the short ¾ mile section *below* Boyds Corners Dam is most interesting. Large browns move up into it in fall, and I have also caught big largemouths at the bottom of the stream in springtime. Although it is not stocked, it is probable that there are some resident trout in this nice looking brook. It is open enough for both spin and fly fishing. Gain access from Rt. 301 just below Kent Cliffs. Parking is no problem.

PLUM BROOK. This is a picturesque little feeder that enters Muscoot Reservoir two miles south of Somers. Park at the Rt. 100 bridge, and gain access to the stream by walking up the cinder path just north of the bridge. This old railroad bed follows the stream for a mile or so.

The best water is from the bridge up to the first lake. There are no eyesore roads here, but there are some nice deep pools shrouded by thick alders in summer. You can count on having Plum brook to yourself much of the time. This particular area is still undeveloped.

HALLOCK'S MILL. The overall character of the Amawalk Outlet extends up into this tributary, and it is a nice brook. It enters the popular Amawalk just below the dam.

Unfortunately, there is now a sewage treatment plant located on the banks of Hallock's Mill. This and the fairly new string of telephone poles and houses have detracted much from this once idyllic-looking stream. Coursing through thick stands of conifers, the lower end of Hallock's Mill may still harbor trout that either reside there or migrate up from the main river. To locate this brook, see the Amawalk Outlet map.

ANGLE FLY BROOK. Judging by the evasive answers and sly glances I got from local residents, this Muscoot Reservoir feeder may be a sleeper. I have long heard that reservoir browns move up into Angle Fly when it is swollen from heavy rains. Yet on a late-season, low-water hike along the stream, I saw many trout darting into the rocks. So there may be a fair number of resident fish, too.

Above Rt. 35, the stream is small, but there are still holding lies . . . even in late summer. You can gain access to the lower end by walking up from Muscoot Reservoir. Or, park along Rt. 35 where you can, and walk up or down. Posting makes access somewhat difficult. Consider asking permission from residents. For location, see the Amawalk Outlet map.

MUSCOOT RIVER (AMAWALK INLET). Amawalk Outlet (Ch. 5) is properly regarded as one of the best streams in the area. At the north end of Amawalk Reservoir there is another stream. It's not as big and it's not as good, but it's not worth ignoring either. Friends who fish it more than I do report occasionally good action, and it does get a stocking of several hundred fish per year. It also gets some fairly heavy pressure, though. Park by the reservoir at Rt. 202 and walk up. There are no roads near this section. Alternatively, you can park near the jct. of Rt. 6 and Mahopac Avenue and fish up or down. While the water is smaller, there still are some nice holding lies. This is more than a little brook, and rightfully it could have been placed in the preceding section.

WACCABUC RIVER. This is a tributary to Cross River (or Cross River Inlet if you prefer) discussed earlier in this chapter. It flows south from Lake Waccabuc and meets the Ward Pound Ridge Reservation a few miles later. This upper section is fairly small, and in many places alder-choked. Access to this part is off of Bouton Road and Post Office

Even many of the small brooks of the Croton Watershed contain trout. All you need is a short rod and a little exploring spirit.

Road just north of Rt. 35. There is a parking space right at Rt. 35 just west of Bouton Road. Here, where the stream goes under the road, is a very nice pool. There is also some nice water above and below Rt. 35, but watch for posted signs. Just below the bridge the stream enters the park. Unfortunately, it is quite swampy and brushy from this point down to where it meets Cross River near the eastern terminus of the park. If you're willing to fight back the brush, you may encounter native brookies or browns in this section.

PART II

MORE GOOD FISHING IN WESTCHESTER AND PUTNAM

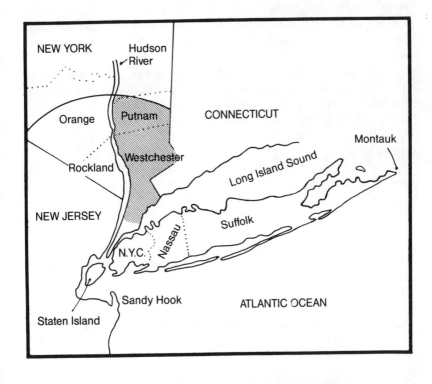

7.
A QUARTET OF
INTERESTING
BROOKS

It's an episode that sits perfect in my memory. I have a witness, too — Artie Venier. He watched it all from the car.

It was pouring, not just drizzling, when we got to the Peekskill Hollow Brook that late April day. Just over the bridge at the mailbox marked "L. Nathan" I parked the old Chevy, then slipped into my rainsuit and started fishing upstream. Through steamy glass, Artie eyed me between gulps of coffee, and I eyed him between flips of my little garden worm. We each knew what the other was thinking.

One of the biggest skills in worm fishing is discerning bottom snags from strikes. This time, though — when I flipped my worm beneath the big rock — there was no doubt.

At once, the battle moved into the fast riffles beneath the boulder, and after ten seconds or so, I knew I was into a weighty fish. There really was no quieter water to lead him into, so I kept trying to maneuver the fish upstream so I could net him as he drifted back down. I'll never forget the moment when I saw that it was a trout, not a sucker. Or the moment when the #8 Eagle Claw popped out of his jaw just as I hoisted him up in the net.

An eighteen-inch brown is a big fish from a little stream . . . especially for a sixteen year old boy. But as my father often reminded me when I was small, "you can't catch fish unless your line is in the water."

THE PEEKSKILL HOLLOW Brook is the largest brook in the area that is *not* part of the Croton Watershed. It rises from a swamp east of the Taconic Parkway and flows on a fairly steady southwesterly course for about 16 miles before meeting the Hudson River near Peekskill.

I wish the report on the Hollow Brook could be better. This was one of the first streams my father took me to when I was a boy, and back then, in the early sixties, it was pretty as a picture. The river itself hasn't changed much, but development in the valley has gone on slowly and relentlessly. There is more garbage in the river now, and more new houses near the river (especially above Adams Corners, the stretch I used to like). Still, plenty of nice browns are caught every year and while it's doubtful that there is much if any natural reproduction, there is certainly considerable holdover of stocked browns (a few rainbows are also planted). How you feel about the Hollow Brook now will depend on how important aesthetics are to you and whether you remember it in its gentler days.

The Hollow Brook is a good bait stream. For much of its length, it is a mountain-type stream – rocky, bubbling and fast flowing. However, there are quiet, silty sections and the upper end is more like a meadow stream. I've never had great luck with lures here. Worms and salted minnows are the first weapons I would deploy. However, good friends do well here with lures and I would certainly knot on a spinner after a good rainstorm.

I've never noticed any fly hatches to speak of. One evening I did see a fair fall of stoneflies. But I'll admit that I fished this stream mainly before I got interested in fly fishing. There may be some modest fly life, even though very, very few fly anglers will be observed.

The lower end of the Hollow Brook is tidal. Poking your way in among the willows and the locust you are apt to catch white perch, blue claw crabs, herring and other brackish creatures in their respective seasons.

Not far above the Hudson, the Hollow Brook already looks like a trout stream. At Gallows Hill Road there is a sharp looking pool and an obliging parking spot on the west side of the creek. From Gallows Hill Road all the way past the drive-in and up to Oregon Corners it is somewhat secluded and woodsy, though some houses and side roads are adjacent. Besides Gallows Hill Road, access to this section is via side streets that run off of Oregon Road. Two of these are Adams Rush St. and Corlandt Avenue, opposite the Hillside Cemetary.

From Oregon Corners upstream to Adams Corners there are several youth camps and a few new houses, but also some nice water. I like the section just above the first bridge above Oregon Corners. You can park by that bridge or else make your first left past the bridge and follow the dirt road down to the stream.

From Adams Corners to Tompkins Corners there are a few remaining farms, but also new houses. As of a recent visit, there were no posted signs at Bryant Pond Road, and there is some nice water at that bridge and downstream from it. Above this road, there are a few old shacks as well as a few new log homes, and there may be some place to peek in among the private sections.

Above Tompkins Corners the Hollow Brook is increasingly swampy and I have often heard of some native brookies in this section. You might try just east and west of the Taconic Parkway. There is plenty of parking here, but watch out for posted signs.

This is one of the very few trout streams in the area with an extended season. You can legally fish the Hollow Brook for trout up to November 30th.

THE SAW MILL

I would give much to know what the Saw Mill River looked like a hundred years ago. Gliding gently through the unspoiled Westchester countryside, it must have been the classic meadow stream: Low gradient, undercut banks, draping foliage much of the way. Its essence remains today, and there are still trout, But all too often nowadays, the prime holding lies are shopping carts.

This stream emanates from a pond just west of the parkway near the village of Chappaqua and flows nearly twenty miles before meeting the Hudson at Yonkers. Let's look at the different sections and what they have to offer.

From Chappaqua down to the middle of Pleasantville, the stream is very small. While there are a few decent pools, this section has recently been upset by new construction. In summer, this piece is very shallow.

PER BRANDIN

From Pleasantville to the Hawthorne Circle, the Saw Mill is a little deeper, especially from the Thornwood traffic light down to the circle, where the stream runs adjacent to Graham Hills Park. As with the upper section, parking is available on nearby village streets.

Definitely the nicest remaining section is from the Hawthorne Circle down to Eastview. Flowing at one point through pretty Rosedale Nurseries, the Saw Mill here rides hard against a steep ridge that forms the eastern limit of the Rockefeller estate. It is very shady and the water runs cool and nice. Parking is where-you-find-it along nearby Rt. 9A (the somewhat difficult parking keeps the fishing pressure light).

At Eastview, the Saw Mill is swallowed by the sprawling Union Carbide complex, and then carefully picks its way through the industrial parks and junkyards that characterize Elmsford. However, just below Elmsford, the stream again becomes a little secluded. Even south of Ardsley, there is some very pretty water.

Maybe the best thing the Saw Mill has going for it these days is the fact that many anglers now "cast beyond it," looking upstate for better fishing. The river still gets an amazing quota of about 3500 fish annually, and many of these trout winter-over very well due to the now light fishing pressure.

A colorful old character named Joe Burla, who took me fishing a lot when I was a kid, really knew how to fish the Saw Mill. He used an old glass flyrod to work his garden worms into and under the hanging brush where the trout lie in wait. Finding the good holding lies and coping with the heavy overgrowth are the secrets here. And what's a shopping cart or two when you're catching trout so close to home!

THE MIANUS RIVER

The Mianus rises just west of Armonk, flows north, turns on itself at the village of Bedford then flows south to eventually empty into Long Island Sound. For the fisherman, the noteworthy reach of this stream is that 2½-mile section lying within the *Mianus River Gorge Wildlife Refuge And Botanical Preserve.*

The privately owned and funded Mianus Gorge is "being maintained as a 'wilderness island' on which nature, including all plants and animals, may live so far as possible free from any interference by man directly or indirectly." Worth a visit even if you don't fish, the gorge is open daily from 9:30 to 5:30 from April 1st-December 1st, and there is no admission charge (do support the Gorge with your contributions, though).

The river is stocked with trout (about 500 annually) and the fishing may be good throughout the preserve in the early season. However, later on, the upper third of the river, in the Preserve, becomes quite thin and suitable holding lies few.

Downstream is another matter. As the river descends into the gorge there are deep pools, rushing water and enough depth even in summer. According to Chief Warden-Naturalist James M. Gibb, the best fishing is in the lower two-thirds of the preserve. Below this the Mianus empties into Mianus Reservoir and there may be some interesting fishing in the inlet area.

There are definitely some bragging-size browns in this stream. In fact warden Gibb once saw an 18-incher and a 21-incher creeled on the same day! Gibb notes that while fly fishermen seem to outnumber bait fishermen, the bait wielders consistently take the largest fish.

The Mianus Gorge is somewhat tricky to find. Look at a road map in the vicinity of southeastern Westchester County near the Fairfield County border. The trail shelter and preserve entrance is on Mianus River Road a bit north of its junction with E. Middle Patent Road.

Outside the preserve – i.e. upstream of it – the Mianus is small but not totally worth ignoring. Here it runs somewhat inky and flows in and out of thick alders. It is also intermittently private, but an inconspicuous young angler should have no problems. There is an especially nice pool just below the bridge where Middle Patent Road meets Pound Ridge Road.

Here, as mentioned, is where the river does an about face. Upstream of Pound Ridge Road the river is quite swampy but it can be accessed via several dirt roads that shoot off of Greenwich Road.

CANOPUS CREEK

Old Joe Burla, in his convoluted half-Italian, half-English accent use to call this "The Odirondock Stream." It is a very pretty brook, not large but reminiscent of the Adirondacks with its steep descent, shrouding conifers and jagged, rocky pools. Trout are stocked, and some fish do holdover. Natural reproduction would seem to be very possible, though DEC reports that they have found none.

Canopus spills out of Canopus Lake in Fahnestock State Park (see Ch. 8). The extreme upper end, from Canopus Lake down to Sunken Mine Road, is very small and rocky, and summer water flows are questionable. As to access, you can park on Rt. 301 and walk down (the Appalachian Trail runs by here), or park at Sunken Mine Rd. and walk up.

From Sunken Mine Rd. down (south) to the park boundary, possibilities improve considerably. Here the stream is very, very rocky, with short pools, boulders and a canopy of cooling conifers. It's very pretty, and far from any car traffic. You can park at Sunken Mine Rd. and

In the secluded Mianus Gorge, the angler can often find peace
and solitude — plus nice-sized browns.

walk down but be forewarned that the dirt roads in this part of the
park are iffy – it's almost jeep terrain. Alternatively, to reach this
section, you can drive to the extreme northern end of Bell Hollow Rd.
This road becomes a jeep trail at the extreme southern terminus of the
park, but there is a little room for parking a car.

The next section is from the park border down to the junction
of Canopus Hill Road and Canopus Hollow Rd. It is much less
steep here, and there are many nice runs, pools and little "ponds."
It's posted in places but some access may be possible. Ask permission
from landowners.

From the above junction down to Albany Post Rd. the water is varied, and most of it is just out of eyesight of roads. The stream here runs through two very wiry little swamps where surprised mallards will greet your presence. It is very deep, but access is difficult because of the swampiness. Still, the best trout are usually found in the most difficult places.

The final leg is from Albany Post Rd. down to stream's end at Annsville Creek (a bay extending off the Hudson River).

8.
PARKS: FUN FOR THE WHOLE FAMILY

It certainly wasn't the first time in its homeric 220,000 miles that my old Chevy convertible had played jeep. But after brief epithets — spat at whatever obscure bureaucrat had allowed the severe gullying of the access road — our thoughts turned anxiously to Stillwater Pond, shimmering up ahead.

There were rises everywhere! "What" and "how big" were the only questions. Jimmy Booth and I tried to recollect the exact results of a previous excursion to Stillwater, many years earlier. Near as we could figure, it was either brookies or rainbows, either eight or twelve inces long, caught either on worms or lures. We hoped to create a more solid memory on this trip.

The surface was alive with eager but very small rainbows, most of which fell off until we switched to smaller lures. It appeared as if an autumn stocking of fingerlings had been made — it was early October — and later research proved that hunch correct.

We fished up and down, high and low, searching for a spring or a deep hole or for some formula that would raise the bigger trout that surely must live in this icewater-clean lake. All the while we groped for the right analogy: Canada, the Adirondacks, Maine. What with the rugged, rocky jags, the hills of Ruffed Grouse laurel and the late season solitude, we allowed there was no finer place to strike out than on Stillwater.

AT 11,000 ACRES, Fahnestock is easily the largest park of those covered in this chapter. It is a place of startling beauty, and on a recent October fishing trip, it let me live out one of my biggest fantasies: Finding a place where I can sit and hear pure quiet (except for natural sounds). I doubt I encountered five other people that day as I drove and hiked around, fished a little, and at least looked at each body of water in the park. Besides lovely Stillwater, there are four other "still waters" as well as a trout stream and a few little tributaries.

Fahnestock is open year-round to fishing in season. While there is no entrance fee, a state fishing license is required. You can bring your own small cartopper and use it at Canopus, Stillwater or John Allen Pond. Only electric-type motors are permitted. Alternatively, you can rent a rowboat on Stillwater (April 1 – open of bass season week-ends only) or on Canopus (opening of bass season to labor day). To launch your own boat a permit is required: $5 for the season.

Overall, my impression of Fahnestock is that the fishing is fair to good, but that the waters are only semi-productive and not nearly as good as the nearby watershed reservoirs. Stillwater is a specially-managed trout lake. Bluegills and even small trout can be caught directly off the wooden dock at the north end of the lake. You're really much better off with a boat, though. This north end is shallow and features a very rocky, rubble-strewn bottom. Stillwater is stocked with brookies and rainbows in good numbers. As trash fish have been eliminated, live minnows are strictly forbidden, so bring worms or artificial lures. When selecting lures, remember that golden shiners are an abundant forage fish here. According to Park Manager Bill Grounds (ever notice how people's names often fit their occupation?) recent gill netting showed that the rainbows reach a maximum size of about three pounds.

Canopus lake is an equally beautiful, shimmering-clean lake that is actually split in half. The north end was raised not long ago to improve swimming conditions, and "the bass in that section are just coming along" according to Grounds. Largemouths of 12-14 inches are now pretty common, though bigger bass are not.

In the south end, largemouths of 4-6 pounds are taken annually and there are also some pickerel, bluegills, crappies and perch. There is better shore-fishing access here than on Stillwater.

Pelton Pond is a man-made pond formed from the damming of a 1930 iron ore mine shaft. It is surrounded by a 1.5 mile self-guided nature trail, and is overlooked by a pavilion and scenic little picnic area. It is very quiet, very picturesque, and the secluded southwest arm is particularly nice. The water is very deep in places, lily-pad covered in others. As casting will be from rocks and small clearings, bring a long-handled net! Seduced infrequently are largemouths of 3-5 pounds and pickerel of better than 24 inches. According to Park Manager Grounds, "the crappie fishing is sometimes quite good in Pelton."

Set deep in the park next to a questionable dirt road is John Allen Pond. It, too, is very scenic and looks to be classic largemouth and pickerel water, with heavy lily pads and shoreline weeds and brush.

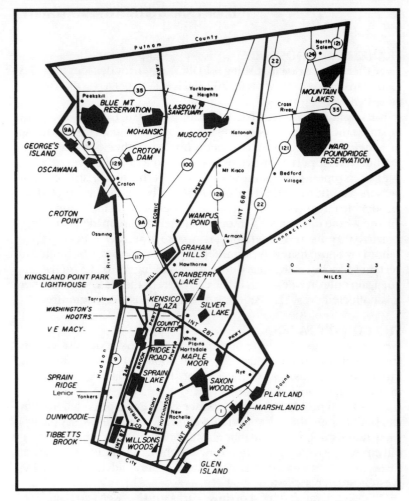

Figure 8-a. Westchester's County Park System. There is fishing in about 17 of these close-to-home parks.

The usual panfish are present.

Duck Pond is very small, yet rumor nonetheless has it that someone wrestled a 5¾-pound largemouth out of here not too long ago. Finally, there is Canopus Creek, covered separately in Ch. 7.

For more information, call or stop at park headquarters, one-half mile west of the Taconic Parkway on Rt. 301. The office is open year-round, and they will give you, free of charge, a map of the park showing the exact location of all waters, roads and trails.

FRANKLIN D. ROOSEVELT

The other state park with fishing is F.D.R., known for decades previous as Mohansic. It is located on Rt. 202 and is easy to get to via the Taconic State Parkway.

You might have noticed bassy-looking Mohansic Lake while driving north on the Taconic. It is, in fact, a good bass lake, and largemouth up to a hefty eight pounds have been boated. Other finny creatures include yellow perch, brown bullheads, and loads of bluegills.

F.D.R. is open year-round with fishing permitted in season. Four persons can fit into the sturdy 14-foot rowboats that are rented for reasonable rates. The fee at present is $1 per hour up to 3 hours, or $6 for the whole day (plus a $15 deposit). Rentals are made from 10:00 a.m. to 6:00 p.m. from about mid May to late June, then every day up to Labor Day. Shore fishing is permitted, though casters may be limited to certain sections by the heavy growth. A parking fee of $2 is charged, but again only on week-ends in the early part of the season. In summer, it is collected every day. Pedestrians and bicyclists can enter free.

THE COUNTY PARKS

Westchester must have one of the finest and most extensive county park systems in the country. There are about 30 parks, comprising thousands of acres, and of these some 18 offer fishing. See fig. 8-a to locate all these county parks.

A common problem that anglers face is finding a place where they can both pursue their devotion *and* entertain (or shall we say pacify) their non-fishing family members. Many of the Big W's parks fit that bill eminently well. Fig. 8-b runs down all the family activities extant at these fishable county parks. First some general advice on utilizing Westchester's park system.

Officials tell me that most of those parks *south* of Kensico Dam Plaza are open strictly to Westchester residents. In most parks north of Kensico, non-residents can enter, but they cannot obtain a county park permit which entitles the bearer to discounts on parking and entrance fees. Currently, this fee is $4 and is good for two years. For more detailed info, call the Westchester County Dept. of Parks, Recreation & Conservation (either "permit information" or the general information number).

Generally speaking, fishing is permitted in all the lakes and streams under the control of the county park system except where signs are displayed against tresspassing. No special fishing permit is needed – just a valid New York State fishing license. Children under 16 years of age are *not* required to have a fishing license in New York. In all these

STATE PARKS WITH FISHING IN WESTCHESTER/PUTNAM

Name of Park	Location	Waters	Family Activities
Clarence Fahnestock Memorial	Taconic Pkwy. at Rt. 301	Canopus Lake Pelton Pond John Allen Pond Duck Pond Stillwater Lake	Picnicking · Snowmobiles Hiking · Bridle Paths Nature Study · Skiing Some Swimming Ski Touring
Franklin D. Roosevelt	Taconic Pkwy. at Rts. 202/35	Lake Mohansic	Picnicking · Golf Swimming · Ice Skating Ball Fields · Ski Touring Hiking · Sledding Snowmobiles

WESTCHESTER COUNTY PARKS WITH FISHING

Croton Point	Croton-on-Hudson, west of tracks	Hudson River	Swimming · Ball Fields Camping · Picnicking Special Events
Blue Mt. Reservation	Welcher Ave., Peekskill	Loundsbury Pd. Peterson's Pond New Pond	Swimming · Picnicking Hiking · Nature Study Ice Skating · Horse Trails Sportsman's Center
Cranberry Lake	New Castle — Orchard St. off Rt. 22	Cranberry Lake	Picnicking · Hiking Nature Study · Ski Touring Small Nature Museum Self-Guided Nature Trail Special Events
George's Island	Dutch St., off Rt. 9A	Hudson River	Picnicking · Nature Study Boat Launch · Ball Field Self-Guided Nature Trail
Glen Island	Pelham Road, New Rochelle	Long Island Sound	Swimming · Picnicking Boat Launch
Kingsland Point	Palmer Ave., off Rt. 9 N. Tarrytown	Hudson River	Ball Field · Picnicking Lighthouse
V. Everit Macy	Saw Mill River Pkwy., Ardsley	Dammed portion of Saw Mill River	Picnicking · Ice Skating Ball Fields

Figure 8-b.

WESTCHESTER COUNTY PARKS WITH FISHING continued

Name of Park	Location	Waters	Family Activities
Oscawanna	Furnace Dock Rd., off Rt. 9A Montrose	Hudson River	Nature Study
Playland	Playland Pkwy. Rye	Long Island Sound	Swimming · Picnicking Hiking · Nature Study Ice Skating · Boating Rides, games, etc.
Saxon Woods	Mamaroneck Ave., White Plains	Mamaroneck River and flood plain of same	Swimming · Golf Picnicking · Hiking Nature Study · Horse Trails
Tibbetts Brook	Midland Ave., Yonkers	Two connected ponds	Swimming · Picnicking Hiking · Nature Study Ice Skating
Wampus Pond	Rt. 128, North Castle	Wampus Pond	Picnicking · Ice Skating Nature Study · Hiking Boating
Ward Pound Ridge	Rts. 35 & 121, Cross River	Cross River and tributaries	Picnicking · Hiking Nature Study · Camping Horse Trails ·Ski Touring Sledding · Nature Museum Snowmobiling Self-Guided Nature Trails
Twin Lakes	California Rd., Eastchester	Two separate lakes	Hiking · Nature Study Ice Skating
Willson's Woods	East Lincoln Ave., Mt. Vernon	One pond	Hiking · Nature Study Ice Skating · Swimming
Mountain Lakes Camp Hemlock	Hawley Road, North Salem	Five Ponds: Spruce, Laurel, Hemlock, Little Pine, Big Pine	Swimming · Picnicking Hiking · Nature Study Ice Skating · Boating Horse Trails · Camping Ball Fields · Ski Touring Sledding
Croton Gorge	Rt. 129, just northeast of village of Croton	Croton River	Picnicking · Nature Study Sledding

Figure 8-b.

parks, seasons, take limits and other regulations established by New York's Dept. of Environmental Conservation are in force.

Croton Point Park is an especially appealing place to fish the Hudson River from shore. You can keep an eye on your propped-up rods while you play softball or frisbee ... all the while revving up an appetite for an al fresco sup prepared among pretty stands of Sycamore and Willow. Off the far west end, big catfish, snapper blues and crabs are gotten in season, along with usually copious numbers of white perch. Striped Bass can be caught off of Teller's Point at the southern tip of the park; try also the rocky northwest corner of the park. Mid-April to mid-May and late September-October are the best times for stripers.

Farther upriver is George's Island park, but here the best fishing and crabbing is a ways off shore. Happily there is a good ramp, from which you can launch a craft of up to about 24 feet. There is usually very good crabbing off George's Island in mid-summer.

Between Croton Pt. and George's Island is Oscawana Park. At present, this is an undeveloped piece of land, but it is right on the river and the scenery is nice. You can bring your family here, but lunch will have to be taken on your lap or on a big flat waters-edge rock if you can find one.

Downriver of these three is what I deem to be the prettiest park *anywhere*: Kingsland Point. Perhaps it's personal nostalgia. I grew up a mile away and first wet a line, at age four, in the little tidal creek that enters the Hudson at Kingsland. Yet I find this park to be very soothing. If you ever *really* object to something I write, you can bring your gripe down to Kingsland in summer, where you will find me writing but more usually fishing, crabbing, loafing or paddling around in my inner tube. If there is a prettier place anywhere for a family picnic, I would certainly like to receive a post card of it. (Note: More information on fishing the Hudson is to be found in Chapters 10-12.)

Both because of its size and its diversity, Ward Pound Ridge Reservation should be singled out as a dandy fishing-family destination. The available fishing is in Cross River Inlet. Since that stream is covered in detail in Ch. 6, we will not discuss it further here. What should be mentioned is the exceptional range of family activities available, as fig. 8-b shows. But in addition to those things listed, there is also a fine "Trailside Nature Museum" and a highly developed schedule that includes many special events.

Croton Gorge Park is, at once, a good fishing spot, a meeting place, a fine picnic niche and a "scenic underlook." Located at the base of Croton Reservoir's Cornell Dam, this little park is bisected by the main branch of the Croton River. The fishing is described in Ch. 6.

If you were ever lucky enough to have been led on a moonlight hike around Cranberry Lake Park, you would have noticed a seductive-looking little bass pond picking up the moonbeams. The pond, of course, is Cranberry Lake, situated askance a real, live cranberry bog. There are, indeed, fish present, and my friend and former park naturalist Craig Stevens can prove it. He showed me pictures he shot at an ice fishing clinic he ran there, and sure enough, flopping on the ice were some good pickerel, yellow perch and bluegills. Bass are also in the lake.

Two parks, Playland and Glen Island, are located on Long Island Sound. For specific information on when to fish the sound for what species, see Chapters 15-17.

At Playland, you can either rent a small boat or fish off the pier. Capt. John Gasparrini's is the boat concession here, where you can rent a 16-foot skiff with outboard for $39.50 per day or $19.50/day if you bring your own motor (1984 prices). Their season runs from about St. Patrick's day to November 30th. Gasparinni's does sell bait and tackle. Call Playland Park for info on when the pier is open.

At Blue Mountain is the well-known "sportsman's center." There is also some fishing for largemouths, crappies, perch and sunnies in three ponds. It is shore fishing only – boats are not allowed. The park is supervised year round, and if the ice is thick enough, officials will let you out to ice fish.

Wampus Pond in the park of that name is very nice looking, and has a bassy reputation. Rowboats are rented here. In versatile Mt. Lakes Park, there are five ponds wherein swim bass, pickerel, perch and sunfish.

In the more southerly parks the fishing is less auspicious, but any fishing is better than none. V.Everit Macy, Willson's Woods, Tibetts Brook, Twin Lakes and Saxon Woods all offer some piscatorial challenges. Inquire by contacting the individual park.

9.
JUST FOR KIDS: FINDING AND FISHING PONDS

The Tarrytown Lakes looked a lot bigger twenty odd years ago, when I was thirteen and Artie was twelve. I still pass by them almost every day, and I still smile when I pass the "bad corner", a spot where I fell in chasing a turtle and where Artie hooked his brother Mattie in the head all on the same day. Just beyond the bad corner is a point of land where Artie and I caught *some* mess of fish one hazy, summer afternoon.

For the point to be exposed, the lake has to be down a few feet, and so it was on the day in question. We started with nightcrawlers, tiny pieces of them, threaded on the fine wire trout hooks Rita at the bait store used to save for me.

Yellow perch! Artie yelled to me and we both admired the fat one writhing and flopping on the sand. But while plain pieces of worm worked OK, things really started to happen when I took a Garcia Abu-Reflex and added a piece of worm to its feathered treble hook. As the late afternoon shadows grew longer, the perch got bigger and bigger. Finally, with daylight fading fast, I hooked "the monster."

In the back room of Nick's Bait & Tackle Shop later that evening, Artie and I cleaned the two dozen big yellows, while Rita and Nick and old Mrs. Morabito (who got most of our panfish) looked on. Everyone agreed that the 15½ incher I'd fooled with a Garcia lure was one heck of a yellow perch.

ALTHOUGH THEY'RE more concentrated in some areas than in others, ponds are found all around the metropolitan area. I learned to fish on a little pond; so did most young boys. Ponds are numerous, close to home and inexpensive to fish. Even very small ponds in this area host some really jumbo largemouth bass. Some have smallmouths, trout, big bullheads, or crappies. Almost all have great supplies of bluegills, yellow perch and eels. There are even a few surprises thrown in here and there.

If you still have only "two wheels" don't despair. A bicycle will put you within reach of a lot of excellent fishing. You may even find many ponds to be within walking distance. First, though, you have to find them.

Even a budding young sportsman should acquaint himself with the topographical maps distributed by the Geological Survey in Washington D.C. (see the reference section for ordering information). Each of these maps covers a very small area, and can therefore show great detail. Almost any pond big enough to hold fish will be depicted on a topo (see fig. 9-a).

All types of maps will be useful to you, not just topos. A regular road map of New York, for example, may have a metropolitan area inset. If the scale is small enough, larger ponds may be depicted. Many town or county highway departments issue maps of their respective municipalities. To find virtually every drop of water big enough to fish, purchase the Hagstrom atlases that are sold by county (Westchester, Fairfield, etc.). These atlases cost about $9, but are incredibly detailed. Further, they are useful even beyond fishing purposes. See the reference section for more map information.

Some ponds are owned or controlled by villages. Therefore, another good way to find nearby ponds is by phoning the parks & recreation

AUTHOR PHOTO

Take a boy fishing — as Gus Montero of Tarrytown is doing here with his son, David. Place: The Tarrytown Lakes.

department of the village in which you live. Some ponds, in fact, are open only to village residents, and inexpensive permits are occasionally needed. They may also set rules and fishing seasons different from state seasons.

The nearest regional office of New York's Dept. of Environmental Conservation can also help you find ponds. They sometimes have free contour maps of ponds and small lakes, as well as stocking reports; they may also be able to provide you with a list of waters in your area. Make your questions very specific if you write for information.

Light spinning is not the only type of tackle for fishing ponds, but it is by far the most popular. With the improvements in Spin Casting and Bait Casting reels over the last ten years, these two methods are challenging spinning. In any case, the weight of your tackle should be light.

My idea of an ideal pond rod is one 6-6½ feet in length. Shorter rods, while usually strong enough, cut way back on your casting distance, and limit the range of lure weights you can use. Pick a rod that can flick a lure as light as about 1/16 oz. and as heavy as about ½ oz. This will cover you for most situations. These capabilities, by the way, are usually inscribed on the rod just above the reel seat. I favor a fairly stiff butt section, a fairly light mid section, and light tip for pond-type angling.

Most all fishermen go through a "light line phase" which lasts until several lost lunkers push them on to the next phase ("catching fish"). Forget 2-lb. test. It's too unmanageable. In very clear water, 4-lb. test may be required to fool wary gamefish. For most pond fishing situations, 6-lb. monofilament line is an excellent all around choice. Remember, though, that light line is simply not necessary in murky waters or at night. At such times, give yourself the benefit of eight, even ten pound test. Extra spinning spools, housing different line weights, are invaluable.

You don't need to bring heaps of other tackle to fish ponds. Foot-high waterproof rubber boots will always be useful. In some places, though, where the shoreline is brushy or very shallow, rubber hip boots can make all the difference, allowing you to wade out to where you can cast. To carry your tackle, the various types of pocketed canvas creels with shoulder straps are much more convenient than tackle boxes. These have compartments for toting your fish. Still, bring a metal stringer for the bigger fish we hope you'll be latching onto. Fig. 9-b gives more advice on tackle and lures for the pond-bound angler.

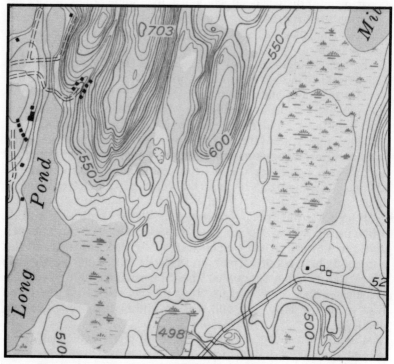

Figure 9-a. An example of the maps distributed by the U.S. Geological Survey (the actual maps are in color). Even the tiniest pond can be located with these maps.

PANFISH

Yellow and white perch, and especially crappies, respond well to live shiners. Keep them small . . . one to one and a half inches long. Fish them on small, unsnelled hooks, size 8-10. When the fish are on top, use a bobber small enough to allow the shiner to pull it along as he struggles on the surface. Many times, especially in hot weather, panfish will seek cooler water down deep. To sink the bait, use only a few small split shot, and leave your bail open after casting. More than occasionally, the strike will come as the bait is sinking.

Bluegills and sunfish, all closely related, are extremely prolific and will be found in most ponds. They have fairly small mouths – keep that in mind when choosing bait. A small piece of worm on an unsnelled #12 hook is a simple but effective terminal rig. As with perch, bluegills

POND FISHING CHECKLIST . . . JUST FOR KIDS

	Ultralight (Panfish only)	Light (Panfish, bass & pickerel)
Best Rod	5 - 6' spinning Lure weight rated 1/32 - 1/16 oz.	6 - 6½' spinning or spin casting Lure weight rated 1/4 oz. minimum, to 5/8 oz.
Best Reel	Ultralight spinning	Light spinning or spin casting
Best line	4-lb. monofilament	6-lb. monofilament
Boots	Twelve-inch all rubber boots with only three top eyelets are often ideal. Hip boots will be a big help, especially where pond is swampy along shore.	Same
Creel	Many still prefer traditional willow creel, which is the best for keeping fish cool and airy. Evaporation-type creels such as Articreel are much more compact and work well.	When angling for bass and pickerel, also carry a stringer.
Hooks	#8-10 for perch #4-6 for crappies #6 for bullheads *Sproat bend unsnelled are recommended. Snelled hooks are good in certain instances only, as when the fisherman cannot see the hook eye too well (low light situations, etc.).	Same as on left, plus: #2-2/0 for bass (use the larger sizes when rigging rubber worms)
Other Terminal Tackle	Assortment of small barrel swivels and snap swivels. Use black, not brass. Swivels disturb the action of many baits/lures, so do not use all the time.	For larger lures, buy the more expensive ball-bearing swivels, such as those made by Sampo. They're worth the price.

Figure 9-b.

POND FISHING CHECKLIST (continued)

	Ultralight (Panfish only)	Light (Panfish, bass & pickerel)
Baits	**Sunfish, Bluegills, Yellow Perch:** Small pieces of nightcrawler, whole small worms, grubs or other larval worms. **White Perch:** Worms or very small baitfish, fished either live or dead. **Crappies:** Small to medium shiners. **Catfish & Eels** (Use natural bait only) Worms, cheese balls or dough balls, or other strong-smelling bait; smallish dead shiners fished on bottom.	**Largemouth Bass:** Medium to large shiners or other baitfish; live frogs. Whole nightcrawlers (in areas where they can be fished without being stolen by panfish.) **Smallmouth Bass:** All of above at certain times. Crawfish is the top bait for smallmouth. **Pickerel:** Same as for largemouth; pickerel have large mouths and will tackle large baits.
Lures	Generally, fish lures weighing 1/16 - 3/8 oz. in weight, depending on the stiffness and rating of the rod. Some good ultralight lures are: • Rocky Junior, Rocky Senior • Colorado Spinner • Small Mepps (#0 and #1) • Small Phoebe and Daredevle • Miniature rubber worms • Other rubber imitations also work well, such as dragonfly, cricket or grasshopper, helgrammite	Generally, fish lures averaging 1/4 - 1/2 oz. in weight. Where large bass are present, lean to the larger lures . . . even up to 5/8 oz. Some good medium weight bass lures are: • Jitterbug, Crazy Crawler • Lead-head jigs • Crawfish imitations • Flatfish • Rubber worms — try different lengths and colors • Spinner Baits • Large Mepps (#2-3)
Other Gear	• Pocket or belt knife • Fisherman's pliers (those that perform several different functions) • Asst. of small bobbers • Extra reel spools with different line weights • Fishing license if you're 16 • or older!	Same as on left, plus you might want to add these under some circumstances: • Asst. of split shot • Asst. of small barrel sinkers ($1/8$ - $1/4$ will be most useful) • Small repair kit: Extra bail spring, tools, reel oil, lube, extra reel handle, ferrule cement

Figure 9-b.

will be pushed deeper by bright sunshine or very hot weather. On such days, look for shaded water, and concentrate your fishing early and late in the day.

An excellent lure for bluegills is a very tiny popper. The smallest poppers, which work best, must be fished with a fly rod. This is superb sport, especially if you get into a pack of plattersized bluegills. Whenever poppers produce, so might small, bushy dry flies. When the fish are a little deeper, tiny wet flies can be dynamic. We've found the darker wets to be better on bluegills.

Many bobber enthusiasts hang on to their technique even when it's not working. Try right on the bottom when you're not having any luck. It's been my experience that yellow perch travel in schools and stay near or on bottom a high percentage of the time. Crappies are very much school fish, too. They love the shade of bridges, but will also hang out near or over submerged brush. Crappies have delicate, paper-like mouths and must be played very carefully.

PICKEREL
The toothy tiger of the weeds is a pond staple. This skinny but powerful fish can survive in ponds that are both very small and very shallow.

A pickerel is a meat-eating gamefish, and any live shiner or other baitfish drifted over his nose is likely to produce a watery explosion. Forget the tiny shiners recommended for panfish; pickerel have gaping, tooth-filled mouths and will quickly reduce any four or five inch baitfish to confetti.

In classic pickerel habitat – lily pads in still, shallow water – weedless lures are more than welcome. A proven, time-tested lure is the weedless Johnson spoon in silver or gold. You can crank this lure through the wiriest salad without getting snagged. Spoons, by the way, seem to outproduce either surface or subsurface plugs. A pork rind strip added to the spoon's treble hook adds an incredibly lifelike, writhing motion that can drive pickerel wild.

LARGEMOUTH BASS
What young fisherman hasn't trembled at his first glimpse of a truly big bass as it passed like a submarine by the edge of a bullfrog pond! There's scarcely a pond around that doesn't have its legendary "scarface" or "old mossysides." When I was twelve, there was nothing more important than trying to catch a 7-lb. bass (my priorities seem to have changed little).

There is no better bass bait in a small pond than a live frog. The frog should be hooked lightly through the lip and be allowed to swim about freely. The explosion that follows will be quick to come if there are any even moderately healthy bass in the vicinity. Perhaps because it simulates a frog, a hula popper seems to be one of the best bass lures in ponds and small lakes. Some of these come weedless. Try fishing the popper *extremely slowly.* Twitch it only slightly after very long pauses. Rubber worms, rigged weedless where necessary, are tough to beat on pond bass. Again, fish them *slowly.* Without question, certain lures work especially well on certain ponds. It always pays to experiment.

Duckweed, the type of free-floating little weed that can completely cover a pond, can be dynamite for bass. A good tactic is to twitch a surface lure through it very slowly. You can tease the unhungriest bass into striking, but you have to do just that: Tease. This principle does not apply strictly to weed fising. The best bass fisherman I knew when I was a kid had tremendous patience. He used to cast for hours in nearly the same place. Eventually, he'd hook a big bass.

CATFISH AND EELS

Some of the most exciting fishing I ever had as a boy was fishing ponds at night for catfish and eels. It was different, productive and filled with action, and the night sounds made it eerie and a little scary, even though my father and the others were there with me.

Brown Bullheads, the type of catfish most common in our waters, and eels are very common in most ponds. But they feed predominantly at night, and we always had our best action after 9:00 p.m. The technique is simple. Fish either good-sized pieces or whole night-walkers right smack on bottom. A ½-oz. barrel sinker will keep you down. Try a pond's deeper water or channel, if you know where that is. Close the bail, and set your rod on a forked stick or against the bridge railing. You'll see the tip bounce if you get a hit.

There are a few other pieces of necessary gear. First, of course, you'll want a good lantern or two. Second, bring a pair of needle nose pliars to extract hooks, as both cats and eels swallow the bait often. *Don't forget rags!* These are slimy fish.

Serena Mateyak looks tentative, while John Cronin is dreaming about a ten pound brown.

PART III

THE UNTAPPED HUDSON...
AND ACROSS THE RIVER

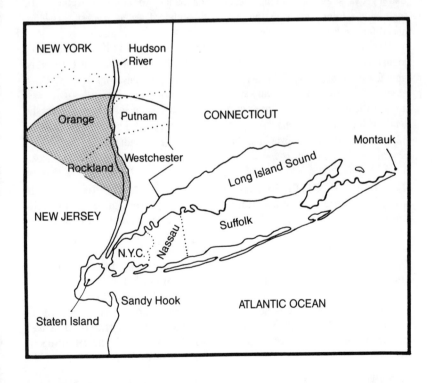

10.
TIPS, TECHNIQUES AND TIMING FOR STRIPERS

Long shadows had already effaced the detail in looming Hook Mountain, and nothing shone now but the forelit faces of black men casting for cats on Crawbuckie Beach. When Haverstraw finally ate the sun, an electric feeling settled over the water. On Croton Bay, in late April, the day begins at sunset.

If you can't measure the depth with your spinning pole, you're using too short a rod. Jimmy Booth proved the point by bouncing his 2½ Merc over the large sandbar that'll get ya' at all but dead high. Just outside the bar, we set up two trolling rods, each with a 6-inch Rebel at the end. With outboard set at slowest speed, we aimed for the Tappan Zee Bridge.

There's nothing cleaner looking than a striper. The first 19-incher that belted my jointed Rebel seemed prettier than usual. Trolling back over the same area, we picked up a few more that size, and one Bullhead on a drifted sandworm.

On Croton Bay, the schooling stripers can be anywhere. You just sort of cast around, when you're not trolling or drifting bait. When Jimmy sort of cast towards the tenth high-tension pole, his 7½ foot rod did a curlycue. You should have seen his 32-tooth grin when he hoisted that big linesider over the gunnel.

THE HUDSON RIVER Estuary, that section up to the Troy Dam, is a major striped bass spawning area. Although the figure is energetically debated, perhaps 10-20% of the entire Atlantic Coast stock is provided by the Hudson. Of the millions of mature stripers that winter-over here, most are thought to do so between Haverstraw Bay and the Tappan Zee (those broad expanses just above and below the bridge). When the water reaches approximately 10° C., bass ascend the river, with many fish gravitating towards the Hudson's tributaries and water that is less salty or even fresh. Most spawning is thought to take place in the river proper, not in the tributaries, between mid-May and mid-June. Eggs hatch within about 48 hours of fertilization, and juveniles remain in the river for one to three years. Most mature fish exit the river after spawning, spending the summer months in the New York Bight, off the coasts of northern New Jersey and south shore Long Island, and in Western Long Island Sound. There is some debate as to how far north and south Hudson stripers roam, though tagged fish have been caught as far north as the Merrimack River in Massachussetts.

Some mature fish, even quite large ones, do remain in the Hudson through summer, in certain pockets. I also believe that striper movements are very much affected by baitfish movements, and that fish may *re-ascend* from time to time to follow schools of baitfish. This past season, for example, excellent catches of stripers were made by locals Joe Leiperte and Midgy Taub off the Croton trestle in early July. Besides baitfish movements, stripers may also respond to strong infusions of fresh water, as when the Croton Dam is overflowing due to heavy rains.

Once the spawning urge bites, stripers become very widely dispersed. Starting at the tip of Manhattan, there is a dandy rip at Spuyten Duyvil where the Hudson branches off. Yet after years of riding commuter trains past this spot, I've still to see a boat plying the waters here. Nonetheless, insiders know that this can be a hotspot, as can be "Hell Gate" farther down.

Not knowing the river, your best bet might be to concentrate around the mouths of tidal tributaries. There are a number of these within 50 miles of Manhattan.

Apparently ignored by anglers is the mouth of the Pocantico River in North Tarrytown. The stream itself is too small to hold bass of any size, but the inflow is quite strong. I can't vouch for the fishing, just for the fact that virtually no one tries here from a boat.

I *can* vouch for the Croton River, the largest tributary to the lower Hudson. This is one of the hottest spots for spring stripers, and fish are caught both in the Croton River proper (all the way up to where it is pure fresh water) and ouside in expansive Croton Bay. Fishing pressure has increased dramatically in the last five years, but the bay is big and there is still plenty of room. Learn where the channels are here, watch the other fishermen, and do not fail to try the rip off of Teller's Point.

Just above the Bear Mt. Bridge is another productive tidal stream, Popolopen Creek. Access is difficult, so plan your strategy and find a parking area ahead of time. Also on the west side of the river, just north of Cornwall, is Moodna Creek, while across the river just south of Beacon is Fishkill Creek. The mouths and tidal sections of these good-sized streams are fine spots for stripers.

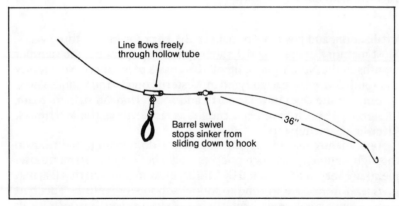

Line flows freely
through hollow tube

Barrel swivel
stops sinker from
sliding down to hook

36"

Figure 10-a. Fish Finder Rig. This versatile rig is useful in many situations and for many species. It's virtue is that when the fish picks up the bait, it can run with it without feeling the weight of the sinker.

By no means does one *have* to fish a tributary to catch stripers in the lower Hudson. The bass, as mentioned, become very well distributed in spring. Big fish are taken annually from "The Yellow Rocks" in North Tarrytown, and from the entire rocky shoreline northward a few miles; off the docks at Scarbrough; from Crawbuckie Beach just north of Ossining; from the rocks at the river bend just south of the Cornwall Yacht Club; at Plum Point; from Little Stony Point just south of Breakneck Ridge; and around Pollepel Island. And these are only some of the better known honeyholes.

The best time to fish, someone once observed, is when you're able to go. While all too true for those who work for a living, this adage does not hold too well with an anadramous fish like the striped bass. By far the best time is early April to late May in that portion of the Hudson covered by this book. Returning stripers can be caught in late September, through October and sometimes even to mid-December. However there are now seasons that you must pay attention to. At this time, the season runs from March 16th to November 30th in the Hudson River upstream of the George Washington Bridge. Here, the size limit is 18 inches. Below the G.W. Bridge, and elsewhere in New York marine waters, the season is April 16th to December 14th and the size limit is 24 inches. With the severe decline of the striper along the Atlantic Coast, these regulations are subject to change. Check before heading out.

I've yet to catch a March striper in the Hudson, though some hotshots have taken bass in Croton Bay as early as March first when the weather warmed up suddenly. One day, around the 20th of that month, I was casting lead-head jigs off the Croton Trestle. With my anxious net man Artie Venier and several others ogling, I played a huge fish for some 10 minutes, all the while phrasing the headline for next day's paper: "Local Man Nails First Big Striper Of The Year." Turned out it was a carp, maybe 25 pounds of him, which I'd apparently snagged while raking the ½-ounce jig over the bottom.

Things happen fast when April rolls round, though, and solid catches are usually reported by April 10th. I would have to place the peak of the action between April 10th and May 15th, with the biggest fish most often taken during the last 15 days of that time frame. Some striper action certainly continues through May and even into June, but it seems to diminish quickly after May 15th. It's important to note that as you go upriver, catches of linesiders continue a little later.

Early in the season, up to about April 15th, whole bloodworms and sandworms can be fished either from shore or boat. By this time, the bait-stealing white perch haven't gotten too bad yet. (There's a joke circulating that local bait dealers stock the river with perch.) If you're in a boat, use a fish-finder rig (fig. 10-a), and drift over rips, sand bars, or rocks where you can find them (stripers do love rocks, but the Hudson is rocky only in certain locales).

By day you catch mostly small stripers. Late afternoon (4:00 p.m. on) can be OK, but the best action on fish of eight pounds or better is from dusk to daylight. That last magical hour before darkness can be explosive.

At dusk, a few techniques are popular. On Croton Bay, for example, anglers often troll a 6-inch Rebel or Redfin until a fish is boated. Then they cast those same lures in that area. If the day is windy, you can quietly drift, casting lead-head jigs, Redfins, or even sandworms. Remember that stripers often circle in tight schools and can be found almost anywhere. Bring binoculars and spy on your neighbors!

Striped bass love herring, and both alewives (*Alosa pseudoharengus*) and blueback herring (*Alosa aestivalis*) make impressive spring runs in the Hudson. Striped bass movements are very significantly influenced by herring movements. There is indeed, no better way to nail a trophy than by livelining a herring at night. If you're strictly a lure man, try a noisy popper during darkness. Swimmers, such as Redfins and Rebels, seem to work well very early in the morning. Lead-head jigs are perenially popular, and yellow seems to be the choice color.

The lightest striper tackle generally seen on the Hudson is a 6½-7½ foot spinning rod with 6 lb. test line. Obviously, for trolling or livelining bait, you will need sturdier equipment. For this type of work I use a battered old Mitchell 300 spooled with 12-lb. mono, on a 7-foot Daiwa with a fairly stiff tip. The ultralight stuff is OK for daytime, but at night you need at least 12-lb. line. Fish of at least 40 pounds have been caught, and every year a few in the 25-30 lb. class are beaten.

On shallow Croton Bay, and doubtless at other locations, fly fishing is a very real possibility. Bob Boyle, author of the fine book on the Hudson, recommends a big (3/0) streamer with a palmered flourescent red hackle collar and a white saddle hackle tail. For the boatless set, one good place to wade and cast is off "Duck Island" at the north end of Crawbuckie Beach (walk down a half-mile or so from the trestle).

The favorite stoveside chitchat of Hudson "river rats" is tides and their affect on striped bass fishing. Upon one point there seems to be universal agreement: An angler must learn the best time of the tide for the specific place he fishes. Tides, and their mechanical effects, vary tremendously from spot to spot. Generally, the top of the tide – near high – is best in the tributaries. This is when baitfish are most likely to be thick. Just outside a tributary, as in Croton Bay, the best time seems to be the last two hours of the rising tide and, especially, the first two of the falling tide. A very good condition is when a rising tide is two hours short of dead high at dusk.

As far as night fishing goes, the darker the night the better. Moonless, cloudy nights are choice, and often they're even choicer if it's also stormy with wind and rain. I have gone on enough in this book about the importance of stormy weather to the fisherman.

AUTHOR PHOTO INSET   PER BRANDIN

By day, expansive Croton Bay is lethargic. But at night, in spring-time, it comes to life!

11.
SUMMER: BLUECLAWS
AND SALTY PANFISH
BY THE PAILFUL

It was late August, and stifling even at four dark bells. The moonlit, muddy channel, though — flat out with the rising tide about to pounce on it — looked deadly. At once, my father and I began the pleasing ritual, the chain of operations we hoped would result in a full, 8-qt. pot of "Crabs Cappy."

The first order of business was black coffee from an all-night diner, though in the heat, I'm sure my father seriously considered a can of "pop top orange juice" instead. Bait the crab traps. Tear a piece of salami off the Italian wedge and place it in the killy trap. Tie the killy trap to an obliging railroad bolt, toss the trap in the water. String up the 5-foot spin poles, tie a one-inch Kastmaster on one, tandem #8 hooks on the other. Then, out in the boat to lower the crab traps. Only then did we relax with coffee, and gloat a little over how we'd timed the tide just right for once.

And the Blue Claws were there! Big ones, six and seven-inchers that got that way because of the mild, 8-parts-per-thousand salt. Between pulls, the killies were put to work on white perch that came in by the pailful; snapper blues hit the wobbling lures like little dynamos. These salty panfish were, in turn, used to rebait the crab traps.

There is a harmonious circle here that non-hunters never get to see. It's like the magic of a mountain breakfast trout: The one you fooled with a fly, tied from the feathers of a grouse you walked twelve miles to shoot last October.

BLUE CLAW CRABS run in the Hudson from about mid-July to early October, but it is a very imprecise calendar. Sometimes the run is early, sometimes late. Sometimes there is even a "split run" with a gap of several weeks between two hot periods. Mature males and immatures of both sexes may winter over right in the river though no one seems to know for sure. In any event, from mid spring to about early July, try deeper. Few crabbers venture forth this early, so you'll have the river to yourself. From mid-July to mid-October, most crabs are taken in waters of three to twenty feet. It should be noted that crab populations fluctuate dramatically. There are occasional years when scarcely a crab will be found in the Hudson, and regretably, 1984 was close to that. The previous seven or eight years had all been good, though.

Exactly where do you crab in the Hudson? First, a few parameters. Pure seawater is about 32 parts per thousand (ppt.) salt, while fresh water is about zero. Essentially, it is a *range* or gradient of salinities that makes for the best blue crab habitat. However during the summer mating period, concentrated in August and September at these latitudes, crabs seem to seek slightly fresher waters. Thus the best crabbing is usually between the Tappan Zee Bridge where summer salinities average 12 ppt. salt, and the Bear Mt. Bridge, where they average 3 ppt. in late summer. Depending on heavy run-offs, or conversely, droughts – conditions which can push the salt line one way or the other – you might find good crabbing all the way down to Spuyten Duyvil or all the way up to Newburgh or even a bit further. Crabbing, then, depends a good deal on rainfall.

The shallower east bank is generally more productive, though good crabbing can be had around Nyack, Piermont, and other shoal areas on the west side. Always check around the mouths of feeder streams, where some of the best combined fishing-crabbing exists.

Here are some proven hotspots on the east bank: From the docks and marinas from Yonkers up to Irvington; in the very shallow flats under and just north of the Tappan Zee Bridge; off the Scarborough docks; in and around the mouth of the Croton River; off of George's Island County Park; over the old oyster beds off Verplanck, where several commercial crabbers operate; in and around Annsville Creek, just outside of Peekskill. Note that crabs are roamers, and may be taken most anywhere from shore in summer. A small boat, though, is needed for some of the above mentioned places.

The omnipresent white perch can also be taken almost anywhere, but again, you'll do best in and around the mouths of tributaries, and in the Hudson's many backwater "ponds." These fish are highly school oriented, so search out the schools for the best action. Besides tribs, they will also congregate around bottom structure.

For bait, you cannot beat small, whole baitfish. Killies, spearing, baby sunfish – all of which you can catch yourself in the Hudson – are dynamic when worked in and around certain rips or in the currents that are created by bridges, feeder streams, narrow passages and sunken bars or other distinct depth differences. Wherever there is a current, the perch will readily suspend off bottom, watching for food to pass by. Though whole baitfish twitched enticingly are best, small silver lures and small pieces of fish can also turn the trick. In calmer

PER BRANDIN

A mixed summer bag from the Hudson: Blue Claw Crabs, White Perch, and Snapper Blues.

waters, where there is very little current, there's no good reason for
fish to suspend; most food will be on bottom. When this is the case,
fish any kind of worm (small pieces) on bottom. White perch are
widely distributed throughout the entire section of the Hudson covered
in this book.

It seems to me that I can recall years when snapper blues were not
so plentiful in the Hudson, but one expert I spoke with says he has
always found them to be abundant. When they're in, they seem to be
everywhere. When they first appear in mid-summer, they are only a
few inches in length. By early September, they've grown to a sportier
six to eight inches. A few years back, large schools of small harbor
blues – 12-16 inches – were roaming the river, and every once in a
while even bigger specimens turn up. Generally, though, bluefish (as
well as weakfish) use the river mainly as a nursery area. Mature fish
would have to be termed strays.

When you're crabbing, take along a 5-foot ultralight spinning pole
or a medium weight fly rod outfit. Even baby blues are great fighters.
The best bait will be small whole baitfish in the currents, small chunks
of fish when on bottom. Depending on tides, currents and other
conditions, snappers can be high, low or in-between. Bring both small
bobbers and small sinkers. Every local tackle shop sells both hooks and
lures made especially for snappers. Ask for them. If you're a fly rod
purist, try small silver or white bucktails.

A cyclic visitor to the Hudson is the Lafayette or "spot" (*Leiostomus
xanthurus*). Reaching a maximum size of 14 inches, spot average only
about six inches in the Hudson. An extremely tolerant and far ranging
Atlantic Coast fish, more common in southern waters, spot will be
found over mud or sand bottom, or over shellfish beds. In the Hudson
we catch them right alongside the perch and snappers, and techniques
are pretty much the same. This, too, is a summertime fish, and they are
usually very abundant in the years when they are present. They are
reported to be good eating.

12.
MORE ESTUARINE SURPRISES

The old black men were gathered at the Cooney Docks that night, and we knew why they were there. Artie and I had hustled home from school, changed, picked up two dozen bloods at Nick's, and were now on the water at 6:00 p.m. Tommy and Danny were there, and they'd filled a pail the night before, Nick said. The log was burning and spitting creosote, and the men were telling stories we didn't understand or really care about. All you cared about in November, when you were 13 years old, lived along the Hudson and loved to fish, was that the "tommies were running."

I rigged up tandem hooks, and pushed small pieces of blood worm into each of them. Then I clambered out onto the barge, pail in one hand, worms in the other. My fingers were already numb.

The first thing I caught was an iceberg. That out of my system, I started yanking out 9-inch Tom Cod two at a time, though it was always hard to wait for the second tug when you knew you had one hooked. I might've filled a pail that night too, if it hadn't been so cold. Most of the time we spent listening to stories, as we huddled around the log that smouldered for weeks till Christmas pushed fishing out of everyone's mind for another year.

THE HUDSON RIVER'S frost fish, the Tommy Cod (*Microgadus tomcod*) arrives at about Halloween and seems to be most plentiful around turkey day. We've bucketed "tommies" on into January, but usually the action dwindles before Christmas. Few stick it out that late anyway, due to very cold weather and ice jams on the river. By the way, the tommy is not a juvenile codfish as some suspect, but a separate species of the cod family. It does resemble its bigger cousin, though.

The Tommy Cod, on its estuarine migratory (and spawning) run is a shallow water, bottom fish. This makes for easy shoreline fishing at a time when most boats are off the water anyway. We wouldn't dream of fishing single hooks – tandem is the rule, and when the fish are thick, you can even catch three at a time. Small pieces of bloodworm are my choice of baits, though sands and to a lesser extent nightwalkers have performed.

Tom Cod are small fish which, according to *McClane's Standard Fishing Encyclopedia* grow only to about 15 inches and perhaps a pound in weight. Most are smaller, though, and in the Hudson they average about 6-11 inches. Thus light spinning or bait casting rods, ¼-½ oz. swivel sinkers, #8 hooks and a bucket to hold your fish are all you need in the way of gear. Just remember to wear *very* warm clothes, and bring a Thermos of something hot. Tommy Cod anglers are habitual fire builders, and there's nothing more pleasant than huddling around a cherry-red log in the November night when this strange little fish bites best.

Catfish and Eels are often spoken of in one breath, since so often these fish are taken by the same bottom-fishing methods. There is a sad footnote now, though: Hudson River eels, being mud dwellers, have been found to be highly contaminated with PCB's (Polychlorinated Biphenyls, one of the Hudson's worst toxic problems). Thus it is illegal to even *possess* an eel from the river. If you catch one, throw it back or you could be subject to a summons.

Bullheads are abundant, and White Catfish up to several pounds are present in good numbers. I have recently heard that there are also occasional Channel Catfish, a fish that is more abundant to the south. At present, Catfish have not been quarantined like the eel. But the health advisories are often unclear and constantly changing. For specific current health information on fish, consult the NYS "Fishing, Small Game Hunting, Trapping Regulations Guide," issued annually. Or, contact the nearest branch of the conservation department.

By far the peak of the action on river cats seems to be May and June, but with fairly steady activity continuing on through the warm months. There is a quiet cult of cat men on the Hudson, and these close-mouthed addicts know that a superb catfish bait is strips of shad or herring. Even if you can't obtain one of these, be sure to stick to natural baits. Like the carp, the catfish feeds primarily by scent. Worms of all types will certainly take their share of catfish, but many of the weird cheese or dough concoctions used on carp will also work on cats.

There are some bruising carp in the river, and in spite of its lackluster or even maligned reputation, old *Cyprinus carpio* has a distinct following here on the Hudson. I am not sure if the carp roams the Hudson at all depths, but I do know that most pursuers concentrate around tributary mouths and in quieter backwaters of the river. There

ANGLING GUIDE TO THE LOWER HUDSON RIVER

Most Common Species	Size Range	General Habitat	Most Available	Recommended Outfit	Best Baits and/or Lures	Closed Seasons or Restrictions
Striped Bass	Up to 40 lbs. 3-5 lbs. typical	Fairly shallow, rocky areas, bars	Apr. - Oct., esp. Apr. 15 - May 15	7½-8½' med. spinning 10-20 lb. lines	Bloodworms, herring; jigs, Rebels	Yes
White Perch	Up to 3/4 lb.	Easily taken from shore	Apr. - Oct.	Light spinning	Whole killies, spearing; small shiny lures	No
Catfish/Bullheads	Up to about 6 lbs.	Muddy bottoms (on bottom)	Apr. 30 - Oct. 20	6-7' medium stiff baitcasting outfit	Strong-smelling natural baits	No
Snapper Blues	4-5" early in season; bigger later	Widely dispersed, easily caught	Aug. 15 - Oct. 1	Light 6' spin or #6 fly rod	Small baitfish, whole or cut; silvery lures	No
Lafayette ("Spot")	6-8"	Widely dispersed	Summer (occurs some years only)	Same as for snappers	Same as for snappers	No
Black Bass	2-5 lbs., occ. larger	Backwaters, in around tribs.	May 15 - Oct. 31	6½-7½' spinning outfit	Wide variety of baits & lures	Yes
Tommy Cod	5-10"	Near bottom, in 15' water or less	Nov. 1 - Jan. 1	Med.-light spin 6-8 lb. line	Small pcs. worm fished tandem	No
Herring	6-14"	In tribs, and often near shore	Apr. 1 - June 15	Ultralight spinning	Small darts, jigs; flies possible	No
Smelt	5-8"	Tributaries	Short, intense runs usually in March	Dip nets	—	No
Blue Claw Crabs	4-8" (point to point)	Shallow water often concentrated by tribs	July 10 - Oct. 20	Box nets, scap nets, handlines	Eel, white perch, snappers, herring	Yes
Yellow Perch, Sunfish	Up to 1/2 lb.	Backwaters in and around tribs	Warm months	Ultralight spinning	Worms, small shiners, very small lures	No

Figure 12-a.

are two primary methods of capture.

The "Fishing Method" centers around long, powerful rods and strong-smelling baits. Remember that these fish may grow to 60 pounds or more in the river, and twenty pounders are fairly common. Tackle must be tough. As for those famous, smelly carp baits: Several commercial types are sold, but true carp men are wont to make their own. Often, these formulas are guarded like the family jewels, and passed down from one generation to the next.

The "Hunting Method" involves the use of bow and arrow. Most Hudson River bowfishermen concentrate on some of the shallower, marshy backwaters.

In the spring, from late March through late May, three important species of baitfish make spawning runs in the Hudson. One of these is a fine food fish in its own right. The other two make excellent striper bait and are thus worth pursuing.

Smelt (*Osmerus mordax*) make a very intense but also very short spring run in the Hudson. Some observers believe the run lasts only about seven to nine days at any given location. In fact there is a joke circulating in certain North Tarrytown gin mills about "the smelt run being on." Seems that certain chaps have been rousted off of comfortable bar stools to such a battle cry, only to arrive at the river and discover that the run was over. The best advice, if you're serious about smelting, is to pick a tributary and check it every night starting around the first of March. All you have to bring is a dip net, a lantern to spot the fish and a bucket. If the smelt are really thick, you'll know it as you approach your chosen stream: There will be a distinct smell of cucumber which the smelt give off! All the effort will be worth it, though, because there is no finer fish – to my taste buds – than smelt that have been batter-dipped and deep-fried. (If only I could get the recipe from Benny D'Agostino, who sometimes serves this delicacy at his popular Irvington, N.Y. eatery, "Benny's Seafood Restaurant.")

The other two anadramous baitfish that spawn here are Blueback Herring and Alewives (yes, these are the same alewives given so much attention in Part I). These two virtually indistinguishable fish would be inedible if cooked by conventional methods due to the high oil content. However they are delicious when smoked or pickled, and the roes of both fish are excellent when sautéed. Additionally, both make top shelf Striped Bass and crab bait, and the bigger herring specimens of 14 inches or so provide good sport in themselves on light tackle. Very small, bucktail-streamers or split-shot head jigs can be used to trick spring-run herring. Again, you can try in or near the tributaries.

Art Venier tries for tom cod off the old Tarrytown docks. Background: The Tappan Zee Bridge.

Many anglers are curious about the famous Hudson River shad runs. Probably several million shad do, in fact, ascend the Hudson to spawn in springtime. In the section of the Hudson covered by this book, the shad are taken almost exclusively by commercial netters. However upriver, especially between Kingston and Catskill, a growing number of anglers are taking shad on jigs, darts and streamers. DEC prints a free brochure on sport fishing for shad in the Hudson. Send to the New Paltz office listed in the reference section. The primary species is the American Shad, but Hickory Shad have also been observed in recent years, especially in late-summer early-autumn.

Occasionally some tidewater brown trout and black bass are taken in the lower Hudson. From Peekskill southward, these odd catches are invariably made in the tribs or at the mouths of the tribs during a period of heavy run-off. The Croton River is one such spot. Of course as you go upriver, especially above the Bear Mt. Bridge, salinities decrease to the point where trout, black bass, pickerel and crappies are taken farther down the tribs and even in the river proper. Popolopen Creek, Fishkill Creek and Moodna Creek are all trout streams in their upper reaches. Some browns may migrate down, and some of these may become true "salters" moving back and forth between river and tributary. To my mind, there is no more exciting fishing than exploring by canoe or small boat these Hudson feeder streams, where any one of a dozen or more different fish might be caught on any given cast.

This by no means completes the roster of fish found in the lower Hudson. Christopher Letts, an educator whose specialty is teaching about the Hudson, loves to fish for Atlantic Needlefish (a long, skinny, gar-like fish) and Jack Crevalle (another small exotic averaging a foot or so in the Hudson). He claims they're both especially good eating, but that they're just not available to most people most of the year. Chris also asserts that fluke are present and are taken by commercial men in shad nets. I would have strong interest in knowing how *many* fluke are out there, though I suspect it's not in vast numbers. There are also two species of sturgeon in the Hudson, but to my knowledge these caviar carriers are taken only by netters as they do not usually respond to rod and reel offerings.

Under the sponsorship of the Hudson River Institute, many river fish (especially stripers) have been tagged. You will be aiding valuable research by returning any fish tags you recover.

13.
THE PRETTY PALISADES

It was a soft, windless day in autumn, and one had to forgive the hills for admiring themselves in the obliging mirrors below. Lake Askoti, our destination, not only looked like an October jewel — it immediately did something that raised our blood pressure.

As Per Brandin and I loaded the boat, a small shiny baitfish began doing the dance of fear on the surface. It was being chased! Then quickly it was gone. I at once chucked a much-too-big Rebel towards the fading wake, let it sit ten seconds, then gave it a sharp twitch. Smack! The fish (not the minnow, certainly) jumped right on it. No metal hit home, though, and no further casting could raise him again. But what the heck — we hadn't even launched the boat yet, and the little lake looked ever nicer as shadows lengthened.

At 41 acres, Askoti is easy to cover, and cover it we did, following a contour map I had to seek out the deeper portions. But besides the boating of several jumbo bluegills, little happened until I cast a Flatfish towards a large, protruding rock at the north end of the lake.

When the 3-lb. bass finally came up, it simply spit the Flatfish back at me. But while Per didn't forgive me — it was the only decent fish of the day — I was certain that the hills did. I imagined they'd seen that kind of thing before.

PRETTY IS INDEED the word for the Palisades Parks. While they're not the first place I would send you to catch a mess of trophy fish, they are a fine place to find out what Wordsworth, Keats, Byron and Shelley were talking about.

The Palisades Interstate Parks comprise a chain of parks and historic sites extending along the west side of the Hudson from Fort Lee in New Jersey northward into Rockland, Orange and portions of Sullivan and Ulster Counties in New York.

FISHING IN BEAR MT./HARRIMAN STATE PARKS

Lake	Principal Gamefish Present	Type of Boats Permitted
Askoti	Trout, Largemouth Bass	None
Brooks Pond	Largemouth and Smallmouth Bass	None
Hessian	Trout, Largemouth Bass	Rowboats
Island Pond	Trout, Largemouth Bass	Rowboats, Canoes
Kanawauke	Largemouth Bass, Pickerel	Rowboats, Canoes
Nawahunta	Largemouth and Smallmouth Bass	None
Silvermine	Largemouth and Smallmouth Bass	Rowboats, Canoes
Sebago	Large & Smallmouth Bass, Pickerel	Rowboats, Sailboats, Canoes
Skannatati	Largemouth Bass, Trout	Rowboats, Canoes
Stahahe	Largemouth Bass, Pickerel	Rowboats, Canoes
Tiorati	Largemouth Bass, Pickerel	Rowboats, Sailboats, Canoes
Welch	Largemouth and Smallmouth Bass	Rowboats, Sailboats, Canoes
Wanoksink	Largemouth Bass	None
Pine Meadow	Largemouth Bass	None

- Panfish: Yellow Perch, Bullheads and Sunfish are generally common to abundant in all these waters. Crappie, Rock Bass and White Perch may be present in some.
- The following lakes are generally closed from mid-June to Labor Day because group camps for children are located on them: Upper Cohasset, Lower Cohasset, Te Ata, Upper Twin and Lower Twin. The Park reports that Largemouth Bass, Pickerel and Perch are present in these lakes.

HIGHLIGHTS OF RULES & REGULATIONS (Also Contact the Park)

1. Fishermen in the Palisades Interstate Parks in New York are governed by N.Y.S. Department of Environmental Conservation Laws regarding licenses, open seasons, sizes and methods of taking. **Special Park Regulations do not extend fishing seasons beyond dates prescribed by the State Conservation Law.**
2. Fishing is **not permitted** in Queensboro Lake, Summit Lake, Turkey Hill Lake or the Letchworth Village Reservoirs.
3. Fishing **after dark is not permitted**.
4. **ROW BOATS** may be rented from the concessionaire at Hessian Lake, Lake Sebago, Lake Welch and Rockland Lake.
5. **PRIVATE BOATS** may be used **by permit only**. All boats must be inspected before a permit will be issued. Inspection sites are located at Tiorati Circle, and Beaver Pond Campground.
6. **A LIFE PRESERVER** that conforms to U.S. Coast Guard standards is **required** by law for each individual using a public or private boat.
7. **TROUT STREAMS** — Queensboro Brook, Tiorati Brook, Ramapo River and Stony Brook — State regulations pertain.
8. **TROUT LIMIT** — Five per day in Hessian Lake, Lake Askoti, Island Pond and Lake Skannatati.
9. **FISH STOCKING** — in Park Commission-owned waters is done by the N.Y.S. Department of Environmental Conservation.
10. **BAIT AND SUPPLIES** — On sale by concessionaire at the Rockland Lake State Park fishing station. No bait or tackle sold in Harriman/Bear Mt. Parks.
11. **ICE FISHING PERMITTED** on Tiorati Lake, Rockland Lake, Hessian Lake, Skannatati Lake, Askoti Lake and Lake Sebago.

This chart adapted from three fliers distributed by Palisades Interstate Park Commission.

Figure 13-a.

The Palisades Interstate Park Commission was created in 1900 to preserve the scenic beauty of the west shore of the lower Hudson River. These parks now comprise more than 80,000 acres wherein lie several dozen bodies of fishable water. All the parks must be considered excellent places for a family outing. Activities are diverse and there are also many special events.

For many people, the Palisades Interstate Parkway will provide the best access to these parks. A beautiful, scenic ride in its own right, the parkway runs 38 miles from the George Washington Bridge to Bear Mountain.

By far the bulk of the fishing lies in the huge contiguous parks of Hariman-Bear Mt. Fig. 13-a, which lists the lakes and streams along with species present, was adapted and revised from flyers obtainable free from the park. These brochures also list the general regulations pertinent to angling. See the end of this chapter.

Before we discuss the fishing, there are a few important things to take note of. First, a current New York State fishing license, resident or non-resident *is* necessary if you're over 16. There is no additional park fishing fee, but there is a boating fee. The only other tote would be for parking at certain of these lakes. Such fees are generally collected only in season, i.e. from Memorial Day to Labor Day. There is no general park entrance fee.

On all those park lakes open to fishing, shore fishing is allowed and access is generally good (though casting conditions may be tough in places). There are a couple of "walk-in" lakes – Wanoksink and Pine Meadow for example – that can only be reached on foot as they are off the road. Here, shore anglers may encounter a little welcome elbow room.

As for boating: Boats are permitted on some park waters only. Moreover, as shown in Fig. 13-a, there are stipulations as to what *types* of craft may be used in which waters (rowboat, sailboat, canoe, etc.). Where boats are permitted, you can launch your own but it must be inspected and you must pay a $5.00 fee (good for the entire season). By the way, electric trolling motors are permitted but outboards are not. Also, inflattable craft are prohibited. If you don't have your own boat, you can rent a rowboat on several of the lakes (Fig. 13-b).

Finally, the best advice overall is this: When in doubt call the park ahead of time. Both Harriman and Bear Mt. are very busy, active parks, and the rules, regulations and conditions are subject to change.

Probably the best finny target in these parks is the Largemouth Bass. But we'll start with trout first.

Only trout are stocked in these parks, and only in these four lakes: Island Pond, Askoti, Hessian and Skannatati.

Island Pond makes for interesting conversation. About six or seven years ago some 10,000 Kokanee Salmon fingerlings were stocked here one time only. However, according to Chief Ranger Tim Sullivan and DEC officials, subsequent electrofishing and netting yielded not one salmon. Nor have any grown-up specimens been reported by anglers, according to Sullivan. Some think the salmon may by simply lying undetected in the depths of Island Pond, which plummets to an amazing 130 feet in places. But considering the lack of any returns whatever, I do not list salmon as being present although the park does in the fishing flyer they distribute.

Nonetheless, Island Pond is interesting. It is deep and it is also one of the more secluded waters in the park, being about 1500 feet off the main road. As with Welch and Tiorati, an "access key" is needed to drive right down to the launch area. Ranger Sullivan reports that he has seen some good-sized trout taken here, meaning that there is at least some holdover of stocked fish.

Askoti is very small, and appears to be typical of these relatively infertile glacial lakes. It has a mud bottom, and very, very little rooted aquatic vegetation – not a good sign. Askoti was drained some years ago to eliminate all rough fish so trout could be stocked. Now, only trout are supposed to be present, though I can personally verify that at least a few bluegills and bass are in there. Overall, it appears that the trout fishing in Askoti is mainly put and take, but at least it does receive the highest stocking quota (about 1600 fish) of any park water.

Right across the street from Askoti is Lake Skannatati. This is known as a fairly good bass lake, but it does receive a small stocking of trout.

Hessian is the other trout lake. Divers here have confirmed that this lake has one rim that drops off a sheer 75 feet. Thus there is depth. But being right next to the Bear Mt. Inn and park headquarters, this smallish lake is assailed by boaters, shore anglers and sun revelers during the summer. On a summer week-end, there are literally hundreds of picnickers and partiers along Hessian's banks. So here again we must assume that trout fishing is mainly put and take. However...

Maybe the trout here become nocturnal because of all the daytime commotion. Maybe the offseason prospector will find some lunkers lurking in the depths. For the serious trouter, Island Pond and Hessian Lake leave some questions unanswered.

Besides trout, there are largemouths and panfish in most of the lakes, and smallmouths in a few. Chain Pickerel do not appear to be an important game fish, although they are found here and there.

In 1978, Welch, Tiorati and Sebago were surveyed by DEC. It's likely that the results of these surveys are still valid.

Lake Welch was shown to have an "abundant" stock of smallmouths and a lesser supply of bigmouths. Further, the ratio of game to non-game fish (1:2.57 by weight) was considered good. Those non-game fish are yellow perch, several species of sunfish, and a few species of catfish. Growth rates for all species were found to be good.

Sebago was found to contain no smallmouths, and the largemouths were less abundant than in Welch. Tiorati was found to have large-mouths in fairly good supply, as well as a very good head of fast-growing panfish. A fine panfish population could be why Tiorati seems to be the busiest of the park's lakes during the ice-fishing season. According to park officials, ice anglers congregate heavily at the west end of the lake.

Ranger Sullivan reports good largemouth action at Kannawauke.

Like Tiorati, this is a fine-looking bass lake worthy of exploration.

There are a few waters listed as trout streams in Harriman-Bear Mt. parks, but these appear to be very marginal. Two of these – Tiorati brook and Queensboro Brook – were found to be nearly bone dry during a late September trip. Most of the small number of trout stocked here are probably (hopefully!) harvested quickly early in the season. However, Ranger Sullivan suggests that Stony Brook/Pine Meadow Brook, which feeds the Ramapo River, has water in it all the time.

In the off season, the throngs of people in these parks greatly diminishes. By October, on weekdays, I have found these huge parks to be almost eerily vacant. Summer's another story. You will find large crowds on week-ends, so fish early in the morning if you have to come on a Saturday or Sunday. Summer weekdays are a little better, but most fishermen prefer a little solitude and quietness. This will only be found before May 31st or after September 5th, when, often, you may well have any given lake to yourself.

PER BRANDIN

The sprawling Palisades Parks are not only pretty – they're dotted with fishable lakes. Before Memorial Day and after Labor Day, solitude is eminently possible.

Certain printed materials, available from the Bear Mt. central office, may prove helpful to you. For all of the following, write to: Palisades Interstate Park Commission, Administration Building, Bear Mt., NY 10911.

1. *Palisades Interstate Parks.* A brochure with charts and a non-detailed map of the park region showing all parks. Free.
2. *Detailed Trail Map* of Harriman-Bear Mt. Parks. Shows all lakes and streams. Send $1.25, they will pay postage.

3. *Fishing Information Sheet.* Shows species present and rules and regulations. Free.
4. *Winter Activities In NYS Parks & Historic Sites.* Free.
5. *Boating Information Sheet.* Shows where (what lakes) boats are allowed and which *types* of boats are allowed where. Free.

There are two other Palisades Parks within the scope of this book that offer fishing. One is Nyack Beach, where the fishing involved is in the Hudson River. See Chapters 10-12. The other is Rockland Lake Park in Rockland County.

Rockland Lake offers some interesting sport to anglers. Since 1980, Tiger Muskellunge ("Norlunge") fingerlings have been stocked here. 3000 were planted in each of 1980 and 1982 and stocking is supposed to take place every two years. In 1982, the first legal 30-incher was already witnessed, in 1983 10-pounders were caught, and in 1984 even bigger specimens were boated. This sterile hybrid does not reproduce, but it does grow *fast!* There are also Largemouth Bass and panfish found here.

There is a private concession on Rockland Lake where you can rent rowboats and buy bait and tackle. On this subject, remember that *no* bait and tackle is available in either Bear Mt. or Harriman State Parks, so plan on bringing everything you need.

14.
OTHER WATERS IN ROCKLAND AND LOWER ORANGE

Mallards and the heady scent of the October uplands were in the air that morning. It is truly a month that tears me many ways, but the Ramapo River and the thought of fishing some brand new trout water quelled the internal battle. We arrived streamside at a leisurely 11 a.m.

On advice, we tried near Sloatsburg first. I rummaged through my vest for a box of terrestrials, patterns that always seem to work well in the sparse-hatch days of late season. After knotting on a fuzzy brown beetle, I clambered down through bug-laden branches that I hoped were dropping their surfeit to the dark riffle below me. A sloppy but accurate roll-cast laid the beetle atop the farshore channel.

It was three or four casts before the first fish rolled and took and powered into one of the Ramapo's numerous brush-jams. I steered him out, but something told me — smallmouth! I sent him back with orders to wake up the browns in the river, but unfortunately, not even bass followed that first fish: Only good-sized chubs that took like trout and fooled me time after time.

Later we drove upstream, where the water looked even nicer. But in this smaller water, too, only chubs responded to our dry flies. Pleasingly off the road, the stream at one point widened into a little pond. Suddenly, as we approached, several mallards burst skyward! The birds immediately veered into a perfect, 30-yard crossing shot, but they felt no sting when I reflexively snapped my 7-foot flyrod to shoulder. It was unloaded.

THE RE ARE ESSENTIALLY four trout streams in Rockland County, not counting those located in the Palisades Parks (all park waters covered in the preceding chapter). The Ramapo River is the most noteworthy, though it still does not compare to any of the three quality streams of the Croton Watershed (Ch. 5). It is stocked with about 900 brook trout and 1800 brown trout annually, and in a recent mid-summer DEC survey – 1983 – a good number of fish stocked that spring were recaptured, indicating good survival. The Ramapo offers to anglers an extended trout season – up to November 30th. It is one of only a handful of streams in this area open for trout that late.

I have fished the section between Tuxedo Park and Sloatsburg, which regulars on the stream tell me is the best section for trout. Below Sloatsburg, trout habitat is increasingly marginal. Access to this section is no problem. Pull off along Rt. 17 wherever you can – there are several empty lots – then just walk the railroad tracks up or down.

By all accounts, the trout appear to be concentrated in certain specific sections of the stream. It will pay you to roam the river until you find these spots. Chubs, dace and smallmouth bass are plentiful. The smallmouth fishing, in fact, is quite good, especially in the several impounded ponds. In 1984, a state record Rock Bass was caught in the Ramapo!

There is also some interesting water upstream, between Tuxedo Park and Arden Valley Road. This upper end is quite rocky and fast in places, and also somewhat inaccessible. A good part of it is contained within the western portion of Harriman Park. There is a DEC fisherman's parking area, by the way, at the bridge just off Village Road in Tuxedo Park.

The state stocks this river *only* between Sloatsburg and Arden Valley Road. The extreme upper end is not stocked because it tends to run warm due to the presence of several little ponds. There is a sewage treatment plant on the upper Ramapo, and some officials think this also has a negative impact on the upper part of the river.

All in all, the Ramapo should be considered a good resource in heavily developed Rockland County. There is a nice mix of water – good flows, deep holes, nice pools and runs, boulders, undercuts, downed trees and overhanging foliage. One problem is the noise! It seems impossible to escape the clamor of the nearby Thruway and Rt. 17. It should be pointed out, though, that its specific location, wedged in among the Thruway, Rt. 17 and the train tracks, provides a type of protection and buffers the river from development.

The nearby Mahwah River is also a stocked trout stream, receiving about 600 brooks and browns annually. It rises in central Rockland County, and flows along the southeastern border of Harriman State Park. The Mahwah eventually joins the Ramapo just south of Suffern in New Jersey. It is stocked from just above Lake Antrim in Suffern up to about Lime Kiln Road. This is the best section for trouters. At one point, the stream flows through Kabiak County Park.

Sparkhill Creek is tucked into crowded southeastern Rockland County, but offers, nonetheless, some fishing opportunity. It rises just east of Blauvelt, about three miles north of the New Jersey border, and eventually joins the Hudson near Piermont at the northern tip of Tallman Mt. State Park. The five miles of the Sparkhill that are stocked receive about 800 browns annually.

The fourth Rockland County trout stream, Minisceongo Creek, was found to have at least some wild brown trout back in 1977. In all likelihood, these wild fish were found in the upper section of the stream. This creek rises in Harriman State Park, actually emanating from Welch Lake, then flows east through Letchworth Village. It then drops into suburbia, picking its way through Thiels, Garnerville and Haverstraw before eventually meeting the Hudson north of Grassy Point. There is a considerable tidal section to this stream by the way, and here you might go exploring for white perch, stripers, crabs and other brackish water creatures. Minisceongo Creek – the north and south branches combined – receives a hefty annual stocking of about 1400 browns. Some holdover does occur.

Two brooks mentioned in the previous chapter, Tiorati and Stony Brook, are part in and part out of the park. Sections of these streams may be stocked outside the park, in the downriver sections where there is a little more water.

ROCKLAND – LAKES
The largest body of water in Rockland County is Lake Deforest Reservoir. It was surveyed in depth by Sr. Aquatic Biologist Mike Gann in 1982.

The survey turned up a sparse population of Largemouth Bass "dominated by extraordinarily large adults." Unfortunately, the non-game to gamefish ratio (24. 5:1) is one of the poorest ever obtained in any water in Region 3. This was attributed to the overabundance of carp and stunted white perch.

Shore fishing only, at six specific sites, is allowed. No boats. A fishing permit is needed, and can be obtained for $1 from the Spring Valley Water Company, 360 West Nyack Rd., West Nyack, NY.

Mainly because of the ban on boating, this large reservoir really offers relatively little opportunity. Even shore fishing is limited because, as mentioned, anglers are restricted to six specific sites and cannot wander the shoreline beyond these. Thus even though nearly 1500 permits are issued every year, angler harvest remains low. Following that 1982 survey, DEC made several recommendations aimed at improving the fishing, including opening the lake for ice fishing.

At this date, though, nothing has really changed. Thus if you care to poke in among the trees to fish Lake Deforest, you are likely to catch mostly undersized panfish. If you do nail a largemouth, though, it is liable to be a real lunker.

The only other lakes of any note in Rockland County are within the Palisades Parks and these are discussed in the preceding chapter. There are, of course, innumerable ponds for the adventuring young angler, who can find many tips for finding and fishing these stillwaters in Ch. 9.

ORANGE — STREAMS

As noted, this book only covers southern New York up to a radius of 50 miles from New York City. Thus not all Orange County waters are included here. Significant waters like the Neversink and the Shawangunk Kill will be covered in the next book in this series.

Of those Orange rivers within the 50-mile circle, the Wallkill is the largest. It is a warm-water river. There are black bass, some pickerel and panfish present but no trout.

Rising in New Jersey, the Wallkill flows northward through Orange and eventually meets the Rondout Creek in Ulster County. The upper section — that is, the section in lower Orange County — flows through agricultural lands, and is more turbid and not as good for fishing as the section north of Rt. 84. Boating is popular on the Wallkill but again mainly in its more downstream section . . . especially north of Montgomery. Though access for boaters is generally good, the water level must be up to make fishing from a boat pleasurable. Canoes are used here, as are small rowboats. Large motorboats would be out of place and not feasible, though some people do use elecric trolling motors.

There is good smallmouth fishing in the Wallkill, and also some largemouth. Redbreast Sunfish are plentiful (this species often thrives where the smallmouth does), and pickerel are found in the upstream section towards New Jersey. The river is characterized by many long, slow pools and often quite turbid water. There is little weediness.

Although there are many little creeks in Orange County, some surely containing native trout, we will discuss only the four notable trout streams. A list of all stocked waters may be found in the reference section.

First is Moodna Creek. This fair-sized steam is put together in central Orange County by a host of smaller brooks. It is stocked primarily in its downstream mileage, below Salisbury Mills. Yearly, Moodna receives a healthy quota of about 2200 brook and brown trout. There are no wild fish reported, but there is some holdover.

Also a viable trout stream is Moodna's main tributary, Woodbury Creek. This brook flows north quite a few miles before meeting Moodna just west of Cornwall. You can see this stream as you drive along the New York State Thruway north of the Harriman Interchange. While I have not fished it, a hunch tells me I should next spring. It flows through some pretty farmland, as yet undeveloped. Woodbury is implanted with more than 2000 brookies and browns annually.

Moodna Creek by the way, is tidal in its lower miles. These brackish sections of trout streams are very often full of surprises. As mentioned in Ch. 10, the mouth (and downstream section) of Moodna is a good place to look for spring stripers.

A little-known but reportedly productive Orange County stream is Rutgers Creek. A tributary to the Wallkill, this stream wanders through the "black dirt" agricultural land of Greenville and Minisink townships. An impressive eight to nine miles of Rutgers is stocked with about 2400 trout annually mainly upriver of the black dirt sector. The really good news here is that the Orange County Federation of Sportsmen's Clubs has worked with landowners to keep this stream open. You'll be pleasantly greeted with "Fishing Permitted" signs on parts of Rutgers Creek.

PER BRANDIN

Rockland County's Ramapo River is a better trout stream than many passing commuters suspect. For much of its length, its fishiness is belied by the flanking Thruway, railroad, and Rt. 17.

Tucked into the southernmost corner of the county is Wawayanda Creek. It is located just west of Greenwood Lake and flows through Warwick. Several miles of this stream are stocked with a total of about 700 browns each year.

ORANGE — LAKES

Greenwood Lake, which Orange County shares with New Jersey's Passaic County, is probably the most interesting stillwater in the vicinity. At 1900 acres it's easily the biggest. Greenwood's other vital statistics are 57 feet maximum depth, length about six miles, and maximum width about one-fourth mile. Note that either a valid New York *or* New Jersey fishing license permits one to fish the entire lake from a boat.

This is a true, two-story reservoir, with two cold-water gamefish – rainbow and brown trout – sharing quarters with three warm-water gamefish: Large and smallmouth bass and pickerel. Made, undoubtedly, nervous by this toothy quintet are several species of panfish that include yellow perch, crappies, rock bass and sunfish. There are even two species of "cats" available: Brown bullhead ("abundant") and White Catfish ("common"). Sawbellies are abundant, too.

While browns are stocked by both states, rainbows are put in only by New Jersey. The rainbow fishery appears to be primarily put-and-take, meaning that few stocked fish make it to the following year. But the 'bows are put in at a good size, many being one and two-year olds. The browns definitely grow and holdover and many nice fish over three pounds are boated.

For those seeking largemouth and pickerel, extensive weed beds are found at both the north and south ends of the lake. Smallmouths, which are not as plentiful here as bucketmouths, are found principally along the rocky areas on the east side of the lake.

Trout hunters should concentrate on the New York side of the lake, where the water is deeper. This is all the more urgent in midsummer when, a survey disclosed, oxygen is insufficient below 30 feet.

A usual hotspot for largemouth is in the weedy area between Storm Island and the eastern shoreline. Another is around Chapel Island at the extreme north end of the lake.

This is a popular ice-fishing lake, and in fact, *all species are open year-round*! It is a rare southern New York water indeed where this is the case.

Of considerable interest to the trout stalker also are Walton Lake and Round Lake, close together stillwaters that are located just outside the village of Monroe.

On Round Lake, the town maintains both parking facilities and a launch for putting out a small boat. No boats are rented and no motors are permitted. This lake receives an annual stocking of only about 1000 brown trout, but they are nice ones: 2-year olds averaging 12 inches or better. Sawbellies fatten them up quickly, and sawbellies are certainly the preferred bait. Round Lake also has some nice largemouth, and I have gotten some recent reports (unverified) of smallmouth and pickerel.

Just down the block, Walton Lake is stocked with a healthy 4000 brown trout annually and DEC biologists say there is some holdover. Fairly rich with weed growth, Walton Lake supports some good largemouths. Pickerel, panfish and alewives are also present. Boats are rented on Walton Lake and electric motors are permitted.

Just southwest of Newburgh is yet another place for trout fishing, Washington Lake. It is allocated some 500 rainbows and 1000 browns per year, and these are oversized 2-year old fish. According to officials, largemouth bass, pickerel and "every panfish known to man" are also present.

Orange County has an abundance of small ponds. Young anglers intent on seeking them out are once again referred to Ch. 9.

PART IV

FERTILE & FISHY WESTERN LONG ISLAND SOUND

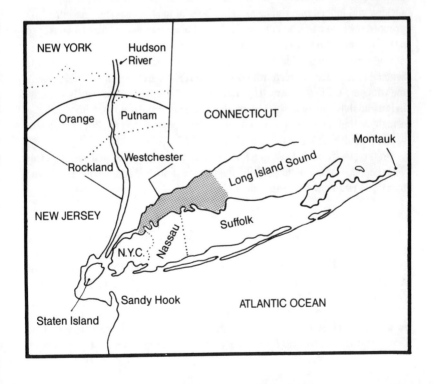

15.
BUNKERS, BLOOD AND BLUEFISH

The cove was greasy-calm at high tide, and as I scanned the water, something Blas Diaz once said came back to me: When the blues are in, there's nothing alive on the surface — no ducks, geese, gulls, nothing! But there *were* schooling bunkers plainly visible on top, and best of all, Nick Morabito was there. A local bait dealer in my hometown of North Tarrytown for years before retiring recently, Nick had a talent for being at Greenwich Cove *only* on the mornings when the fish were in. With these encouragements, my buddy Roger Mostar and I shouldered in among the line of anglers, and lobbed big, clunky-looking pieces of mossbunker into the brine. As I propped my pole up on a bent sapling, I saw the gruesome remains of a bunker cut neatly in half by some awesome pair of jaws.

God save the seas if bluefish ever grow as big as sharks! The next hour of that September morning in Greenwich Cove epitomized the excitement of Bluefishing. As the choppers made their way back into the cove, one by one the big Harnells and Daiwas doubled up, and expressions changed from pre-dawn blank, to smiling, to actually scared as reel bushings smoked and lines popped. And the fish were all nice: twelve-pounders at lot of them, a few of them fifteen.

On the bloody bank, I saw one Bluefish with a huge chunk ripped out of its side. What happened was, another bluefish flopping on shore had attacked it. I decided not to try and clean any of the fish for several hours.

WESTERN LONG ISLAND SOUND – the area from Bridgeport, Ct. and Port Jefferson, N.Y. westward to the New York City line – probably has one of the heaviest concentrations of sport fishermen on the Atlantic Coast. Yet in spite of the pressures, it remains quite productive.

The great range of water depths and bottom types make it attractive to a wide variety of species. You can fish shallows along shore or find bottom more than 200 feet below you. The deepest area is the trench

PER BRANDIN

Big blues are very much available to the boatless angler.
September is the best month.

separating buoy 28A (formerly 24C) and buoy 11B. These lie midway between the west end of the Norwalk Islands and Eaton's Neck on Long Island. The mainland shoreline is largely mud, clay or rock whereas sandy beaches characterize most North Shore Long Island areas.

Of all the species taken by sportsmen, only flounders, blackfish and lobsters can be considered non-migratory populations. Lobsters are included because the area provides a very productive commercial fishery and many sportsmen like to put out a few pots.

Most of the migratory species enter Western Long Island Sound from the east, but many menhaden (mossbunker) schools and most striped bass arrive by the way of New York Harbor and the East River.

Because the area is so heavily developed, shore access is quite limited. Still, there is some good shore fishing and Chapter 17 will help you find it. For consistent fishing success, though, Sound sportsmen are heavily dependent upon boats: private or open party boats, or skiffs rented from the several rowboat liveries along the Sound (there are a few charter boats as well).

Anyone planning to spend much time fishing Western Long Island Sound should purchase NOAA Nautical Chart 12364 of New Haven Harbor Entrance and Port Jefferson to Throgs Neck. This government printed publication is available at most larger marine dealers and sporting goods stores (see also "Other Resources" in the reference section). Although the scale of the foldout design is 1:40,000 rather than the 1:20,000 of the large individual charts, the foldout is much easier to use, especially if you are in a small boat.

There usually is an arrival of small to medium size blues between late May and mid June. These fish stay from a few days to six weeks and normally a period of slow action follows before the fishing begins to build toward the late summer peak. September is the best month for the big "alligators". Then bluefishing tapers off through October with few fish remaining by the end of the month.

Trolling is the most popular fishing method and although some downriggers are used, the vast majority of fishermen rely upon wire line. An "umbrella" or "coathanger" is the usual rig although a trolled subsurface plug can be deadly, especially with bigger fish. Dependent upon the water depth and the feeding level of the fish, the length of troll can vary from 100 to 300 feet. A rule of thumb for wire line is that it sinks 10 feet for each 100 feet let out.

One of the most exciting forms of bluefishing is casting lures to surface feeding fish. Popping plugs, subsurface swimmers and metal lures such as the Hopkins all are effective.

The open party boats rely primarily upon jigging, actually the only practical method with fishermen lined shoulder to shoulder along the rail. This technique is extremely effective with small school fish. However, the approach usually is not as productive when fishing from a private boat. Apparently, much of the party boat's success is due to the fact that 40 or more jigs flashing up and down in the water at once excite the blues into a feeding frenzy. A couple of lures beneath a small boat is not enough to hold the school below you.

Still fishing or drifting with cut bait also can be very rewarding. Use a little weight to hold the bait near the bottom. When drifting, a fillet strip is preferable to a chunk as it moves through the water more naturally and does not spin.

In late summer and early fall, there is no better way of taking a big bluefish than by swimming a live bunker (Fig. 17-c). The alligators tend to follow the bunker schools and the most productive locations usually are around the mouths of harbors and rivers. More often than not, the action is not directly in the bunker schools but somewhere else in the vicinity. Even when they are not actively feeding, big blues cannot resist the temptation to grab a struggling bunker.

The smaller fish will gorge on sand eels, shrimp and juvenile herring or menhaden and usually are found in the open Sound. But the biggest bluefish normally are close to shore harassing the menhaden schools which have sought refuge in harbors and rivers. Among the most consistently productive areas for school blues are the K racing buoy between Mamaroneck and Hempstead Harbor, outside of Captain's Island at Greenwich and Center Island Reef off Bayville. The Eaton's Neck triangle bounded by buoy 11B, buoy 13 and the obstruction buoy is heavily fished as is the inner Smithtown Bay area from the LILCO power plant to the Nissequogue River. Popular spots further east include Crane's Neck northeastward to the Middle Ground, buoy 11 outside of Port Jefferson Harbor and buoys 18 and 20 off Stratford.

STRIPED BASS
Although a few bass winter in power plant warm water outfalls, (especially the LILCO facility at Northport) and some sheltered coves, the majority of stripers are part of a migratory population.

The earliest action usually occurs to the west around Turtle Cove behind City Island and across the Sound in Little Neck Bay. Occasional fish are taken as early as Washington's Birthday in a mild winter, but it normally is late March or early April before there is any consistency to fishing around the New York City line. As you move eastward, action begins later and almost invariably, it is the last half of May before the

bass are distributed through the whole area of the Sound discussed here.

Good fishing continues through the summer and ends with the migration of striped bass, primarily school fish, westward through the Sound in October and November. These are fish heading toward their Hudson River wintering grounds around Haverstraw Bay.

Although some fish (notably large cows) of the main Atlantic Coast migration enter Western Long Island Sound from the east, Fisheries Director Robert Jones of the Connecticut Dept. of Environmental Protection estimates that 90% of the striped bass in the area west of Bridgeport are part of the Hudson River population. The happy result of this is that Long Island Sound, especially the western portion, is one of the few areas on the Atlantic Coast where striped bass still are plentiful. As a consequence of the 1976 closure of the Hudson River to commercial fishing (due to PCB contamination) and several extremely successful spawning seasons during subsequent years, the Hudson population is at one of the highest levels ever recorded. This contrasts sharply with the Chesapeake Bay population upon which the rest of the East Coast is primarily dependent. Statistics indicate that the Chesapeake fish would represent about 80% of the Atlantic Coast total under normal circumstances. However, there hasn't been a dominant year class in that area since the early 1970s and there is no indication of improvement in the near future.

Although many consider striped bass a wary game fish, they will respond to a wide variety of baits and lures. All of the following methods have proven successful: trolling sandworms with or without a turkey bone lure or spinner; drifting sandworms beneath a float; trolling umbrella rigs, plugs or tube lures (a piece of tailhook porkrind behind the tube increases effectiveness); casting streamer flies or plugs; and jigging. Jigging usually is most effective during the fall migration when the bass are schooling in deeper water. At most other times, the fish are found from a depth of 20 feet right up to the shore and this shallow water does not lend itself to jigging. Fishing cut bait on the bottom or livelining a mossbunker are the methods most likely to put a big cow bass in the boat.

Striped bass tend to spread out over the whole shore line and few areas can be written off as a waste of time. Obviously, there will be more fish where the baitfish concentrate. As a result, the sedge and rocks around river mouths, coves and reefs produce more consistently than open sandy beaches.

During the fall migration, large schools tend to remain in certain areas for days or even weeks. Among the most consistent hotspots are buoys 18 and 20 off Stratford; the area from buoy 11B to buoy 13 and the obstruction buoy off Eaton's Neck; and Prospect Point at the west side of Hempstead Harbor.

WEAKFISH

The first weakfish usually are taken around the end of May, but late June through mid-September normally is the most productive period.

Weakfish are extremely cyclical and the excellent fishing which began around 1973 tapered off as we entered the 1980s. Each year saw fewer, but bigger, weaks – an indication that we were fishing on the same year classes season after season. In recent summers, not too many have fished specifically for weakfish. Most fish taken were incidental catches for those seeking striped bass, bluefish or even porgies.

Weakfish will respond to trolled or cast plugs and jigging is productive if a school is located in deep water. However, sandworms or jelly worms drifted near the bottom around dawn or dusk probably is the most consistently effective technique.

Although Greenwich Harbor, Cockenoe Island off Norwalk, Penfield Reef at the west side of Black Rock Harbor and buoys 18 and 20 west of the Housatonic River often produce well, North Shore Long Island locations seem more consistent. These include Matinicock Point at the mouth of Hempstead Harbor; Center Island Reef off Bayville; inside of buoy 15 at Lloyd's; the obstruction buoy in front of Eaton's Neck; Crane's Neck at the east side of Smithtown Bay; and buoy 11 outside of Port Jefferson Harbor.

MACKEREL

When the Atlantic Coast population was at a very low ebb during the late 1960s and early 1970s due to heavy pressure from foreign trawlers, spring mackerel fishing was fantastically good in Western Long Island Sound. However, as the numbers recovered in the 1980s after the enactment of the 200 Mile Limit, the Sound runs became smaller and of shorter duration each year. There is no logical explanation for this inverse ratio. Possibly, availability of food prompted a change in migratory patterns.

Mackerel usually make their first appearance between the last week of April and the middle of May and remain in the area from a few days

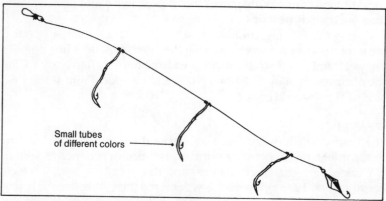

Small tubes
of different colors ⟶

Figure 15-a. "Mackerel Tree" Rig.

Thick schools of Atlantic Mackerel visit metro waters nearly every spring. It's possible to catch two hundred or even more in a day's outing.

to a month. A few small schools stay through the summer and there sometimes is a fall run of tinkers (young of the year). However, in Western Long Island Sound, mackerel are primarily a springtime species.

By far the commonest rig is a mackerel tree (Fig. 15-a). This consists of a jig with three or four very small tube lures spaced at about 8-inch intervals above it. It can be trolled, but drifting and jigging usually is more productive once you have located the schools. For jigging to be really effective, there must be enough wind or tide to move the boat at a fairly good rate. Normally, a very short line, no more than 20-30 feet, is best since the fish almost invariably are near the surface when feeding. Mackerel will only hit a fast moving lure, so continuous jigging is a must.

The mackerel arrive from the east and the first catches are made in the area just west of the Middle Ground. The schools gradually move westward, often as far as Execution Rocks off New Rochelle. It is difficult to predict a season's hot spots in advance, but mid-Sound from buoy 32A between Greenwich and Oyster Bay eastward is most likely to provide consistent action.

16.
BOUNCING FOR FLOUNDER
...AND OTHER EASY
CELLAR DWELLERS

The Italian deli was warm with the smells of fresh espresso, as well as provolones and pepperonis that hung from stainless steel hooks. But the steamy front window was being rattled by the last chill breath of winter. April 20th — not exactly swimming weather. Still, it was spring, a time when a young man's fancy turns to . . . what else — flounder!

Lunches in hand, we pushed off from the simple public ramp at the end of Milton Point in Rye. The Scotch Caps, well-known reefs just outside Milton Harbor, positively stunk of Striped Bass. Too cold for that, though. We skirted the caps on the inside and tied up to the raft that bobbed in the 15-knot breeze.

One thing about flounder, Jimmy Booth observed, is that the tide has to be moving. How right he was, based on all my experiences in the Sound and up at Quincy Bay. Luckily, the slack tide soon started to ebb, and the flounders started biting. There were several doubleheaders, and at least a few fish of Quincy Bay proportions. Almost all were big enough to filet.

We figured we caught $35 worth of fish that afternoon. And we didn't spend much because for bait, we used nightcrawlers we caught ourselves. All we really spent was six bucks for two salami & cheese wedges, and two coffees that were quickly put on ice by winter's last hurrah.

WITH THE POSSIBLE EXCEPTION of bluefish, flounders are the most popular sport fish in Western Long Island Sound. The stringent restrictions on trawling west of Longitude 73:00 (about midway between Bridgeport and New Haven) enacted by Connecticut in 1983 have had a strong positive impact on flounder fishing. This is basically a non-migratory species which moves only seasonally between the deep waters and the inshore areas of the Sound.

Flounder provide the first fishing in the spring and are among the last species caught in the fall. The best spring fishing is from late

March through the middle of May. Action tends to begin and end a little earlier in the westernmost portions. The flatfish return in the fall as the water begins to cool, and they provide good sport from early October well into November.

Although some catches are made at a depth of 30-50 feet when the flounders are moving in or out, most fishing is done in 20 feet of water or less. Often, the biggest flounders will be found next to shore in only a few feet of water.

Flounders prefer a mud botom, but sometimes can be found on sand or cobble. The bigger fish often feed on a cobble bottom or next to a reef.

A bit of sand or bloodworm on a small, long shank Chestertown or beak hook with enough weight to hold bottom is the usual rig. Flounder can be taken while at anchor or when drifting. If the fish are scattered and the wind is not too strong, drifting can be more productive. Chumming with crushed mussels, corn (dried or canned) and cat food will increase the catch if you are anchored.

Good flounder fishing is available throughout Western Long Island Sound. However, the hot spots in any particular area vary from year to year. Thus, it is best to secure guidance from local bait and tackle shops or other anglers when you are ready to fish. Most of the more consistently productive areas have two common characteristics – a clean, soft bottom and a depth of 10-20 feet.

BLACKFISH
Many are put off by the slightly slimy feel and ugly looks of these shellfish feeders. But blacks provide tremendous sport and fantastic

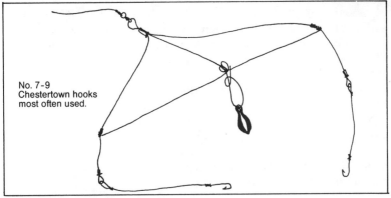

No. 7-9
Chestertown hooks
most often used.

Figure 16-a. Flounder Spreader.

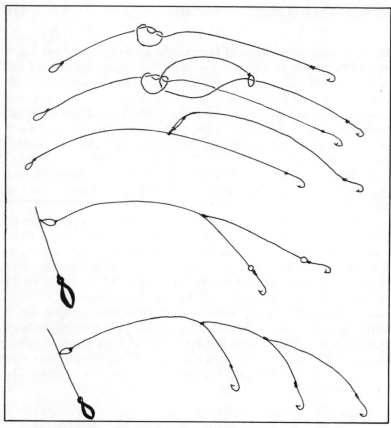

Figure 16-b. "No Hardware" tandem flounder rig. The third hook is optional, but will cause more tangles. Some fishermen attach the hooks only an inch or two above the sinker.

eating. They are not oily or "fishy" tasting and they freeze well.

The blackfish is another of the Sound's non-migratory species and, like the flounder, merely moves between deep and shallow water with the seasons.

Tradition has it that spring blackfishing begins when the dogwood blooms and this is a pretty good rule of thumb.

Normally, blackfish are found only in rocky areas. There are a few exceptions, such as the oyster beds inside the Norwalk Islands.

The spring run starts in April and builds until spawning takes place about the end of May. It then tapers off as the Sound warms to summertime temperatures.

Around the end of September, the blackfish again begin moving toward shore and there is good fishing in the shallower areas until the beginning of November. However, the best fall fishing, especially for larger fish, is to be found on the outside reefs at a depth of 30-60 feet. This action runs from the middle of October to the end of November. Experienced fishermen will bring back large catches with most of the fish in the 4-8 pound range.

Green crabs, fiddlers and soft clams are the commonly used baits. Blackfishing experts seeking big fish normally prefer half of a green crab although fiddlers or clams sometimes are more productive in early spring. The commonest hook is the Virginia style and this is what you will be given if you ask for blackfish hooks in a tackle shop. However, many of the serious fishermen seeking big fish use a 5/0 or 6/0 Sproat.

Successful blackfishing requires that the bait remain still on the bottom; blacks are wary feeders and easily spooked. Because of this, you need enough lead to hold bottom without rolling and this can mean up to 12 ounces on the deeper reefs when the tide is fast.

In spring and early fall, almost any inshore rocky area is a prospect although those where the reef extends out to deeper water produce more consistently.

Among the best locations for fall, deep water blackfishing are the outer portion of Execution Rocks off New Rochelle; the deeper water at the south side of Hen and Chickens at Larchmont; the reefs east of buoy 42 off the end of Rye's Scotch Caps; buoy 32A in mid-Sound between Greenwich and Oyster Bay; and Sound Reef which lies about midway between 32A and the Stamford Harbor entrance. Some of the best fishing, especially late in the season, can be found at Cable and Anchor Reef which begins on the east side of buoy 28A (formerly 24C) between Norwalk's Green's Ledge Light and Huntington Harbor; buoy 11B off Eaton's Neck; and the Middle Ground area in mid-Sound between Bridgeport and Port Jefferson. Apparently the fish migrate from the west since the more easterly locations seem to provide the best action as Thanksgiving approaches.

PORGY

Although the first porgy catches usually are reported in June, the best fishing is from mid-July until early October.

Like the flounder, porgies have benefited from the Connecticut restrictions on trawling in Western Long Island Sound. Another boost is that dragging in New York waters west of Eaton's Neck has been

Flounder! It's one of the premier sport fish of the party boat fleet. Flounder are easy, accessible, and there's no better tasting fish.

banned from April 1 to November 1 for many years.

Although striped bass worm trollers sometimes take big porgies close to shore, especially around dusk or dawn, most fishing is done in water with a depth of 20-60 feet. Hard or cobble bottom normally is most productive. Porgies are bottom feeders and the usual rig is a snelled hook tied into the line six to eight inches above the sinker. Often, a second hook, the length of a snell above the first, is used.

Sandworms or bloodworms are excellent bait, but thieving bergalls make use expensive and frustrating. In addition, porgies are adept bait stealers themselves. Solution? For many porgy chasers it's a strip of squid which is tough and difficult to tear from the hook.

By August, porgies are dispersed over most of Long Island Sound.

However, a few locations are more consistently productive. One of the most popular porgy fishing grounds is the whole area eastward from Huntington Harbor to buoy 11 off Port Jefferson including Eaton's Neck, the LILCO loading platform in the middle of Smithtown bay, Crane's Neck and Oldfield Point.

OTHER SPECIES

FLUKE. When the overall coastal population is high, North Shore Long Island can provide good fluke fishing. Since fluke prefer a sandy bottom, numbers usually are not sufficient to prompt one to fish specifically for them along the Westchester and Connecticut shoreline.

The commonest technique is bottom drifting on a moving tide. Preferred baits are a squid strip, a squid and sand eel combination or a live killie (mummichog minnow). Some of the biggest doormat size fish are taken on live snappers. Other baits are used as well, and the fish sometimes respond to lead head jigs and big streamer flies. Unlike flounders, fluke are aggressive predators and prefer a moving bait or lure. See also Part V.

Among the best areas are Matinicock Point on the east side of Hempstead Harbor to Center Island Reef and the mouth of Oyster Bay; Lloyd's Neck (buoy 15) eastward to Huntington Harbor; and the Eaton's Neck area. Popular fluke grounds further east include Crane's Neck and the area inside of buoy 11 at Port Jefferson.

DANIELLE BRANDIN

Blackfish, called Tautog further north, are superb table fish. They abound all around New York salt waters.

TOMCOD. This small member of the codfish family is subject to extreme fluctuation in levels of abundance. When plentiful, many are taken by flounder fishermen, especially in late afternoon. As a rule, they feed most actively from the last daylight hours into the night. Most sportfishing takes place from late October to early December when they move into stream mouths to spawn. During the spawning run, they often can be taken with a long-handled frog spear or in a trap with the opening facing downstream.

HERRING. Several species of herring, in addition to menhaden, can be found in the Sound but primarily during the colder months. Of these, only the alewife is fairly plentiful. During their late April spawning run, alewives often are taken in large numbers with dip nets when they concentrate at an obstruction such as the dam in the Mianus River just above U.S. Route 1 in Cos Cob.

SMELT. This is another extremely cyclical cold water fish which often virtually disappears for a decade or more. Most sportfishing activity occurs in the fall (mid-October into November) or during the spring spawning runs. At these times, the fish concentrate in the brackish water at the mouth of a stream.

WHITING AND LING. Although there has not been a good run of ling in Western Long Island Sound since the 1940s, whiting have been plentiful intermittently over the years. Both species prefer colder water and provide end-of-season action. Whiting pursue bait along the beaches on still, early winter nights and feed so aggressively that they sometimes ground themselves and freeze when they are unable to flop back into the water.

BUTTERFISH. This is another cyclical species which became very plentiful in the 1980s. Most sportfishing occurs in late September and October when the schools move into coves and streams.

EELS. Although eels are fairly plentiful every year, many regard them as a slimy nuisance. What a shame. Gourmands know that they are excellent in rich fish stews, and even better when smoked. Many do pursue eels, though, and the usual method is a long shanked Chestertown flounder hook baited with a bit of sandworm. Whole small killies, spearing or sand eels are sometimes used too. Since eels are primarily bottom feeders, the hook snell should be attached directly above the sinker.

Spearing used to be a very popular method of taking eels although few do it any more. On a calm summer night, a small boat with a downward pointing jacklight would be poled along the shallows, especially the edges of marshes and sedge banks. During the winter months, eels concentrate in areas with a soft muddy bottom.

17.
DETAILED ACCESS GUIDE FOR THE SHORE FISHERMAN

Gasparinni's old wooden skiffs bobbed musically in the cold, April breeze, while gulls out on the reef picked their teeth after some fine, low-tide dining. Out on the playland pier, we prepared a meal of different sorts: Fiddler crabs — just the right size, Frank Rhotko said. I was only twelve then, and wouldn't have known a good blackfish bait if it bit me (which, it seemed apparent, *this* bait was eminently capable of doing).

With disappearing fingers, I gentled the odd bait down into the rocks, then waited patiently for a tug. If it was like fishing crawdads for bass — which I'd done — I figured that I'd be hung up in seconds. So, shutting out the world like only a child can, I guided the bait with x-ray vision past each and every potential snag and towards the mouth of the waiting mystery fish.

I gave it a good shot, too. About ten minutes. Then, swayed by the flatties I saw flying over the rail, I switched over to a flounder outfit. Only thing is, I caught a blackfish! On the first cast, on a worm.

You can never tell what's going to happen in fishing. But if it's April, you can bet that a raw, damp northeaster is going to be biting.

THE WESTCHESTER-CONNECTICUT shoreline of Western Long Island Sound is possibly the most intensely developed section of the Atlantic seaboard. Not only are there houses, summer houses and commercial development aplenty, there are entire peninsulas that the wealthy have usurped and closed off to the public. In spite of this, an enterprising angler can enjoy good fishing here even if he/she can't afford to own a boat. Before we name some 25 specific locations between the Housatonic River and Throg's Neck (which really comprise about 35 different spots), some general advice on gaining access to and fishing the Sound would be in order:

1. During the off-season – generally mid September to mid May – access is much easier. Many parks open only to residents of

specific municipalities *in season* will explicity or implicity allow you in off-season. (Some parks have a longer "in-season" running from about May 1st to October 15th.) Many of the spots in this chapter are off-limits to non-residents, at least part of the time. But to qualify the exact situation at each and every spot would've taken more asterisks than a Roger Maris scorecard. Take a ride to the place – you'll quickly find out what the story is.

2. At the fringes of the season, i.e. April-May and September-November, try to get permission from private landowners to fish.

3. Look for reefs, rivermouths, eelgrass, docks and piers, bridges – anything to break up the monotony. Plain stretches of flat bottom with no obstructions usually hold few fish.

4. Talk to other fishermen to learn new spots. Sunday is a good day. It's amazing how much you can learn this way – not only where-to but when and how.

5. Arrange to be dropped off. Very often, fishing may be allowed but parking may not. Or, use a bicycle!

6. From a fishing standpoint, spring and fall will *generally* be more productive than the middle of the summer.

7. The access points depicted and described in this chapter can be eliminated in any of a number of ways (though the parks remain pretty constant). Try to check a spot out before an actual outing.

8. Jetties are not only potentially dangerous places that should be given respect, they are also very much exposed to the elements. Bring extra clothes and don't be caught on a bar by a rising tide.

9. Generally, laws allow a fisherman to walk or wade nearly *anywhere* along the sound below the high water mark.

The locations of the following spots are roughly shown on Fig. 17-a. For each quadrant, the fishing locations are numbered from east to west and correspond to the text.

In keeping with the approach of this book, only minimal directions are provided. This is to allow room to talk about the actual fishing. It is assumed that the reader will use this book *in conjunction* with a good map. Do not attempt to find all these spots through the directions given in the book without a map, as you will sometimes get lost.

Although a county road map would be good, highly recommended are the Hagstrom Atlases. For the Connecticut spots, use the Hagstrom *Fairfield County Atlas;* for the Westchester shoreline, use the Hagstrom *Westchester County Atlas;* for spots in the Bronx, use the Hagstrom *New York City 5 Borough Atlas.* In a pinch, a standard road map will help, but a full-size state map will not be detailed. Look for a

"Metropolitan Area" road map.

One last note: References to I-95 refer to Interstate Rt. 95. This is called the Connecticut Turnpike in Connecticut, the New England Thruway in New York. *Some Ct. exit numbers may be the same as N.Y. exit numbers!*

QUADRANT I — THE HOUSATONIC RIVER WEST TO PENFIELD REEF

1. MILFORD: CARTEN'S GRAVEL PIT. In Milford, take Naugatuck Avenue to Caswell Avenue. Go west on Caswell to the end. Although this spot is really on the lower Housatonic, it is a good place to try for big bluefish. At the end of Caswell Road, and just north of the A.J. Carten Sand & Gravel Co., cross the railroad tracks and take the cinder road into some abandoned fields. Big blues often linger here, by Pope's Flat (an island) and are taken in late summer and early fall. Other salt and brackish water fish may be present.

2. STRATFORD: SHORT BEACH. Exit 31 on I-95. Take South Street to Main Street, follow it to Short Beach Park.

Any place where a freshwater river enters the salt is liable to be a hotspot. This wide peninsula is at the mouth of the Housatonic River ... one of Connecticut's largest. To fish Short Beach, bring waders. The main attraction here is a long bar that can be waded for two hours before and two hours after low tide. Flounder are caught off the beach, while the bar yields stripers, blues and occasional weaks, mackerel and fluke.

3. STRATFORD: POINT NO POINT. Exit 30 on I-95. Take Lordship Blvd. to the end of the point. Park along Beach Drive.

There are really three separate spots here. Russian Beach stretches almost all the way from Stratford Point back to the rocks at Hillside Avenue. In late summer and early fall, surfcasters catch blues that sporadically hit the beaches. An occasional weak or fluke spices the action. Flounder flurries can be quite good right off the rocks along Beach Drive. If it's cold, you can sit in your car between bites! Further up is Long Beach, where in addition to blues and flatties, anglers take some stripers and blackfish.

4. PLEASURE BEACH. Exit 29 off I-95. Take Seaview Avenue to the clankety wooden bridge that connects this little island to the mainland.

This is a very pleasant spot to fish, and an interesting one. Park in the big lot just over the bridge; a little refreshment stand and bait shop is open in season.

Bluefish of up to 20 pounds have been snared from the front beach. There is also a very long, rocky breakwater and a wooden fishing pier.

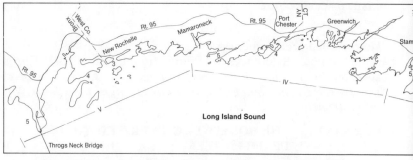

Figure 17-a. Access to the Westchester-Connecticut shoreline of Western Long Island Sound is difficult but not impossible.

5. PENFIELD REEF. Exit 21 off I-95. Take Reef Road all the way to the end. Park anywhere you can along Beach Road or vicinity.

This is a long reef that stretches nearly out to the lighthouse, and it is one of the best access points on the sound. The best time is from two hours before and two hours after low tide, when the reef is fully exposed. With waders, you can fish the fuller portions of the tide, but currents are strong. BE CAREFUL!!

Blues, stripers, weaks and blacks are all taken off this long reef. It is advisable to fish with a partner and study the tide tables so you do not get caught.

QUADRANT II — SOUTHPORT HARBOR WEST TO THE SAUGATUCK RIVER

1. SOUTHPORT HARBOR JETTY. Exit 20 on I-95. Take Sasco Hill Road to the end. In season, this beach is for Fairfield township residents only, and a parking sticker is required. Before mid-May and after mid-September, non-residents can probably park here without any problems, for purposes of fishing. Walk the beach (Sasco Beach) west about 200 yards to get to the long jetty at the mouth of the Mill River. This is Southport Harbor.

While not one of the most dynamic shore fishing spots on the sound, big blues are nonetheless taken here at times. Bunkers are frequently bunched up, and can be snagged for bluefish or striper bait. Early morning is the best time here, September and October the best months. Small stripers and some flounders are also caught.

2. FROST POINT. Exit 18 on I-95. Take Greens Farms Rd. east to Burial Hill Beach. Walk east a few hundred yards along the beach to Frost Point. In the off season, you may be able to park at the private beach lot at the end of Burying Hill Rd. At other times, park by Greens Farm train station and walk down. Or, take a bicycle. You can enter through a gate just above the large concrete reinforcing wall on

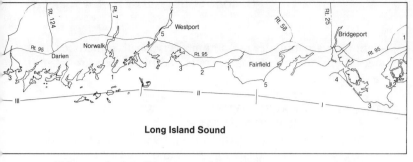

This map depicts 25 access points, which comprise some 35 different fishing locations. These quadrants are keyed to the text.

Beachside Avenue.

Blues are taken here in season, as are good-sized striper schoolies. Blackfish are also sometimes caught from this rocky point.

3. SHERWOOD ISLAND STATE PARK. Exit 18 off I-95. The park is open year-round to residents and non-residents, and while it closes at dark, fishermen who stay later are usually not harassed. A $2 parking fee is charged.

Billy's Rock is the point that divides the park neatly in two. Flounders and blacks are taken in season. Passing blues are occasionally caught, too. Good-sized stripers are nailed by early-morning pluggers from the little beach west of the point. At the eastern boundary, blue crabs, snappers and perhaps other fish are taken from the wooden breakwater at little Mill Creek.

4. COMPO. Exit 17 off I-95. Take Bridge St. over the Saugatuck River, turn right on Compo Road. At the highway divider turn right onto Compo Beach Road.

Westport residents can get a free parking sticker from the Town of Westport Parks & Recreation Commission. For non-residents, hefty parking fees are charged. Fees are collected May 1 to Oct. 15 only.

Big stripers are gaffed here, some in the 30-40 lb. class. East Beach is popular for linesiders. Bluefishing is also very good at times, and you can frequently snag your own bunker for bait. Off the south beach, there is a rocky jetty from which flounder and blues are caught.

5. IN AND AROUND THE SAUGATUCK. Exit 17 off I-95. Here we speak of the lower tidal section, which flows right through downtown Westport.

Despite a rash of new construction along the Saugatuck, there are still a few places to fish. One good one is from the Rt. 1 bridge. Another is from the little park opposite the Sunoco Station on Riverside Avenue. A third is from the old steel bridge (Bridge St.) just above the Thruway. For this latter spot, park in the little pull-off just east of the bridge.

Caught here are flounder (sometimes very small, sometimes o.k.), snappers, crabs and occasional stripers and blues. Eels are taken in very good numbers.

QUADRANT III — CALF PASTURE BEACH WEST TO
KOSCIUSKO PARK

1. CALF PASTURE BEACH. Exit 15 from I-95. Take East Ave. south. The name changes twice to Gregory Blvd. and Calf Pasture Beach Rd. There are two jogs to the left at the far end of the triangular park just beyond the railroad and around the monument at the end of Gregory Blvd. This is a Norwalk city beach and there are non-resident restrictions during the bathing season. Flounders, snappers and some blackfish are available. Occasional excellent bluefish action in late summer and early fall when the bunkers are cornered against shore.

2. VETERANS MEMORIAL PARK. Exit 14 from the northbound I-95. South through South Norwalk business district. Park is on your

APPROXIMATE TIMETABLE FOR INSHORE FISHING
IN LOCAL SALT WATERS

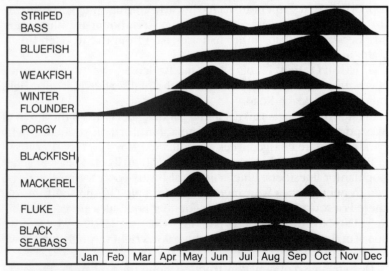

Figure 17-b. This is, as labeled, an *approximation*. The bight, the south shore, the western sound, and especially Montauk all have their own particular calendar. When-to information pertinent to each area is found throughout the text.

right when you cross the Norwalk River bridge. Flounders, eels and snappers are available. Large bluefish often are in the river, particularly adjacent to the highway bridge abutments, at night or just after daylight. They are attracted by the bunker schools which are in the lower Norwalk River during most of the summer. It often is possible to snag bunkers for bait between the launching ramp and the bridge.

3. COVE ISLAND PARK/WEED BEACH. For Cove Island Park, take Exit 9 off I-95. Take Seaside Avenue to the end, turn left onto cove Rd., follow to park. This is a Stamford park and a resident parking sticker is required. To get to Weed Beach, take Exit 10 off I-95, then take Noroton Ave. to Nearwater Lane. Make a right on Brush Island Road which takes you to the beach.

These two adjacent locations are connected by a tidal dam which can be walked across at low water. Both small and large flounder are caught here, along with a few weakfish. The nice-looking rocks also hold some stripers. Schools of blues group up here, and there have been reports of a few 10-lb. plus doormat fluke (unconfirmed). These are literally "flukes", though, and no one fishes this area specifically for this species.

4. CUMMINGS PARK/WEST BEACH. Exit 8 off I-95. Take Shippan Ave. south for a half-mile or so until you see Cummings Park on your left. The West Beach entrance is about a half-mile further south on Shippan Ave.

These are city beaches divided by the lagoon leading to Marina Bay and the Halloween Yacht Club. A resident parking permit is required during the bathing season, approximately Memorial Day to Labor Day.

Cummings Park can be fished from the pier at the right side of the beach or along the lagoon. Fishing at West Beach is largely restricted to the area adjacent to the launching ramp.

Flounders, tomcod, and butterfish are taken here, and there is usually fantastic snapper fishing in August-September. When bunkers are in the area, there can be good bluefishing from the pier or in the mouth of the lagoon.

5. KOSCIUSKO PARK. Exit 7 off I-95. Take Washington Blvd. south to Dyke Lane to the end.

Fishermen often refer to this park as "The Dyke." It divides the east and west channels of Stamford Harbor. Most fishing is done from the hurricane barrier in the East Channel to the point at the south end. Parking is available adjacent to this area.

Flounders, eels, tomcod, snappers and an occasional striped bass are coolered. There can be periods of excellent action with bluefish.

QUADRANT IV — GREENWICH POINT PARK WEST TO MILTON POINT

1. GREENWICH POINT PARK. Exit 5 off I-95. It is a ways from the Thruway. Ask directions, or refer to a Hagstrom Fairfield County street atlas.

At 147 acres, this is probably the largest shoreline park along that section of the sound discussed in this chapter. High and low tides are posted here at the Gatehouse Entranceway.

There is a reef off Greenwich Point where blues are caught. Flounder and blacks are reportedly taken here, too. Blues, in fact, may be taken anywhere around this elbow-shaped peninsula. Around the other side of the park, fishing is conducted from Flat Neck Point.

Beach rules are strictly enforced here, and no vehicles are allowed on the several trails or footpaths. This park is off-limits to non-residents most if not all of the year.

2. STEAMBOAT ROAD. Exit 3 off I-95. Take Steamboat Road past the Showboat Nightclub to the end at the water. Parking is on Steamboat Road just before it ends.

This is one of the more popular Western Sound shore spots. The problem is the crowding. When the blues are in for a few days, everybody knows about it and the pier is crowded. Weekdays are better, of course, and you can also find elbow room during the mid-day hours. Unfortunately, mid-day only seems to pan out when it's rainy and stormy. At other times, very early a.m. is the best time for those big blues, some of which hit 20 lbs.

Besides the hit-or-miss bluefish of late summer and early fall, flounder, snappers and eels are caught off this large concrete pier. Snapper chasers can catch their own bait here in the form of spearing. Bring along an umbrella net.

3. GREENWICH HARBOR. (Directions are same as for Steamboat Road.) In some years, the bluefish that are caught off of Steamboat Road work their way back into the harbor. In fact, in the 70's, when both bunker and blues were very plentiful, we had our best action all the way back in off Arch St., practically within spitting distance of the Connecticut Turnpike. There is a little park back here, and I've never seen fishermen harassed fishing from the banks of this park. We liked this spot because the pier at Steamboat Road is always crowded and back here there is elbow room. It's a fine place to snag bunker, too. Whether or not this spot produces seems to be directly related to the abundance of bunker in the sound in any given year. The full portion of the tide is best.

4. PLAYLAND. There is a large pier here that could make a super fishing platform for scores of local fishermen. Unfortunately, the pier is in a bad state of repair, and even after a recent fix-up, only part of the pier is open for anglers.

This is mainly a flounder spot, though smallish blacks are also taken. As with almost any Western Long Island Sound shore point, any of a number of surprises is possible. If you plan to come here, call the Playland Amusement Park Office to find out when the pier is open. During the season, you can buy bait and tackle from Gasparrini's boat livery, located right near the pier.

5. MILTON POINT. Exit 11 off the New England Thruway. Take the Playland Parkway towards Playland for about one mile. Before the amusement park, take a right onto Milton Pt. Road, which will merge into Stuyvesant Ave. Follow to the end.

Here, just before the American Yacht Club, is a small ramp and parking lot. There is also a little rock jetty. This is a nice little spot, but the problem is parking. The lot is very small, and when the fish are biting it quickly fills. This means that you may not have room to leave your trailer, or simply no place to park if you want to shore fish. There is some additional parking on local streets, but this is a ways back. If there were two of you, one could drop off the gear, then go back and park. The walk is not unreasonable.

This is a good place for flounders, both in the spring and fall. Small blackfish, eels, and snappers are also taken, and there is always the chance big blues could move in if schools of bunker are present. Stripers are also taken here occasionally.

QUADRANT V — MAMARONECK HARBOR TO THE BRONX

1. MAMARONECK HARBOR. New York Exit 10 off I-95. Take Mamaroneck Avenue south to its end.

The outer rim of this harbor is mostly exclusive homes and clubs. Thus unless you have some kind of an "in", you will be restricted to Hudson Park on the inside of the harbor. Taken mainly are bottom fish like flounder and some blacks off the rockier sections. Tom cod and snappers can also be gathered in season. As with Greenwich Harbor, jumbo alligator blues can drift in from time to time chasing schools of bunker. In fact, Mamaroneck Harbor is part of the local "bluefish circuit", and serious chopper chasers will check this spot out when Steamboat Road is not producing.

2. HUDSON PARK. (Different park than the one named above.) New York Exit 8 off the I-95. Take North Avenue south to Pelham Road.

While whole, live bunker is without equal for big bass and blues, it is not always readily available. A good substitute, and one that is easier to fish, is chunk bait. Bunker or mackerel are most often used.

Turn left (east) onto Pelham Rd., then bear right onto Hudson Park Rd.

To fish this City of New Rochelle park in season, a park permit is required. Only city residents may obtain this permit. In the off season, non-residents may enter. The Park is open daily from 6:00 a.m. to 10:00 p.m.

Fishing here is conducted from a fairly high seawall often referred to as "The Sundeck." Thus a long gaff or preferably net would be recommended. Gamefish such as blues and bass are caught on chunk bait and sometimes lures, and there is normally some flounder action is spring and fall. The usual assorted sound species such as snapper blues and tom cod may be encountered in their respective seasons.

3. GLEN ISLAND. New York Exit 7 off I-95. Take Weyman Avenue to its end at the park.

Some fishing is done from the base of the mainland side of the bridge, at the end of Fort Slocum Road. Chiefly at night, anglers cast chunk bait (usually bunker or mackerel) for blues and bass that sometimes run to good sizes. Snappers are also sometimes quite abundant in late August and September. To fish the shores of the island itself, a Westchester County Park permit (county residents only may apply) is required between Memorial Day and Labor Day. While gamefish are taken in the sluiceway beneath the bridge, mostly bottom

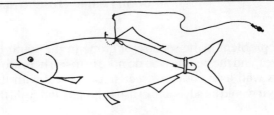

LIVELINING BUNKER
By Ted Keatley

More often than not, a big bluefish will chop off the tail of a bunker and then return to finish the meal in a leisurely manner. Thus, an effective bluefish rig should include a tail hook and nylon coated cable leader. While many use big 2X strong hooks, smaller, needle sharp styles such as a 7/0 Sproat penetrates much more readily. Snell the first hook with 10-12 inches of cable and then attach a second piece about five inches long to the shank of the hook. If the sleeve is snubbed up tightly before crimping, the hook barb will keep it from slipping off. Attach a hook to the short snell and the rig is complete.

When rigging the bunker, insert the first hook under the dorsal fin of the bunker and lay the second hook along the tail. The second hook is not inserted in the bunker. It is held in place by a small rubber bank slipped over the tail.

While many use treble hooks, more and more fishermen have become convinced that single hooks are just as effective. An added benefit is that they also increase the survival chances of a fish which breaks off.

Figure 17-c.

fish are caught from the island. However big blues or bass can never be ruled out, here or anywhere else along the sound.

4. CITY ISLAND AREA. New York Exit 6 off I-95 onto the Hutchinson River Pkwy. Then follow signs to City Island.

City Island and its environs is the best shore fishing location in the populous Bronx. Although there are bait & tackle shops and party boats on the island itself, access to the private shoreline is extremely difficult unless you know somebody. However, fishing is done from the base of the City Island Bridge, where anglers catch flounders, blackfish, snappers and even sometimes porgy in season. Giant bluefish, too, are a possibility, especially from late August through early October.

On the land side of this bridge is sprawling Pelham Bay Park. Fishing for flounder can be good off Orchard Beach, and blacks are caught off both rocky areas that brace this beach. Around back, fishermen hit Turtle Cove for flounder and stripers, the latter especially at night. In the "Lagoon" inside the park, flounder are reeled in. Access to this sheltered lagoon is from either Park Drive or Pelham Bridge Road.

5. MISC. BRONX SPOTS. The Bronx shoreline between Pelham Bay Park and Randall's Island offers relatively little access for the shore fisherman. And, while none of the waters immediately in contact with the five boroughs is especially clean, this stretch can be quite dirty.

Another problem is the spectre of crime in the south Bronx: It's a rough area, and the people who do nose in to fish here are mostly local residents who have enough street sense to deal with the situation. Certainly it would be advisable to fish in groups and avoid the nighttime hours.

What little access there is in this segment is mostly between Pelham Bay Park and the Whitestone Bridge. Anglers cast from the Bronx base of both the Throgs Neck and Whitestone Bridges, but recent reports have been that access is increasingly difficult. This action is overwhelmingly on fairly small striped bass, most of which will fall short of the new 24" size limit. Occasional chopper blues, blackfish where there are rocks, snapper blues, porgies, eels, tom cod and even whiting are other Bronx shoreline possibilities.

UNUSUAL SPECIES OF THE WESTERN SOUND

Many other species are taken in Western Long Island Sound each year, but not in numbers sufficient to justify fishing for them. Among these are seabass, bonito, kingfish (northern whiting) and sheepshead porgies. The "northern whiting" is not to be confused with the "whiting" of this area which actually is a silver hake.

Occasional bonito are taken each year by bluefishermen, usually during September. But with the exception of a few seasons in the early 1960s, these fish of the open ocean have only been chance visitors.

For several years around 1965, a fair number of small market cod were in the area during November, primarily in the vicinity of Eaton's Neck and Execution Rocks. Few have been reported in subsequent seasons.

In the late 1970s, Lafayette (Norfolk Spot) were extremely plentiful during late summer and sometimes represented more than half of a snapper fisherman's catch. However, we are at the northern extreme of their range and after a few seasons, they disappeared again.

Some sharks are always with us. Dogfish are common and there usually are a few reports of the bigger varieties each summer, primarily sand sharks, blue sharks and porbeagles (mackerel sharks).

PART V

ISLAND
CORNUCOPIA

18.
TROUT STREAMS —OUT HERE?

It was October at its most splendid, mid-month with maples ablazing. Per Brandin turned the van off the Sprain Brook Parkway, and onto the buzzing New England Thruway, and soon we were on the Throgs Neck Bridge with the Manhattan skyline off to starboard. Once across the bridge, it was a simple hop from the Cross Island to the Long Island Expressway to the Sagtikos Parkway. We knew it was going to be a good day of trout fishing.

"You've got beat #12 . . . it's nice. Try these wets. Try small muddlers. Try dries if you want to. Wets work better."

As Per coached me, two huge buck deer popped out of the brush, and a flock of semi-wild turkeys ran out ahead of us. There were hawks soaring above, and cottontail rabbits bouncing about. Connetquot River State Park is a beautiful place, indeed.

A belted kingfisher laughed at my first catch — a good-sized oak tree. Backcasting conditions are not delightful. But on my second drift, my #14 Adams curved beautifully through the thick, swaying mats of water starwort, and a 13-inch brownie gave it a slam. I killed the fish and gently laid it on the variegated autumn carpet of oak, alder and maple. Then I sat back to drink in the solitude, and said out loud to myself: I *can't* be on Long Island.

A muskrat swimming by offered no argument.

IF EVER A place could be called an oasis, Connetquot River State Park Preserve would have to be it. Located a bit west of mid-island, its 3400 acres are wedged in among droning highways, bustling towns, and Orwellian shopping malls that seem to clone themselves weekly in their all-out effort to reach Montauk via Rt. 27. Set among this – should I say it, madness – the Connetquot is a morning of refuge, an afternoon of tranquility.

This is a spring creek, meaning that is born of seepages of ground water rather than surface water as in the case of a freestone stream. Like most spring creeks, it is very stable – water levels seldom drop much, and murkiness very rarely occurs, even after a hard rain. Further, temperatures remain quite constant. The water emerges from the ground at about 52 degrees F. and seldom goes higher than the mid-sixties.

The fishing regulations are somewhat unusual. We'll cover the

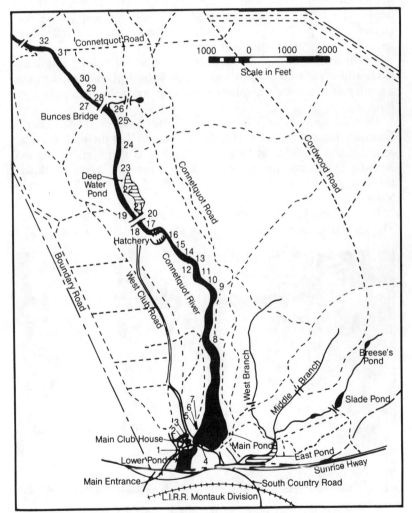

Figure 18-a. Beat Guide To The Connetquot

highlights here, but you should also call the park for the latest word.

As of early 1985, the fee for fishing is $7 per session per rod. This entitles you to fish any one of the three daily sesions: 7:00-11:00 a.m., 12:00-4:00 p.m., and 5:00-sunset (the latter only from April-September). You should call to reserve a spot, and they will take reservations any day in a month for *up to* the last day of the next month. You cannot reserve a particular beat, however. These are given out on a strictly first-come first-served basis about 20 minutes before a session is to begin. This is fun, though. The anglers for the upcoming session all gather in one parking lot and exchange pleasantries and tales about their favorite beat. It lends a European flavor to it all.

It is fly fishing only, and your hooks must be barbless. If you've just tied a zillion patterns on good old Mustad 94840's, don't despair. Bring a small pair of needlenose pliars and crimp down the barb before you knot on a fly.

Although the park is open year-round, fishing is allowed only between February 1st and October 31st. Note, though, that the park is closed Monday and Tuesday in February, March and October, and closed Monday from April through September. Currently, you are allowed three trout per session, and the *unofficial* size limit is 9 inches. Most of the stocked fish are bigger than this anyway.

Trout are stocked at frequent intervals throughout the fishing season. The fish come from a hatchery located right within the park, and in

PER BRANDIN

Whitetail deer are only one of many animals that cavort freely around the grounds of Connetquot State Park.

fact, one of the highlights of any trip to the Connetquot is a few minutes spent gawking at the hatchery pools. Don't miss it.

Annually, the park stocks an average of 40-50,000 brook, brown and rainbow trout. Brookies make up the bulk of this. There is also some natural reproduction of brookies, especially in the upper sections of the river above beat #25. (see Fig. 18-a). Both DEC and the park speculate that there may be some wild brown trout, but neither source seemed able to confirm this. In addition, there are some searun trout, as discussed towards the end of this chapter.

There are 32 beats on the river, as depicted on the map. Twenty three of these are on the stream, while nine are on three little ponds: Lower Pond, Main Pond and Deepwater Pond. If you choose either Main or Deepwater Pond, you have the free use of a rowboat. Some very large trout may be found here, witness the 14-lb. 10-oz. brown yielded by Main Pond. Park Manager Gil Bergen asserts that this is the largest trout he knows of being taken in Connetquot Park.

I think the 7-foot 3-inch Fisher glass rod I custom made is a perfect length for the Conny. Backcasting conditions are tight, and a longer rod will only aggravate the problem. On my Fisher I hang a Hardy Featherweight reel spooled with a DT4F line. On this smallish stream I favor shortish leaders of 7½ to 8 feet.

There is a platform at each beat from which casting can be done, thus waders are not strictly necessary. But I feel this approach makes me too visible to the fish, so I prefer wading. Chest-high waders are needed; hip boots won't do it.

Especially on the narrower upper beats, a classic upstream approach is very, very difficult. I fish downstream, wading slowly and carefully to keep commotion to a minimum. When I reach the bottom of my beat, I simply walk back up to the top and repeat the scenario.

The beautiful, undulating clumps of water starwort and wild celery are themselves fine holding lies here. In this sense, weeds take the place of rocks which are almost totally absent. Trout also lie behind and in front of the many deflector dams, under occasional sunken logs and drooping foliage, and around the platforms. In autumn, trout will hide in off-channel backwaters beneath collecting leaves.

One of the most important trout foods in this stream is *Gammaris*, a fresh-water shrimp (often called "scud"). Immitations of this crustacean seem to be most effective early in the season. The Connetquot is also rich in fly life. Although there may be even earlier hatches, the Early Brown Stonefly comes off here sporadically around the last two weeks of March. Then, along about the second week of April, Gordon Quills pop up as do Little Blue Quills in a size #18. This latter fly is a good solid hatch that generally gets going when the water is at 50° or better for three days. It hatches quite dependably for about a month, and comes off at the gentlemanly hours of about 10:00 a.m.-3:00 p.m.

In early May there are Hendricksons, followed by Sulphurs, size 16-18, in late May. The hot weather of August brings on a variety of Diptera (midges), and caddis are sprinkled in with the others for much of the season. One notable caddis is a blackish one, size 18, that materializes, usually, around the second week of May.

There are a couple of other less common fly hatches on the Connetquot. One is the Little Green Damselfly, a slow water and pond insect that nonetheless may be seen on the stream in early season. Interestingly, this is a multi-brood fly and it usually appears again in June. Often appearing *three* times in one season is the little Callibaetis, 16-18. Curiously, the later broods appear to get a little smaller (16 down to 18).

The park is to be commended for providing fishing areas for the handicapped. Five special platforms have been erected on beats 16-20, and these are reserved for persons who have physically limited abilities. This would include persons in wheelchairs. Such individuals can indeed catch trout from these platforms.

All in all, the Connetquot is a beautiful place to fish. Among the amazing array of wildlife perhaps most notable is the avian representation. More than 200 species of birds have been identified here, including osprey, kingfisher, and several species of hawks. For those interested, Connetquot Park is also rich in botanical life.

The entrance is right on Rt. 27. From the city, take the Southern State Parkway almost to its terminus at the Hecksher Spur. Then get on Rt. 27 for a mile or two more heading east. The park entrance is easy to miss – watch closely for it. From eastern Long Island, take the Sunrise Highway. Fig 19-b will further help you locate this park.

THE NISSEQUOGUE
Much of what is said about the Connetquot can also be said for the Nissequogue. It is another spring creek, of about the same size, and it too lies within a state park: 543-acre Caleb Smith (formerly Nissequogue River State Park). However the Nissequogue has less vegetation and more riffle-pool development than either the Connetquot or the Carman's.

Regulations are quite similar to those on the Connetquot. The fee is $7 per session, and again, you are allowed three fish of nine inches or better. The times of the sessions are a little different, though, so you should call about these.

TROUT STREAMS — OUT HERE?

AUTHOR PHOTO

Fly fishing is the method of the day on the Connetquot. The gent above is fishing in the legal section, just below the off-limits hatchery area.

PER BRANDIN

There are only eight stream sites, but each one is about 400-450 feet long – a good deal more spacious than on the Connetquot. In addition, there are five pond sites. Unlike the Conny, there are no boats on the ponds. All fishing is done from platforms, and there are two platforms at each site. There is also a separate pond reserved especially for children.

The Nissequogue receives its fish from the Connetquot hatchery. Approximately 7,000 brook, brown and rainbow trout are stocked each year, but brook trout predominate. The stocked fish are large, averaging about 12-14 inches, and they grow very well here. According to Park Manager Michael Venuti, quite a few fish of 2½-3 pounds are taken, with a few even larger ones nailed from time to time. To augment the stocked fish is a modest crop of naturally spawned brook trout.

Stocking quantities here are determined by fishing pressure. April to August is the busiest season, and during this time frame trout are stocked every week. Reservations can be made up to a month ahead, and it *is* advisable to do so, especially in spring and early summer.

To me, the Nissequogue water is more interesting than the Connetquot. For one thing, it has less of a manicured look, and certain beats are actually out of sight of the main path. There are even a few of what might be termed pools, as well as a variety of runs, glides and even little islands. The Nissequogue has more character, or definition or whatever you might want to call it.

Caleb Smith State Park is located in Suffolk County, in the town of Smithtown. The park entrance is from the Jericho Turnpike (Rt. 25). See Fig. 19-b.

THE CARMAN'S RIVER

This spring creek rises in Brookhaven Township in the vicinity of Middle Island and flows southward into Great South Bay. A good part of it lies within Southaven County Park, and another part of it lies within a wildlife refuge. The vulnerable stretch is the headwater area where battles are currently being waged concerning land use and development. Right now, this upper end is not intensely built-up, but proposed development in the Middle Island area could greatly affect the lower protected mileage. Fortunately, DEC has designated the Carman's, as well as the Connetquot and Nissequogue, under the *Wild, Scenic & Recreational Rivers Act* which affords them a good deal of protection.

The Carmans is stocked with rainbow and brown trout, and there is some fairly good carryover. It also has a substantial wild brook trout fishery that is superior to either the Connetquot or Nissequogue. The season here runs to November 30th, except in Southaven Park where the season is shorter.

The extreme upper end is above Upper Yaphank Lake. While the water is not large here, it is capable of holding fish. Both Upper and Lower Yaphank Lakes (impounded ponds on the river) are stocked, and recently I've gotten reports of browns up to 18 inches being taken. These are certainly holdover fish.

I like the section between the two lakes. Although it is extremely brushy and fairly narrow, it is canoed, but I prefer wading this section. After the foliage appears, wading and fishing downstream is really the only tactic for fly fishing, since false casting would be impossible.

This reach of water is cleaned up every year by the Art Flick Chapter of Trout Unlimited, a group which meets in a building right near the stream. Recently, this chapter has gotten approval from DEC to do stream improvement work on the Carmans, and that work will commence in 1985, within Southaven Park.

At the bottom of Lower Yaphank Lake, the stream enters Southaven County park. From this northern border of the park downstream about two miles to the big stone dam, fly fishing only is permitted. Although Southaven is effectively closed to non-Suffolk County residents, anyone can enter for fishing purposes. Although canoeing in the park is permitted two days a week, fishing from canoes is not allowed. Fishing is permitted, though, from the rowboats that are rented on Hard's Lake at the southern end of the park. Trout are stocked here, too, and some nice ones are recovered. Unfortunately, the boats on Hard's Lake are also open to non-fishermen, so there may often be considerable disturbance on this impounded part of the Carmans.

If you'd like to fish inside the park, it's strongly recommended that you call for up to the minute information on permits, boat rentals and so on.

South of the park, the stream grows wider; eventually it empties into the Bellport Bay area of Great South Bay. A good part of this lower mileage lies within Wertheim National Wildlife Refuge. Anglers have access here, and in 1985 DEC will be installing a parking lot for fishermen and canoeists.

Within Wertheim, the Carmans becomes brackish. It is in this lower end, south of Rt. 27, that DEC plans to stock sea-run trout for the first time since the 1960's. Also, since this lower stream segment is salty, anglers may encounter white perch (especially in March and April) all the way up to the dam at Hard's Lake. The state record White Perch, in fact, was taken from the Carmans in June of 1982. It weighed 2 lb. 14 oz. Stripers, blue crabs, largemouth bass, huge chain pickerel and perhaps other species may also be encountered in the lower Carmans. If you don't own a canoe, you can rent one from Carman's River Canoe, located on Rt. 27 right by the stream. They also sell fishing tackle and bait.

By far the best trout fishing opportunity on Long Island is in the three rivers we've just discussed. But there are actually three other trout possibilities on the island: In several ponds (see Ch. 19), in a few little brooks in Suffolk County where native brook trout still persist and in several small stocked streams. These latter streams are listed in the stocking reports in the reference section.

LONG ISLAND'S SEA-RUN TROUT
Sea-run trout, also called "salters," are trout that live primarily in the brackish section of a tidal stream but that commonly migrate back and forth between fresh and salt water. There have always been some natural sea-run brook trout in Long Island waters, stream fish that for some unclear reason forsake their brethren and take to the sea. However, shoreline development and the construction of mill-dams blocked upstream migration routes to spawning habitat. Then, about 20 years ago, New York's Dept. of Environmental Conservation began to stock fingerling trout with a genetic proclivity to become sea-run. This program has been on-again, off-again for all that time, but in recent years the efforts have intensified. In 1984, for example, 41,000 fingerlings were stocked: 26,000 in the Connetquot, 10,000 in the Nissequogue and the remainder divided up among about a half-dozen of the smaller brooks. As mentioned, in 1985 the lower Carmans River will receive a stock of sea-run hopefuls, and there is even talk of

erecting fish ladders on this river to abet the sea-run trout effort.

By far, the best returns of sea-run trout have been from the Connetquot, and browns of 4-7 pounds have showed up; some returns of Kamloops Rainbows have also been made. On the Connetquot, sea-runs can ascend beyond Bubbles Falls and all the way up through the park. On the Nissequogue, salters can also make it up through the park, as the dam just south of Rt. 25 at Phillips Mill Pond does not stop them (this dam is the limit of tidal influence). On the Carmans, the fish can ascend as far as the base of the dam at Hards lake — in other words, they are stopped just short of Southaven Park.

Salters may drift back and forth between south shore bays, or Long Island Sound, and the rivers in arbitrary fashion. However October is probably the best month because of the fish's spawning urge. Some experts believe that salters begin to group up at the mouth of "their" tidal stream in early October. Then, when the first good rain comes, the fish ascend. These trout, which average 2-4 pounds but can get much bigger, fight hard and take on a notably silver sheen. Long-rodders try for them with flashy bucktails and streamers, while spin enthusiasts use small Mepps or Colorado Spinners and smallish Rebels and Rapalas. Killies are a natural bait for salters, and during the rains of October, the good old nightcrawler seems to work as well as anything.

One nice thing about sea-run trout is that they can be pursued year-round on Long Island. You can legally take sea-runs at anytime in any river up to the first barrier that stops the tidal flow. There is a 9-inch size limit and 10 fish/day creel limit, and these help protect the fall stocked fingerlings.

19.
PONDS: NO SALT
BUT A LOT
OF SPICE

It was a good year for Hampton beach revelers, the sun bleating hot well into October. And with the ocean on our mind, it was very hard to tear away from those nasty blues that had been camped off Ponquogue Beach. But the harvest moon nights had been cool enough to put down the thick Cabomba weed, and now, we'd heard, the Peconic was just right for fishing. We pushed our canoe off at Edwards Avenue behind some boy scouts, who were about to see what Long Island looked like before it yielded so much of its sand-rooted beauty to the hand of man.

We drifted under the road, and past a few houses where fat, hand-fed mallards were watching balefully. Then we lazied with the current into the quiet of another world.

The reeds brushed softly against our boat, and the only noise was the occasional pop of a load of fours that raised pleasant thoughts of another gunning season. But as I tied on an appropriate bass lure, something seemed out of place. I really almost felt like putting out a few crab cages, or perhaps a killy trap or two. I had to keep convincing myself that this was indeed fresh water.

We worked our spinnerbaits and rubber worms with sincerity, but it became apparent early on that, like any other place, you had to learn the water to score. Eventually we drifted into Forge Pond, but here the weeds weren't fully down yet, and the fishing was even tougher. Fishing-wise, the most excitement was a medium-sized largemouth that came up for my lure and then said "Nah."

As we reached the end of our float near Riverhead, a faint scent of salt wafted in off Flanders Bay, and mixed strangely with the sweet smell of the alders. On Long Island, the land belongs to the sea, which does not let you forget that fact for too long.

LONG ISLAND, certainly better known for its salt water fishing, nonetheless offers a fairly spicy mix of sweet-water sport. Besides the several trout streams discussed in the previous chapter, Long Island has 526 ponds and lakes ranging in size from puddles of less than an acre to 243-acre Lake Ronkonkoma. Some 50 of the more noteworthy of these ponds are listed in Fig. 19-a, with their rough location depicted in Fig. 19-b. The exact location of several of these still waters can be noted from the Montauk Map, Fig. 23-a. All those ponds *not* pinpointed verbally in this chapter may be found with help of a road map or a Hagstrom street atlas.

The largemouth bass is the premier gamefish in Long Island fresh waters, and this warm-water fish grows to good proportions thanks in large part to Long Island's relatively mild winters. Many fish of over 6 pounds are caught annually, and there are a few on record of up to nine pounds! That's a big bucketmouth anywhere north of the Mason-Dixon line. Smallmouths are found in only a couple of waters, namely Fort Pond in Montauk Village and Fresh Pond on Shelter Island.

Many Long Island ponds are shallow, weedy and about perfect for chain pickerel. This skinny but strong fighter is the other important warm-water gamefish. Pickerel here can grow almost as large as pickerel come, and a good many 6-lb. and better fish are reeled in. Redfin pickerel – an eastern sub species of the grass pickerel – are also present in LI waters, but this fish seldom exceeds 13 inches.

Brook, brown and rainbow trout are stocked in about fourteen Long Island ponds by New York's Dept. of Environmental Conservation. In most cases, this is put-and-take fishing, i.e. most fish are caught in the year in which they are stocked. In a few ponds, there is so-called "put-grow-take" fishing, meaning that larger trout are available because they "holdover" from one season to the next. In a few mill ponds, there may even be natural reproduction, especially when the pond sits on a good stream. The stocking reports in the reference section give a complete run-down of state stocked waters. Certain other private ponds may be stocked by rod & gun clubs or other groups, but these are generally off bounds unless you are a member of that club.

There are several so-called "rough fish" in Long Island waters. It's a shame that these species have been so maligned, because there is a lot of good eating here. Eels are present almost everywhere, and can be cooked in a variety of ways. They are nothing short of sensational when smoked. The one catfish found on Long Island, the Brown Bullhead, is also scorned as a food fish up north. Southerners, though, know better. As shown in the list, carp inhabit many Long Island waters, and these sneered-at fish are also good chow when handled properly.

Panfish are most likely present in every single Long Island pond. Here we are talking about two species of sunfish – bluegill and pumkinseed – yellow perch, white perch, and less commonly, black crappie. These are all easily caught fish, and thus the best targets when teaching a kid to fish.

FRESHWATER FISHING ON LONG ISLAND

Ponds	Acres	Nature of Access	Trout	Large-mouth Bass	Small-mouth Bass	Chain Pickerel	Carp	Panfish
SUFFOLK COUNTY								
1 Avon Manor Pond, Amityville	3	Town Park	X					X
2 Belmont Lake	19	L.I.S.P.R.C.		X		X	X	X
3 Southards Pond	19	Town Park	X	X		X	X	X
4 Blydenburg Lake	100	S.C.P.		X				X
5 Lake Ronkonkoma[1][5]	243	D.E.C.		X		X	X	X
6 Mill Pond, Sayville	6	Private	X					X
7 West Lake	20	Private	X					X
8 Canaan Lake[5]	26	Private	X	X		X		X
9 Patchogue Lake[5]	40	Private		X		X		X
10 Swan Lake	30	Private	X					X
11 Artist Lake[5]	30	Town Park		X		X		X
12 Upper Yaphank Lake	19	Town Park	X	X				X
13 Lower Yapank Lake[5]	25	Private	X	X				X
14 Hards Lake	30	S.C.P.	X	X				X
15 Kahlers Pond	13	Town Park	X	X			X	X
16 Navy Coop Ponds	60	F.W.M.A.		X		X		X
17 Forge Pond	120	Private		X		X		X
18 Upper Mill Pond, Peconic River	60	D.E.C.		X		X	X	X
19 Wildwood Lake[5]	64	Private[4]	X	X		X		X
20 Laurel Lake[2][5]	30	D.E.C.	X	X		X		X
21 Sears & Bellows Ponds	30	S.C.P.		X		X		X
22 Penny Pond	13	S.C.P.		X				X
23 Great Pond	50	Private		X				X
24 Big Fresh Pond[5]	64	Private[4]		X				X
25 Litte Fresh Pond	19	Private[4]		X				X
26 Agawan Lake	40	Private[4]		X			X	X
27 Fresh Pond, Shelter Island[5]	15	Private			X		X	X
28 Long Pond	58	Private[4]		X				X
29 Kellis Pond	19	Private[4]		X		X		X
30 Poxabogue Pond	44	S.C.P.		X				X
31 Hook Pond	64	Private[4]		X			X	X
32 Fresh Pond, Hither Hills[5]	35	L.I.S.P.R.C.		X				X
33 Fort Pond[3][5]	192	D.E.C.		X	X		X	X
34 Big Reed Pond[2]	45	S.C.P.		X				X
NASSAU COUNTY (No boats)								
1 Grant Park Pond	6	N.C.P.						X
2 Hempstead Lake[5]	236	L.I.S.P.R.C.		X		X	X	X
3 Smith Lake	20	Town Park		X		X	X	X
4 Roosevelt Park Pond	15	N.C.P.				X		X
5 Mill Pond, Wantagh	19	N.C.P.						X
6 Mill Pond, Oyster Bay	7	U.S.F.W.S.	X					X
7 Massapequa Reservoir[5]	20	N.C.P.	X	X			X	X
8 Massapequa Lake	40	N.C.P.		X			X	X
STREAMS								
① Massapequa Creek		N.C.P.	X					
② Carlls River		Private	X					
③ Orowock Creek		Private	X					
④ Champlins Creek		Private	X					
⑤ Connetquot River		L.I.S.P.R.C.	X[6]					
⑥ Nissequogue River		L.I.S.P.R.C.	X[6]					
⑦ Swan Creek		Private	X[6]					
⑧ Beaverdam Creek		Private	X[6]					
⑨ Carmans River		S.C.P.	X[6]					
⑩ Peconic River		F.W.M.A.		X		X	X	X

Figure 19-a.

COMPLIMENTS NYS DEPARTMENT ENVIRONMENTAL CONSERVATION

Footnotes

[1] No outboard motors permitted; tiger muskellunge stocked in fall of 1982, may be available by 1985.

[2] No gasoline powered motors.

[3] No gasoline powered motos or electric motors over 1/3 h.p.; hybrid striped bass stocked in 1982 and 1983, should reach keeper size in 1984.

[4] Currently Southampton Town restricts fishing within its boundaries to town residents and non-residents with licensed guides. This policy is currently in litigation. No gasoline powered motors allowed in Southhampton waters.

[5] Bottom contour maps available upon request. Write to Stony Brook Office of DEC.

[6] Tidal sections of these streams support sea-run fisheries.

Access Codes

Private — These waters are privately owned. Fishing access is often from unposted town roads. Shore fishing is limited to unposted land. Respect private property rights.

D.E.C. — These access sites are owned and provided by the New York State Department of Environmental Conservation for the launching of cartop boats. Adjacent lands may be private and landowner's rights should be protected.

N.C.P. — Nassau County Park. Open to general public. No boats are allowed on any Nassau County Park ponds.

Town Park — Non-residents permitted, but may have to pay parking fee. Contact specific town regarding regulations.

S.C.P. — Suffolk County Park. These parks are generally open only to Suffolk County residents and their guests, with the exception of Hard's Lake and the Carmans River in Southaven County Park. Special regulations and user fees may apply and vary from park to park. For more information contact individual park offices, call (516) 567-1700.

Access Codes continued

F.W.M.A. — Special Fish and Wildlife Management Area. These waters are open to the public through the Fish and Wildlife Management Act. User permit is required. For permits and information contact the D.E.C. Regional Office at Stony Brook, NY, (516) 751-7900.

N.Y.C.D.P.R. — New York City Department of Parks and Recreation. Open to the public. No boats allowed. Not all Central Park Ponds are open for fishing. Contact New York City Parks regarding regulations.

USFWS — Oyster Bay National Wildlife Refuge. No boats allowed.

L.I.S.P.R.C. — Long Island State Parks and Recreation Commission. Special regulations apply and vary from park to park. Connetquot and Caleb Smith State Parks, require reservations for day use trout fishing; fly fishing only. For more information about fishing waters in these and other state parks, call the individual state park.

LONG ISLAND FRESH WATER LOCATOR
(Keyed To Chart On Facing Page)

Figure 19-b.

COMPLIMENTS NYS DEPARTMENT ENVIRONMENTAL CONSERVATION

There are three types of ponds on Long Island. One is the glacial "kettle hole," basically a hole where a big hunk of ice-age ice melted. This is the deepest of the three, even though some kettle holes on the island are quite shallow. The second is the "mill pond," nothing but an impounded pond on one of the island's many spring creeks. Mill ponds are seldom more than eight to ten feet deep. The third is the "beach pond," originally salt water but cut off from the ocean by the building up of a barrier beach.

Every year, DEC tries to survey at least two fresh-water ponds with the purpose of creating contour maps. Now, many of these maps are available free to fishermen, as footnoted on Fig. 19-b. Simply write to DEC Stony Brook requesting them.

Believe it or not, there are several fish holding ponds in Staten Island, Queens, Brooklyn, the Bronx and yes, even Manhattan. These waters, though, are covered separately in Ch. 21.

NASSAU COUNTY
In highly developed Nassau County, fresh-water opportunities are extremely limited. Some lakes and streams are known to be polluted, and in fact there are special health advisories posted on certain Nassau waters. See the inside cover of the current fish & game syllabus. Because of regulations enforced by several different municipalities, no boats are permitted on any lakes (except private ponds) in Nassau County. It is shore fishing only.

Hempstead Reservoir is the largest still water in Nassau County, but even on this 236-acre lake the fishing is not spectacular. Water levels tend to fluctuate extremely, and there is refuse in and along the shore. Further, the lake is very shallow and there is a decided absence of fishholding structure. To help the situation, DEC recently implanted brush structures at the south end of the lake.

The gamefish present are largemouth bass and chain pickerel. Pickerel actually seem to predominate, but most are under 20 inches. Largemouth seem to average around 12-14 inches, but some 2-3 pounders are collected. Present also are bluegills, yellow perch and bullheads, but they are very small and appear to be stunted. A few years ago, DEC experimented with tiger muskellunge (Norlunge) in Hempstead Reservoir. These gamefish did not take. Additional largemouth bass will be stocked though, to augment the natural stock.

It is not unreasonable to advise the fisherman to check with either DEC or local health officials on any New York City or Nassau County water before eating it's fish. Massapequa Reservoir, for example, currently has posted on it an "eat none" advisory. Ill rumors are likewise heard Freeport Reservoir. At the same time, it should be noted that certain Nassau ponds may be unpolluted and their fish perfectly fine to eat.

SUFFOLK COUNTY
It is in much larger and much less developed Suffolk County where most of the island's fresh water opportunities exist. We'll start with one of the most important bodies of fresh water, one that is neither a river nor a pond but a little of each.

THE PECONIC RIVER. Like the trout streams discussed in Ch. 18, this river garners its flow primarily from springs. However there are certain factors that make the Peconic different: Lower gradient, more surrounding wetlands, and more impoundments. All this makes for

PER BRANDIN

Chain pickerel is one of the reasons why fishermen like to canoe the Peconic.

warmer water, and in fact, only warm water fish are found in the
Peconic. Like so many Long Island streams, it has been dammed in
several places, creating a series of ponds connected by relatively short
sections of free-flowing river. On the Peconic, the best fishing may, in
fact, be in the ponds, the most notable being "Forge Pond" or "Peconic
Lake."

Largemouth bass and chain pickerel are the main objects of interest.
A special "Angler Cooperator" program has been run here (as well as
on Lake Ronkonkoma and Fort Pond) by DEC Senior Aquatic Biologist
Charles Guthrie. These detailed angler diaries reveal some interesting
facts about the Peconic. For example, in 1983 60% of the bass caught
in one section were over the legal size of 12 inches. In another section,
the figure was 50%. This was an improvement over previous seasons,
though it should be noted that in 1984 figures were not as good.
Still, the program has demonstrated that both the bass and pickerel
populations are healthy and stable in the Peconic. As far as sizes, the
study showed that the largest bass taken by participants in 1983 was a
lunker of just over 22 inches. The largest pickerel was 24 inches.
Other fish present in the Peconic include sunfish, black crappie, white
perch, bullhead and carp. By the way if you'd like to participate as an
Angler Cooperator, contact Guthrie at the Stony Brook office of DEC.

Because of swampiness, and also because of private ownership of
much of the banks of the Peconic, most anglers use canoes from which
to launch their piscatorial attack. If you don't have your own canoe,
you can rent one from the Peconic Paddler, which is located right on
the river in downtown Riverhead. Whether you bring your own or
rent, the people at the Paddler will take you upriver for a fee so you can
float back to your car. This eliminates the need for two cars. Note that
the Peconic becomes very difficult to fish in midsummer due to the
blossoming of plant growth, especially the notorius water weed
Cabomba. For this reason the most pleasant and productive times
to fish the river are May-June and then again after mid September.

The Peconic rises in the vicinity of Brookhaven National Labs, near
the border of Riverhead and Brookhaven townships. The headwaters
comprise a series of ponds and connecting brooks, and here there is
some interesting fishing. Much of this takes place on land owned by
the U.S. Navy but managed for fishing and hunting by DEC under a Fish
& Wildlife Management Act Cooperative agreement. As with the
better-known hunting "Co-Ops" upstate, there are a number of restrictions including check-in stations, parking in certain areas only and so
forth. In some cases, reasonable fees are collected. Some of the ponds

are Prestons Pond, Peasys Pond, Duck Pond, Sandy Pond, Grassy Pond, Jones Pond and Zeeks Pond. Note that this is all warm water fishing: Bass, pickerel and panfish but no trout. For more detailed info, write to DEC Stony Brook (see reference section) for the bulletin titled *Information And Regulations For Fishing On Navy Department Unit FWMA Cooperative Area.*

Most of the better fishing takes place on the lower Peconic. Generally, the most upriver point where fishermen put in is at Connecticut Avenue, where there is a canoe launch area. This creates a leisurely 6-hour fishing float and allows one to see the pretty Brown's Bog area. The best bass and pickerel fishing is further down, though, and many serious rod and reelers put in at Edwards Avenue. This will give you a good 4-hour float. Just below Edwards Ave. is probably the prettiest stretch of water and the best for angling. I like the run from just above the Long Island Expressway (which you go under) down to Forge Pond. Some of the best bass and pickerel fishing on the entire river is in Forge Pond itself.

Even below Forge Pond there is good fishing, albeit more civilization. Parking, by the way, is no problem in Riverhead, the end of your journey.

FORT POND. (For location, see Fig. 23-a in Ch. 23.) Fort Pond is perhaps the most dynamic still water on the island. It is also more than a little strange. Located right in Montauk, only a stone's throw from the ocean, it looks and feels like it should be an arm of the sea. Rest assured, though, that it is sweet and so can the fishing be. Hybrid striped bass (one crossed with a white bass) are stocked annually in Fort Pond. By summer of '85, the 1982 and '83 year classes should be 18 inches and 14 inches in length respectively. The legal size for hybrid stripers here is 14 inches. They have the potential to exceed ten pounds.

Largemouth and smallmouth bass are the primary gamefish present in Fort Pond. Populations are not large, but the size distribution is very good. Many smallies of 2-3 pounds are caught, and largemouths of over 5 lbs. are not at all uncommon. In 1982, alewives were stocked and may help both species of black bass along. A fairly new size limit of 15 inches has been imposed on both smallmouth and largemouth. Note that the bass season in Suffolk is a long one – currently from the first Saturday in June to March 15th.

Fort Pond has an abundant stock of white perch, but these panfish are decidedly stunted (usually a result of overpopulation brought on by too few gamefish present).

On productive Fort Pond in Montauk, DEC has constructed a fisherman's access consisting of a parking lot and dirt ramp.

BIG REED POND. (For location, see Fig. 23-a in Ch. 23.) This unusual 45-acre pond is located within Montauk County Park, and so only Suffolk County residents or their guests may fish. Anglers must both sign in and out at the park office.

Unlike Fort Pond, where shore casting and wading are very possible techniques, Big Reed really must be fished from a boat. In fact, it pays to wear hip boots or at least low rubber boots to push off a craft from the swampy shoreline. Gas motors are prohibited, while electric motors are OK (but not really necessary).

The prime attraction here, besides the pretty surroundings, is largemouth bass. The fish do not run large, most being under 15 inches, but there are plenty of them. Lunkers are occasionally boated, though. Very small pumkinseed sunfish are abundant in Big Reed, as are large white perch.

This is a very shallow lake, only about seven feet at the deepest. It is also very weedy, and the rooted vegetation often reaches to the top or just short of it. All these features create a situation where top-water spin tactics are very effective; fly-rodding with bass bugs or small poppers would also be a good method to deploy on Big Reed.

FRESH POND. (For location, see Fig. 23-a in Ch. 23.) There are as many "Fresh" Ponds on Long Island as there are "Mill" Ponds. The one we speak of here is a little jewel tucked into a corner of Hither Hills State Park.

I've also heard this small, 35-acre pond call "Artist Lake" or "Hidden

Pond." This pictographic language is, in either case, more than appropriate. It is very pretty with no hint of civilization anywhere near it. The pond is located in the northern part of the park, north of Rt. 27, and the only road that goes near it is a questionable dirt one where I personally wouldn't take my '70 Chevelle Convertible (which I bought new and have since navigated a quarter million miles through some God-awful places in search of fish and game). If you've a 4-wheeler or high off the ground truck, turn north from Rt. 27 just west of where Old Montauk Highway branches off. Go about a mile, then turn left over the RR tracks. Then make a second left right away onto a narrow dirt road marked by a sign that says "access." This will take you down to the pond. If you feel the road is too tough for your particular vehicle, there is a suitable pull-off just after you've turned north off Rt. 27. The hike in will take you about 25 minutes.

Appropriate here would be a small jonboat or canoe. Outboards are prohibited but some may want an electric motor to deal with the breezes that blow quite fresh across Fresh Pond. Wading here is a possibility, but watch out for the quicksand-like ooze that will suck you down.

In here are largemouth bass, most of which will be under 16 inches, and many of which will be under the legal size of 12 inches. There are pretty good numbers, though. Yellow perch, some of them of a very stocky size, are also present in very good numbers.

WILDWOOD LAKE. (For location of this and all the following ponds, see Fig. 19-b.) This nice, 49-foot deep pond is located in Southampton Township, and that brings up a topic of concern to all local anglers. Since the 1970's, the Town of Southampton has claimed exclusive jurisdiction over its fresh waters and closed them off to all but town residents or non-residents who hire a guide. The DEC's Division of Fish & Wildlife has taken Southampton Town to court on this matter, and the case is expected to go to trial in the spring of 1985. According to officials close to the case, though, no early resolution is expected.

Wildwood is a two-story fishery, with largemouth bass and pickerel living side by side with stocked brown trout. This fairly deep kettle hole does offer some good trout fishing, and holdover browns are taken.

Besides Wildwood, other good, fishable ponds lying within the current Southampton hassle are Big Fresh Pond, Long Pond, Kellis Pond and others.

LAUREL LAKE. Lying within Southold Township, this is another nice, two-story pond. There is good bass and pickerel, and trout are stocked annually. Some of the browns grow to good sizes. Anglers visiting Laurel Lake have the benefit of guaranteed state access. No boats are rented, but you can launch your own small cartopper. Note, though, that there is about a hundred foot carry from parking area to water's edge.

KAHLER'S POND. Located in the Moriches area of Brookhaven Township, this small, 13-acre mill pond offers lots of action on small bass. It is also stocked with about 600 rainbow trout each year. In evidence, too, are carp, sunfish, yellow perch and brown bullhead.

PATCHOGUE PONDS. These three mill ponds are all located in the Patchogue area. In East and West Lakes, trout is the primary quarry. The former gets about 1000 rainbows and browns each year, while the latter receives about 1600 'bows and browns. Some carryover is reported in West Lake.

Patchogue Lake is the third one of this trio. It has good populations of bass and pickerel, and panfish – especially yellow perch – are abundant. This is one of the more popular ice-fishing destinations on the island.

BLYDENBURGH LAKE. (Also called "New Mill Pond" or "Stump Pond.") By Long Island standards, this is a big lake at 120-acres. Unfortunately for some, it sits within a Suffolk County Park and thus is open only to Suffolk residents or their guests. There is a livery here where rowboats can be rented, and like Hard's Lake in Southaven Park, this creates a situation where more than just fishermen are on the water much of the time.

Although recently largemouth bass of 5¾ and 6¼ pounds have been reported, most fish are much smaller. You will have to wade through a lot of 8-inch largemouths before you connect with the odd lunker. Besides bass, Blydenburgh sports a good head of big yellow perch.

LAKE RONKONKOMA. Comprising 234-acres, this lake is Long Island's largest and also one of its deepest (60 feet). There is a fine state access site here, consisting of a concrete launch ramp and a good-sized parking lot (which nonetheless fills up at certain times). Only rowboats or canoes are permitted. Electric trolling motors may be used, but gasoline outboards may not.

Ronkonkoma is well known for a fine largemouth bass population. Recently, catch-per-hour has gone down but size has gone up. This was the exact result desired from the special regs in effect here: Possession of bass over 15 inches or under 11 inches only permitted. Possession of fish between 11 inches and 15 inches prohibited. The season runs from the 1st Saturday in June through March 15th; ice fishing is permitted. Bass of up to 8 pounds are caught, and 3-4 pounders are not uncommon for experienced fishermen.

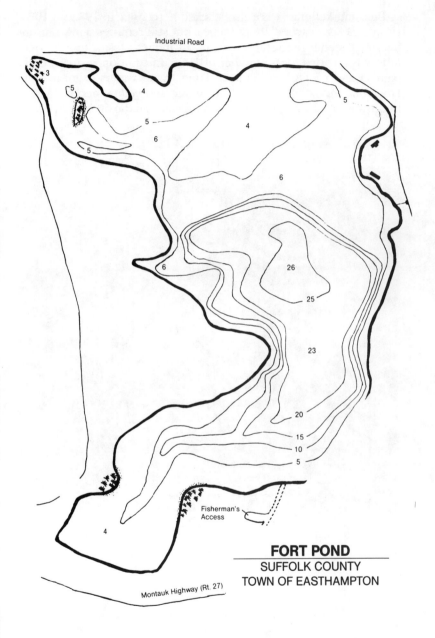

FORT POND
SUFFOLK COUNTY
TOWN OF EASTHAMPTON

Figure 19-c.

COMPLIMENTS NYS DEPARTMENT ENVIRONMENTAL CONSERVATION

Tiger muskellunge were also stocked here, once in 1982. In 1984, this year class reached 18-22 inches, but still required a few seasons before reaching the legal length of 30 inches. Restocking of Tiger Musky is planned for September of 1985. In addition, virtually every panfish and rough fish found in Long Island waters swim in Ronkonkoma. Included here are both white and yellow perch, sunfish, bullheads, black crappie (far less abundant than the others) and carp.

PER BRANDIN

20.
OCEANSIDE: A WORLD OF GOOD FISHING IN SURF AND BAY

There were only a weak scattering of Christmas lights in Freeport Harbor, but more than a few hawkers, whose anxious words froze on contact with the early morning air. They didn't have a chance with us that day, though. Our chartered boat, the Dock I, was revving up in her slip. Bobby Nikitopoulos and I were to be the guests of a Long Island friend.

December 14th, a cold snap, and the word was out — the cod had started! Very best of all, they were close. No marathon boat trips. Our captain said they were just about six miles out, and that really good action was expected any day.

The first five skimmer clams were picked off by dogfish. Then the cod started biting like no tomorrow. Eight pounders, twelve pounders, then eighteen pounders. The mate couldn't keep track, so he started slashing all possible pool fish. By 1:00 p.m. the seas were up to six feet, but the fish box was overflowing and there was really no place to stand for the codfish flopping about on the deck.

"Unbelievable," I said to Bobby Nick as we unloaded near a quarter ton of cod onto the dock later on. "Best cod trip I ever had."

"Whaddya mean. It was your *first* cod trip. And you were hangin' over the rail half the time."

"I know. But I feel great now," I smiled, as I took a long drag on a can of Budweiser.

THE SOUTH SHORE OF Long Island is truly a world of fishing unto itself. Stressing shore access, this chapter will give an overview of that section from Shinnecock Bay westward to East Rockaway Inlet. Montauk Pt. is discussed in Ch. 23 while Jamaica Bay and Gateway are discussed in Ch. 21.

Long Island's south shore might be said to have several *zones* of interest. The very back sections of the bays, especially where tidal streams enter, are where young boys seek out blue claw crabs and white perch. Sea-run trout, snapper blues and small flounder add spice to this back bay action. Farther out, in the main bays, loads of winter flounder and blacks (in pockets) are the cold water staples while fluke is the exciting summertime news. Two other summer delicacies, blowfish and porgies, are also available to rod and reelers, but mainly in Great South Bay. Blowfish seem to be trying to make a comeback in recent years, while porgy, never as big here as in the Peconics, are fairly steady every year. Kingfish and sea bass are also important in certain areas when they are abundant. That has not been the case in recent years, however.

Weakfish and bluefish can also be taken inside the barrier islands. Normally, best action on the big tiderunner weaks is May and June, with a second body of smaller weaks moving into certain areas in summer. Bluefish, migrating north from warmer climes, usually show about Memorial Day, but action is typically sporadic until July. Best bluefish months, both for consistency and size, are August through October, but action has continued later in recent years. By and large, most blues taken within these shallow bays range from snappers to cocktails of about two to four pounds. Encounters with bigger fish are always possible, though.

The inlets of these south shore bays comprise yet another zone of interest, the most dynamic one of all. Predatory fish – fluke, blues, stripers, and weaks – hang in and on both ends of these turbulent channels, watching for food being swept by. These inlet-hugging gamefish can be big – as big as they get in Long Island waters. That includes cow bass over 50, doormat fluke over 15, gorilla blues over 20, and tiderunner weaks better than 15 pounds. While the inlets can hold fish at any time from spring through fall, they take on particular significance in summer when the monotonous beaches of the south shore hold relatively few fish. These broad beaches are best during the gamefish migration periods in fall, and to a much lesser extent in spring.

The next zone would be the world of the surf, though this zone would certainly overlap the inlets. Fortunately, access is much better on the south side than on the north side of the island, thanks largely to the many public parks and beaches. Surfcasters devote by far the bulk of their attention to stripers, blues and weaks, and they use bait as well as the usual range of plugs and tins. Access for south shore surfmen will be discussed in specific terms as we cover the bays in an east to west direction.

Finally we come to the waters just outside the barrier islands. The happy codfish trip related earlier is a good illustration that this important species is not strictly an offshore commodity. Cod can be

Beefsteak of the sea! Cold water cod are about as good a tasting fish as you're going to find.

taken within a few miles of the south shore, both on wrecks and reefs and (at times) on open bottom from December through March. But these inshore waters aren't only for codfish buffs. Large blues, blackfish, porgies, mackerel, fluke, whiting, sea bass and other species in season are pursued by boats sailing from south shore ports. An approximate timetable for inshore species may be found in Ch. 17.

True blue-water fishing is not within the focus of this book, but it should be mentioned that many south shore party and charter boats specialize in offshore and canyon trips. Big-game salt water fishing is not the private domain of Montauk.

SHINNECOCK BAY
(All number references in this chapter are keyed to Figures 20-a and 20-b.) Like Moriches Bay, Shinnecock is much smaller and much less windy than Great South Bay. Thus, even though the fishing is less

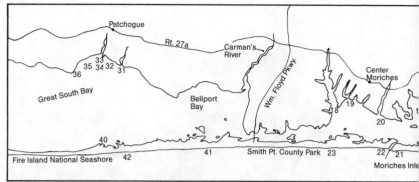

Figure 20-a. South shore Long Island, east.

diverse than on Great South, these two smaller bays are excellent destinations for the small-boat angler. Of course the wind can always kick up, but normally even a wide-beamed 14-foot aluminum boat can negotiate this sheltered bay. A 16-footer with a 10-15 h.p. outboard would be perfectly fine. Such rigs can, in fact, be rented from a number of liveries located around the bay. If you have your own boat, you can launch at most of these liveries for a reasonable fee. There are also a couple of so-so public ramps.

Flounder, fluke and bluefish are the main targets here. Some of the earliest flatfish action on the entire island gets underway in the Shinnecock Canal (1) and in the Quogue (2) and Quantuck (3) Canals. In truth, there isn't any winter month in which flounder haven't been caught in these spots. But depending on the severity of the temperatures, and on icing conditions, there is little effort expended between Christmas and late February. It isn't long after Washington's Birthday, though, that cabin fever bit sportsmen start "canal hopping." Note that this early in the season, the weather is extremely critical. A warm day, with the sun bouncing off the walls of the canal to warm the water, can turn the fish on. The next day, cloudiness can turn them right off again. Pick the sunny side of the canal! And, if possible, pick a sunny warm day with no wind.

Shinnecock Canal is county property, and currently the west bank is open to fishermen with no permits or stickers necessary. There is a big parking lot here, and the fuller it is, the better the flounder are biting! Access to Quogue Canal is very tough in summer, because of a lack of parking, but in early season, you can usually park on adjacent side streets and fish without being hassled.

As March advances, flounder action improves in the bay, but April and early May is the best time. Like Moriches Bay, winter flounder persist very late, and smart fishermen who know the holes can catch

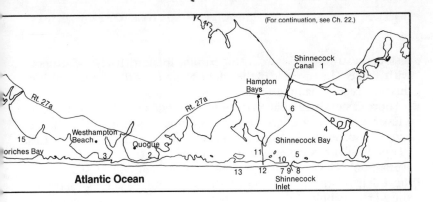

some flounder all summer. Most anglers switch to fluke, though, and what flounder are taken in summer are usually of a diminished size.

The most popular area for flounder is a large expanse of the bay known as "The Basket" (4). This is just off the Indian Reservation. Although nautical charts show this area to be a fairly uniform 10 feet deep, experts with depth finders will seek out subtle depressions where flounder collect at certain times. Flounder are also pursued by the bridge and around the Coast Guard Station, but this entire area is currently being disturbed by the construction of the new Ponquogue Bridge.

Summer flounder, usually called fluke, take over in Shinnecock as the flounder begin to taper. Fluke may be seen as early as May at the inlets, but the best fishing is usually June through September. Fluke must be 14 inches to keep, and in some years it's mostly throwbacks. In other years, the ratio of keepers is better.

Almost any day in fluke season a few four pounders are seen dockside at day's end. Bigger fish are by no means common, but those doormats of seven, ten and even fifteen pounds are out there. Most of the rental fleet use squid and sand eel or spearing combinations, but many Shinnecock locals prefer live killies with Aberdeen hooks and very light sinkers. Snapper blues also make dynamite doormat bait, but they're tough to keep alive. Whatever baits you use, though, bring some white and yellow lead-head jigs. It's all you need at certain times.

The two best-known fluke spots are in the boat channel just inside the inlet (5) and in the channel just south of Shinnecock Canal (6). These locales, though, are very difficult to fish on weekends due to boat traffic and heavy fishing pressure. Weekday and or early morning fluke fishermen have a big advantage.

The west bank of Shinnecock Inlet (7) is a fine shore access spot. It lies within Shinnecock Inlet County Park, but there are no non-resident restrictions. There is a big parking lot here that is always open with no fee. The east side of the inlet (8) is part of that same park, but this side is seasonally restricted to county residents.

Shore casters have a ball in the inlet on bluefish of all sizes. At night, a few big stripers are taken on live eels and plugs, and fluke can be caught, too. Small blacks are picked away at both off the rocky jetties (9) and off the rocks just inside and west of the inlet (10). They average only a few pounds. In fall, bluefish can really blitz this area – in the inlet, off the jetties and in the surrounding surf. Weakfish is another possibility in this area, but weaks are never common even though they migrate through here to reach the Peconics in spring. Sometimes there is a flurry, usually in the canal, but it is very brief.

One of the most popular south shore access points used to be the old Ponquogue Bridge (11). At this writing, the new bridge is about half up, but all that pile-driving can't be doing the fishing much good. There have been reports that when the new bridge is up, the old one will be left in tact as a platform for anglers.

SURF FISHING. On the east side of the inlet, all the way east to Southampton, it is mostly private beaches. To run this section with a buggy, you need not only a Suffolk County Permit but also a special Southampton permit. The exception is the area immediately adjacent to the inlet (8), which is part of the county park. Only a county pass would be needed here. Though non-residents are seasonally restricted

PER BRANDIN

The west side of Shinnecock Inlet is one of the best access points on the south shore. It is open to everyone, and no fee or permit is necessary. Bluefish are common in late summer and fall, while stripers, weaks and fluke are other possibilities.

here, it is an excellent spot, especially for outsized stripers at night. On the west bank of the inlet, the picture is a little brighter for surf fishermen. A good spot is right around the inlet, but surfmen can roam the shoreline west for several miles (no beach vehicles). In the off season, you can simply park in the Ponquogue Beach (12) or Tiana Beach (13) parking lot and fish. These are public beaches. During the bathing season, hefty parking fees are collected. Even west of Tiana Beach, there is some public beach interspersed with private houses. These are also many little pull-offs along this stretch of beach, from the inlet all the way west to Quogue.

MORICHES BAY
This body of water bears much resemblance to Shinnecock Bay. But though it is even shallower, averaging only about 3-5 feet at low tide, it holds the edge over Shinnecock in flatfish production. Often billed as the year-round flounder capital of the island, it well deserves this regard. It is one of the few places where fairly good numbers of blackbacks can be caught all through summer. There is a concession to size, though; most of the bigger flounder appear to exit to the ocean during the doldrums.

The northern (inner) part of this bay is primarily mud, while the southerly part is primarily sand. Thus the mud-loving flounder will be found largely in the inner bay, north of the main east-west boating channel.

In March, the best flattie action will be in the deeper water at the east end of the bay, in the canals and in several very deep holes. It is in these same holes where 7-12 pound weakfish will sometimes group up in September and October. From April through June, most fish will be taken from the flats in four or five feet of water. Some of these flats are off Haven's Point (14), Remsenburg (15) and Harts Cove (16). This early, the fish are dispersed so chumming is recommended. From July to September, flounder move into or adjacent to the channels (17) and since they are already concentrated here, no chumming is needed. Even though the channels are marked, a depth finder will be extremely helpful. The best advice, though, is to check with livery owners to see where the action has been good. Too, these liveries will invariably have helpful handout maps.

Late May to late September is the time for Moriches fluke. The average size is about 14-16 inches, but some years the fish are bigger than others. While the smaller fish are typically on the flats or in the channels, the biggest doormats often lie at the edges of the channels. There is an excellent book titled *Fishing For Fluke* by Scott Simons and Don Kamienski. It is available through *The Fisherman* magazine (see reference section).

Four pound fluke are fairly common here, but much bigger ones have been recorded. One day Gary Grunseich, prop. of Silly Lilly Fishing Station on the bay, hooked into three monsters. The one he landed was 17 pounds, but the two that got away at the boat were just as big. In addition, a man fishing in another boat near him hooked several of the same size. Where this incredible nest of doormat fluke came from is anybody's guess, but it proves that it can happen. Big fluke often run together.

As with Shinnecock, bluefish are liable to be roaming the bay any time from June onward. Cocktail blues will predominate, with the fish often concentrated at the edges of bars where they entrap baitfish. Bigger blues are found mainly near the inlet. Some of the biggest fluke may also be found near the inlet, but beware of these treacherous waters and *do not* enter them with a small boat!

Blackfish are found around rock and other structure, and there is not a heck of a lot of either in any of these south shore bays. In Moriches, as in Shinnecock, some blacks are taken off the rocks at the inlet. The size never compares to those taken on Long Island's north shore or in east end waters, though.

Blue claw crabs have been abundant in the past few years. Oddly, it's been a very late run, with the best action in late October and November. Crabs are garnered both in and around the mouths of Moriches tributaries, and in the bay proper.

Shore angling in Moriches Bay, on the mainland side, is not limited so much by access but by the fact that shore fishing is just not that good. Most flounder are at least 200-300 feet off shore, and that goes for fluke, too. Shore-based rod and reelers catch mostly snapper blues, crabs, small flounder and at times, white perch. A few spots are off the pier in Forge River (18), off the town dock at the end of Union Ave. (19), at the end of Bay Road (20) and at many other roads that dead end at the water. The basic rule holds: In the off season, both access and parking are relatively easy. In summer, non-residents and even residents may get shut out, usually due to parking restrictions or limitations.

SURF FISHING. The news for surf fishermen is good or bad, depending on where you live. The beach east of Moriches Inlet is mostly private, although the area immediately adjacent to the inlet is Cupsogue Beach County Park (21). This area offers surf fishing, including off-road travel, but a Suffolk County permit is required. The west bank is also a county park, Smith Point, which provides a good six miles for

PER BRANDIN

A pair of fat, Moriches Bay flounder. This is *the* bay to head to if you'd like a fine filet dinner.

beach vehicles to roam. Again, you must be a Suffolk resident to obtain the necessary $25 vehicle permit. Alternatively, buggy-less residents can hoof it in after parking in the big parking lot just over the Smith Point Bridge.

Like all the south shore inlets, Moriches Inlet can be an exceptionally good place to fish. As mentioned, all the major gamefish species will relate to inlets, and blackfish like the rocks. At present, Moriches Inlet is difficult to navigate, and it can even be treacherous due to turbulence and ever-shifting sand bars. Shore fishing at the inlet is also potentially dangerous, since an angler could easily be knocked off the jagged

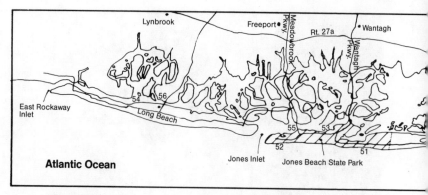

Figure 20-b. South shore Long Island, west.

rocks by a strong wave. Extreme caution is recommended for fishing in or around this inlet.

For those with the necessary permit, the stretch of shore from the inlet west to the Smith Point Bridge can be a very productive one. Off the inlet itself there is a deep hole where weakfish can sometimes be taken all summer long. About one-half to one mile west of the inlet is a spot usually referred to as West Bar (22). Then, about three miles west of the inlet, is Musso Point (23). You won't find this on most maps, but regulars here know that there is a long bar that holds gamefish. Then of course there are smaller bars that come and go with storms and strong tides, and that applies to the entire south shore. The oft repeated advice to check out the beach in daylight before fishing is sound advice.

GREAT SOUTH BAY
Great South Bay is a big body of water, easily riled by the wind. To seriously fish its waters you will need a seaworthy craft. Don't go out on the open part of this bay with a small boat unless you know these waters or are an experienced, knowledgeable boater!

This enormous inland waterway stretches 32 miles, all the way from Smith Point in the east to past the Robert Moses Causeway in the west. Somewhere around Elder Island, behind Gilgo Beach, begins South Oyster Bay; this is part of the same contiguous body of water, though.

Great South's average depth is greater than either Moriches or Shinnecock. Much of the bay is about 10 feet deep though some dredged channels measure 15 feet or a little better. On the other hand, there are extensive flats capable of gulching your boat. Anyone heading to this or any other south shore bay should really have the coast guard nautical charts mentioned elsewhere in this book and listed in the reference section.

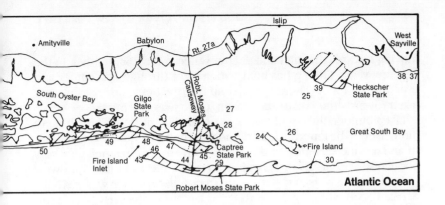

Overall, the fishing here is a good deal more varied than on the more easterly bays. Certainly, one of the big attractions is flounder. Flats are heavily fished not only by rod and reelers but also by commercial netters. Sportsmen who don't have a boat, or a big enough one, can still cash in on Great South's fine flatfishing via the Captree party boat fleet. Described fully in the reference section, Captree is a full-service port from which dozens of party and charter boats sail, for flounder as well as a plethora of other bay and ocean species. A few for-hire boats also operate from mainland points such as Bayshore.

Flounder here follow the basic south shore pattern. In early spring, they are in the deepest holes and channels. Then as the weather gradually warms, they move up onto the mud flats. In summer, smaller fish move into holes or channels within the bay, while most larger fish exit the bay to cooler water in the ocean. There is less summer action on flounder here than in either Moriches or Shinnecock, probably because Great South warms to higher temperatures. In fall, flounder move back into shallower water, and there is generally another good run in October and November. A good flounder rule of thumb in these parts is that the spring run is steady and fairly prolonged while the fall run is shorter but often more intense.

Hot flounder spots change from year to year, and besides that, the fish are very well dispersed during much of their season. For late reports on where the fish are hitting, check with any of the bait & tackle shops along Old Montauk Highway or with the boat liveries on the bay.

Fluke have been seen a bit earlier in south shore bays in recent years, and this may be another subtle effect of the 100-year warming trend we are said to be in. Now, these summer flounder are even caught in May, and by the first week of June the action may already be cooking. Fishing remains good through the summer, with the fish normally moving towards the inlet and deeper water in early September. In the past few years, fluking has held strong right through September and even into October. There is an axiom that the best doormat fluke are taken towards the end of the season, often near the inlets.

Like flounder, fluke will hang out on the flats at times, but they are more likely to be found around rips formed by underwater obstructions, in and around channels and in areas with strong currents. One very popular spot in Great South Bay is in West Channel (24), just southwest of little West Fire Island. This is also a popular spot for weakfish.

Like Peconic Bay, Great South Bay is famous for its early season run of big tiderunner weakfish. And, as they do with the Peconics, weaks use Great South as a spawning area. When the fish are abundant, there is normally a very strong run in this bay, primarily in May and early June. They will use the flats for spawning, but the channels and inlet area for feeding, so there is considerable bottom on which they may be found. A venerable weakfish spot in this bay is the Heckscher Flats (25) just off Heckscher State Park (also a popular spot for flounder). Weaks will also hold on the Fire Island Flats (26), in West Channel, and in Dickerson (27) and Snakehill Channels (28). One of the best spots is the main east-west boating channel just north of Fire Island. Weaks may also be taken in some of the other old or remnant channels which are shown on the nautical charts previously mentioned. For bait, sandworms are choice, and they are often wielded from a drifting boat. For lures, jelly worms are among the most popular.

Besides the early tiderunners, which depart after spawning in spring,

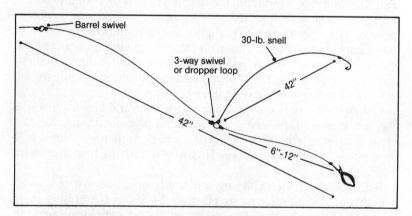

Figure 20-c. Single Hook Fluke Rig. Fluke and other species. Often baited with "ham and eggs", squid strip along with spearing or sand eel.

Great South sees a second infusion of smaller weaks in summer. These fish average about one to three pounds, and provide considerable sport and lots of good eating.

Blackfish are a little more plentiful here than in the bays to the east. As always, you must find rock or other structure that will hold the shellfish blacks dine on. A top spot is Kismet Reef (29) just north of the little hamlet of that name on Fire Island. From this point eastward to Ocean Bay park is the east-west boating channel cited above (30). Besides weaks, fluke, seabass and porgies are taken with regularity from this channel.

PER BRANDIN

Fish for sale at Captree boat basin. Even if you don't fish, stop by in late afternoon for some bargains.

Striped bass have hardly been worth talking about in recent years. Some generally small bass are taken in the estuarine portions of the larger Great South Bay tributaries, and experts believe there is a native population that winters over in these brackish waters. But in the expansive waters of the bay proper, few stripers are taken. Best action is at the inlet, which we'll get to in a moment, with some secondary action in a few other spots.

Bluefish are a summer and fall staple in this bay. It's largely cocktail blues in the main bay, and these roaming maulers are liable to be taken anywhere. They are true pelagic fish, constantly prowling in search of food. Best chance on large choppers is around the inlet and in the surf. Snapper blues are usually very abundant, especially around the tribs and back bays where they are readily available to shore fishermen from late August through September.

Seabass, kingfish and blowfish were all more abundant in past years. All three species seem to be trying to make comebacks. Blowfish or "sea squabs" (delicious eating) have shown well enough in the past several years to inspire at least some reborn commercial effort. However all three of these fish, like porgies, are often taken incidentally by anglers pursuing weaks, blacks, fluke or flounder. On this point it should be noted that Great South Bay party boats often advertise and provide several species at once. You won't get that kind of variety in the more easterly bays.

As with Moriches, shore fishing on the mainland side is not spectacular. Snapper blues, blue claw crabs, small stripers and flounder (usually small) are caught, and often the best locations are in the tributaries or at the mouths of these tribs. A few shore spots are as follows: Off the dock at the mouth of the Swan River (31); from the dock at the end of South Ocean Avenue in Patchogue (32); at the park dock at the mouth of the Patchogue River (33); from the bulkheads at the mouth of Tuthills Creek (34); from the dock at the mouth of Cory Creek (35); off of Blue Point Dock at the end of Blue Point Avenue (36); from the jetties at Sayville Beach (37); off West Sayville Dock at the end of West Avenue (38); off the beaches at Heckscher State Park (39).

SURF FISHING. Immediately west of Smith Point Park is some six miles of federal property within the Fire Island National Seashore. This undeveloped stretch of barrier beach is open to the public, and that includes surf fishermen. This stretch, coupled with Smith Point Park, enables Suffolk residents to run their beach vehicles a full 12 miles, with only one break approximately in the middle. To run a buggy on the federal property only, a free permit must be obtained

PER BRANDIN

Bluefish have filled the void left by the declining striper. The south shore of Long Island was literally awash with 5-8 pound blues in the fall of '84.

from the check-in station just over the Smith Point Bridge. It is available to all persons with qualified vehicles.

While you can walk in to fish anytime you choose, day or night, beach vehicles are only allowed at certain times. Currently, no beach buggies are allowed at all between June 14th and September 14th. At the fringes of summer, daytime use is greatly curtailed. Best advice is to stop at the check-in station. Or, you can send for their literature by writing to the National Park Service, 120 Laurel St., Patchogue, N.Y. 11772.

There is no camping on Fire Island except at one point, Watch Hill (40). This campground must be reached by boat, either ferry or private boat. There are docking facilities. For more information, write to Watch Hill Camping at the Patchogue address just given.

Surf fishing from the six odd miles of the national seashore can be excellent, and sandbars are what you want to look for here. Daylight investigation at low tide is crucial for success on these unbroken beaches, because bars come and go. Nonetheless, there are often good fish holding formations in front of Old Inlet (41) and in front of Long Cove (42).

From a point just east of Watch Hill all the way to the western boundary of the National Seashore, recreational vehicles are forbidden. Only Fire Island residents or contractors may use the beach, and only for working transportation. Along this beach section, which consists of exclusive villages interspersed with federal property, the surf fishing is done almost exclusively by Fire Island residents since access from the mainland is by ferry only.

At the extreme western tip of Fire Island, surfmen can cast from Robert Moses State Park including Democrat Point (43) where 4-wheel vehicles are allowed under permit. See Fig. 23-b in Ch. 23 for more on state park permits. Here you can cast to the waters of Fire Island Inlet (44), a very productive waterway where all the major gamefish as well as certain bottom fish congregate.

On the inside of Fire Island Inlet is another State Park, Captree (see "ports" in the reference section). Some shore fishing is done here from two special docks (45) reserved just for fishermen. In season, there is a cafeteria and bait & tackle shop right in back of the fishing area. Parking fees are collected at certain times.

Fire Island Inlet (see map) is another extremely important south shore waterway. As with all these inlets, small boats are warned of strong currents complicated by heavy boat traffic. Fluke, stripers and blues are the main gamefish quarries within the inlet, with weakfish also available at times. Drift fishing from a boat is the best fluke tactic,

A "BEST BET" SALTWATER CALENDAR
FOR INSHORE LONG ISLAND WATERS

JANUARY	FEBRUARY	MARCH
• Power plants • Ling and Whiting	• More Codfishing if weather is better	• Good Cod month • White Perch
• Codfish when boats can sail	• Eel spearing through the ice	• Flounder unofficially opens St. Paddy's Day; still localized
	• White Perch in and around tribs • Earliest Flounder in very select spots	• Flounder in east end canals

APRIL	MAY	JUNE
• Good Flounder month	• First real Stripers • Good Weakfish month • First Fluke at inlets	• First real Bluefish; small and action hit or miss • Flounder taper quickly
	• Mackerel peaks • Excellent Blackfish	• Fluke can already be excellent • Seabass
• Blackfish build quickly • Earliest Mackerel	• Porgies build to late May/early June peak • Cod, Pollack at Montauk	• Spring Stripers but not as good as autumn

JULY	AUGUST	SEPTEMBER
• Porgy may continue good all summer	• First real Snapper Blues • Blue Claw Crabs but small • Blues may be deep	• Snapper Blues peak • Bluefish everywhere • Look for Porgies eastward
• Excellent Fluke month • Flounder may persist in Moriches Bay		• Fluke have remained strong in recent years • Weakfish pick up
• Bluefish build, but may be in and out • Seabass	• Bluefish bust loose – close and available • Fluke edge towards inlets	• Early showing of Flounder in select locations • Scattered Stripers • Blackfish, but still small

OCTOBER	NOVEMBER	DECEMBER
• Porgies may continue • Crabs have run late in recent years	• Stripers can be excellent, especially Montauk • Blackfish remain strong	• Both Flounder and Stripers may be available pending • the weather • Tommy Cod and Cod
• Excellent Flounder mid-month on • Pollack build	• Flounder can continue excellent if not too cold • Stripers in the sound, too	• Chance of Stripers in the bight • Whiting and Ling
• Famous Striper surf fishing at Montauk	• Excellent Pollack month • Don't give up on Stripers too soon!	• Shop for next year's tackle!

This chart reflects traditional trends, but does take into consideration fishing patterns over the past 5 years.

Figure 20-d.

while stripers are more accessible to shore casters. Besides at Democrat Point, surf fishermen cast for bass on the north side of Robert Moses Park (46) and of course into the surf. On the other side of the inlet, anglers try for gamefish as well as blacks off the "sore thumb" (47), a man-made rock and dirt jetty (open only to Town of Babylon residents). In the lee of the sore thumb, the so called sore thumb pocket, excellent flounder and fluke catches are made at times. The flounder action, in particular, can be good here in late spring when the fish group up prior to their departure to the ocean.

Within this complex waterway there are many good spots, some of them within old channels or the edges of these disappearing channels. Nautical charts are far from foolproof here. Any boat would greatly benefit from having a depth finder.

JONES BEACH VICINITY
The Jones Beach area offers both quality and variety to the landbased salt water sportsman; there is also very good boat fishing in the maze of channels and little bays between Jones Beach and the mainland. There are miles of beach for surf casting, a powerful inlet where both shore and boat angling is good, and fishing piers projecting out into calm, protected backwaters. There are also bridge abtuments from which bay fishing can be practiced. In this case we'll begin with the oceanfront, starting where we left off in the preceding section.

SURF FISHING. Immediately east of Captree State Park is a stretch of beach that is still very much affected by the powerful waters of Fire Island Inlet. Oak Beach (48) facing the inlet can be very productive, as can be Cedar Beach (49), where prominent sandbars build seaward. However Cedar, like nearby Gilgo Beach (50), is a Babylon Town beach open only to residents (walk-on or beach vehicle access, but not during bathing hours). At Gilgo, there is a large parking lot north of the road that is unattended after the summer season and thus open to all at that time. At Cedar, restrictions may be even tighter.

Luckily, interspersed with this semi-restricted terrain is Gilgo State Park, as shown on the map. At present there are no parking facilities, only access for beach vehicles. The permits summarized in Figure 23-c pertain. Buggy-less surfmen can at times park in the above-named Babylon beach lots and walk in.

Just west of Gilgo, there is again a little bit of restricted beach, and then begins the sprawling Jones Beach complex, a state park open to all. Beach vehicles are not allowed but there is walk-in access for surf casters at Field 6 (51) and West End (52). At West End, you can cast not only into the surf but into the swift waters of Jones Inlet. Much of what has been said about the other south shore inlets may be said for Jones, only here the boat traffic is even heavier. Fishing can be good off the inlet jetty at West End, and there can also be some fine action in the pocket that forms on the east side of the jetty. This latter spot is best in fall when migrating baitfish moving from east to west group up in this pocket.

Short-rodders can also have a field day at Jones, specifically at Field 10 (53) where there are several fishing piers projecting out into the waters of the state boat channel. These popular (and sometimes quite crowded) piers provide fine platforms for anglers who catch flounder, blackfish, fluke, snapper blues, kingfish, sea bass and other bottom fish in season. At times, small to medium bluefish are garnered, while big tiderunner weaks occasionally brighten the scene.

There are restrooms here, and a bait and tackle store open in season.

WEST END WATERS
From Jones Inlet west, the landward side of the barrier island becomes less like a bay and more like a jigsaw puzzle comprised of many islands separated by relatively narrow channels, guts and drains. This mosaic of land and water is very fishy, but is mostly for the boat fisherman. Here, some of the best fishing is in Reynolds Channel, the main east-west waterway between Jones Inlet and East Rockaway Inlet. For boaters, some of the top locations are at the various "crossroads" where north-south channels meet Reynolds. Two of these are Broad Channel (54) and Swift Creek (55). From shore, an excellent fishing site is the Magnolia Boulevard Pier (56). The possible variety here is impressive: Flounder, fluke, porgy, blackfish, snappers, crabs, sea bass, cocktail and bigger blues, and more.

Further east, and on the ocean side, is the Silver Point jetty in Atlantic Beach. Large and small bass, as well as weaks and at times blues, are taken from this jetty which borders East Rockaway (Deb's) Inlet.

21.
LUNCH BREAK LUNKERS: AROUND THE FIVE BOROUGHS

It was like a Norman Rockwell painting, dockside of a warm summer evening, and a young boy posing with this impossibly big bluefish. I soaked in all the things that make me love to be around salty ports: The inevitable rubble of nets and buoys and lobster pots, the head of a striped bass twitching to the work of several crabs in a greasy backwater. With the happy smells of Emmons Avenue wafting down, the bay felt as New York as the easter parade. There is only one Brooklyn and only one Sheepshead Bay.

Beer cans began to pop as our group took over the erstwhile party boat we'd rented for the evening. Then, with anchors aweigh, the skipper "pernted" the bow towards the Ambrose Light Tower.

There's two things I hate on a tipsy ocean. One is the smell of gas fumes and the other is the look of sloppy chum. The mate ladled away, though, making sure I saw every gruesome spoonful. I tried to focus on the battling tiger that surely had to be out there in the night, out there chewing up the ocean beneath the swells that slapped against the mist.

It was a long boat ride, and twenty-five souls were grateful when their mackerel chunks were finally pulling tight against the drifting boat. The first bluefish caught me and Bob and Steve; crowded boats were never something I found wonderful. But an eventual sack of ferocious choppers made the occasional bird's nest worth the trouble, and a couple extra cans of Shlitz made me forget about my stomach.

It seems like all the famous people come from Brooklyn, but not a one was up and waiting for us at half past one. On the old west side highway heading home the painting was a different sort, a modern art miracle of a million lights on a black canvas.

WITH FOUR OF New York's five boroughs sitting on islands – Staten Island to the south, Brooklyn and Queens on Long Island, and Manhattan on an island of its own – residents of the world's most grandiose city should certainly not have to buy their fish. Most do, though, and that's a shame, because some amazingly fine saltwater angling is no more than a cast away from seven million people.

The waters around the city are sometimes collectively called the New York Bight, though technically the bight is the entire "dent" in the Atlantic Coastline defined approximately by Montauk, New York City and Cape May. In any event, the several attached bodies of salt water we will discuss here are: The lower Hudson, the East River, the Upper New York Bay, Jamaica Inlet and Jamaica Bay, and the lower New York Bay out to a line roughly drawn between Sandy Hook and Breezy Point.

STATEN ISLAND'S SHORE FISHING

On New York City's southernmost borough, Staten Island, shore fishermen have over twelve miles of sandy beaches from which to cast. Running south from the Verrazano Narrows Bridge, these beaches are paralleled by Hylan Boulevard and extend to Tottenville. Along the way, there are some great fishing locations that are often underutilized.

Right under the Verrazano Narrows Bridge is Fort Wadsworth. Fishermen can enter through the main gate on Bay Street just north of the bridge and enjoy casting for and catching striped bass, bluefish, and weakfish from May through October. During the colder months, flounder can be caught about a mile north of the main entrance gate of Cliffwood Beach off Bay Street on Clifton Avenue, or at the exact end of Hylan Blvd. Working south from this location, anglers come to South Beach, Midland Beach, New Dorp Beach, and Great Kills Park, all of which now make up the Staten Island Unit of the *Gateway National Recreational Area*. This National Park is spread out over a wide area, and encompasses four geographically separated units: Sandy Hook in New Jersey, this area on Staten Island, Breezy Point and Jamaica Bay in the borough of Brooklyn (see Fig. 21-a).

Along the beaches of Gateway on Staten Island, anglers have a horn of plenty to choose from, including flounder, eels, porgies, kingfish, sea robins, black sea bass, blackfish, striped bass, weakfish, bluefish, blue claw crabs, and fluke. Of this group, only the striper can sometimes be caught year round. The other species are more seasonal, their comings and goings largely determined by water temperature. As for bait & tackle, there are many stores on the island with the more accessible ones being found on Hylan Blvd. and by the harbor at Great Kills Bay.

One of the most popular points in this area is Crookes Point in Great Kills Park. Anglers wishing to fish here must first obtain a free parking permit, which can be acquired from the main office of the recreational center housed at Miller Field just off Hylan Blvd. With the permit, you can park at Crookes Point and have your choice of surf, jetty, harbor bulkhead, or the inlet, all of which are readily accessible.

Fishermen here like to use cut bunker for bait for giant bluefish and tide-runner weakfish. The best of this action runs from late-May through October. Fishing is conducted 24 hours a day, with dawn and dusk the preferred periods. Also at this spot, fluke may be taken from area beaches all summer long. Just offshore, boats pound away at pockets of fluke, and unless the wind is especially bad, even a 14-foot tin boat will suffice. The most common fluke baits fished in this area are squid strips, fluke belly, sandeels, and killies. Note that fluke are predatory fish and prefer a moving bait, so don't set your rod in a sand spike. Rather, simply cast one of these baits out as far as you can, then slowly retrieve the offering back to the beach.

South of Gateway, Hylan Blvd. brings anglers to the fine fishing beaches of Huguenot, Arbutus, Seguine Point on Princess Bay, and Tottenville. Cartop boats can be launched from these beaches. Trailered boats can be launched at Seguine Point. The area is characterized by tree-lined streets leading down to sandy beaches. Park your car and fish!

Species pursued here include porgies, blackfish, sea bass, fluke, striped bass, weakfish, and bluefish. Surf fishing is done off all area beaches. Basically, in the spring while the water is cold anglers prefer bait. Then, as the water warms, tactics become more active and lures are more in evidence.

THE BIGHT FROM A BOAT

Fishing the bight from a boat can be very productive. The hotspots along the Staten Island coast include Princess Bay off Seguine Point, Great Kills Bay, and of course many spots within the lower New York City Bay. The primary species boaters key in on are bluefish, weakfish, striped bass, and fluke.

In Princess Bay, bluefish are caught while trolling single red Lancer Tubes, mini-umbrella rigs, flat metals, and AVA 007 diamond jigs. Trollers work the flats off the Dental Works, the area's channels, and the territory between Staten Island and Keyport, N.J. Channel marker #20 on the Raritan Bay West Reach can be counted on to give up good catches of weakfish and bluefish. Strong running tides guarantee daily cooperation early in the morning and again late in the afternoon. Bluefish often remain present and active all day long.

At Great Kills Harbor, the out-going tide usually carries many small baitfish and crustaceans out of the inlet to the waiting gamefish. Here, fluke are caught by the thousands and bluefish, weakfish, and striped bass may be caught daily from late May through October. Fresh bunker can be snatched near the inlet and then fished live or in pieces for the major gamefish species. For the fluke, try a ½-ounce white bucktail adorned with a live killie.

Many party boats fish in this area. They come from such ports as Tottenville, Perth Amboy, Bayonne, and Hoboken. On occasion, party boats from Sheepshead Bay fish here, too.

Boaters fishing the Lower Bay often concentrate along the beaches of Gateway. Bluefish, weakfish, and fluke are the primary targets. Heavy currents and much bait make for excellent catches in this area. Two good spots to try are Hoffman and Swinburne Islands. For fluke, drift along about 10 yards off shore, while for weaks, blues, and stripers troll your lures right along the rock seawalls which encircle the islands. Be careful of the tricky currents! If after fluke, remember there is a 14"

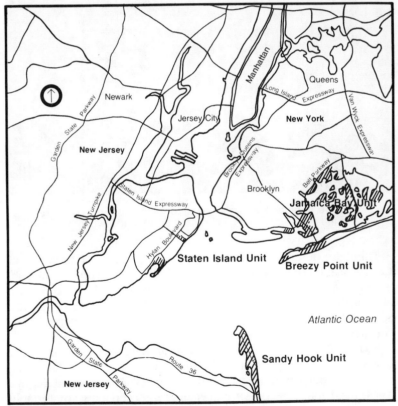

Figure 21-a. Gateway And The New York Bight

size limit. Though one hundred fish days are common, typically you will catch 4 throwbacks under 14" for every legal fish caught.

The Verrazano Narrows and the bridge of that name are just above these islands. Directly under the bridge, boats often drift for bluefish and striped bass with live bunker, eels and sandworms. The last two hours of an out-going tide are considered best.

From the bridge south, blackfish, sea bass, and flounder can be caught during the months of April-May and October-November. Flounder may be caught on into December. Whiting and ling may also be caught during the winter in this vicinity.

RICH GIESSUEBEL

With the angular Manhattan skyline for a backdrop, boaters can find some fine fishing in both the upper and lower harbors.

There are other productive locations for boaters, for example off Coney Island, Rockaway Point, and Jacob Riis Park. Stripers, bluefish, weakfish, fluke, porgies, sea bass, blackfish, whiting, ling, and cod are all available in season. Hot locations include the Tin Can Grounds, Scallop Ridge, Ambrose Light, and an area commonly referred to as "between the channels."

Boats sail daily out of Sheepshead Bay for these species. Some of the boats that call this port home include the Amberjack V, Tampa IV, Brooklyn V, Betty W II, Past Time II, Apache IV, Rainbow, and Zephyr. These head boats have gotten bigger and bigger and more comfortable in recent years. Other party boats that hit the bight sail from Gerritsen

Creek and Freeport. They sail daily for the available species. The morning boats depart around 7:00 a.m. Half day boats leave around 7:00 a.m. and again around 1:30 p.m. Often, night boats are available for bluefish or whiting depending upon season. These boats sail around 7:00 p.m.

Not to be overlooked are the flats lying off Coney Island and around to Gravesend Bay. Between these two better known locations is Norton's Point where giant weakfish, bluefish, and striped bass are waiting to test your skills. A fisherman's arsenal here would include diamonds, umbrella rigs, live bait, and bucktails.

Moving north under the Verrazano Narrows Bridge will leave you afloat on the Upper New York Bay. The best locations here include Governor's Island, Robbin's Reef, the Statue of Liberty and Ellis Island. At the latter two spots, anglers drift behind the islands, out of the main current, or they drift worms over the shoals. They fish high-low worm rigs (see Fig. 21-b), and often a flat of worms will be consumed in a day's fishing.

Bucktails, AVA diamonds, and Hopkins metals are excellent lures for striped bass, the most important gamefish in the upper bay. Simply drop the lure, then raise it to a point several inches above the bottom. Then begin jigging it up and down several feet. As the lure settles, that is when a striper is likely to engulf it.

Probably the best location in the Upper Bay is Governor's Island. From Fort Jay to the point of the island facing Manhattan, *Bass Feed Daily!* This is not a holding area, it is a major feeding station. Don't try to get too close to land here though. Large underwater boulders can and will do a number on your motor. Rather, stay off the seawall and cast your offerings up to it. Then, reel back to you and once it is near the bottom and directly under you, drift along with it. The best tide to fish here is the incoming.

Up the East River you can fish at all the major bridge abutments, along Roosevelt Island, and at Hell Gate. Stripers are the main quarry, even though few legal sized fish are caught. In New York waters, the striper must be 24" from tip of snout to end (not fork) of tail in order to be legal, except for above the George Washington Bridge in the Hudson where a legal fish must be over 18".

BROOKLYN

There is much good shoreline fishing in Brooklyn. For example, all along the Belt Parkway in Gravesend Bay is a concrete seawall where you can cast for your favorite species. Seawall anglers often employ large surf rods approaching 11 feet in length. Snapper blues, blues, flounder, fluke, weakfish and bass can all be caught, in season, at almost any point along the wall.

At Coney Island, there is a fishing pier, sandy beaches, and jetties. Fishermen have the surf early in the morning before bathers arrive. After that, rod and reelers can utilize the fishing pier which has undergone renovation during the winter of '84-'85. Pier fishermen catch lafayettes, sand porgies, and fluke most consistently. Bluefish and weakfish are occasionally taken, and on winter nights in December there is often fine action on whiting. Most fish can be lifted directly from the water up onto the pier. Of course, all rockpiles give up good blackfish catches every spring and fall.

The best way to fish these beaches is by casting flat metal lures like the Hopkins and Kastmaster, early in the morning or right at dusk. For weakfish, retrieve these lures slowly. For stripers, increase the speed slightly and for bluefish reel as fast as you can! One good terminal rig is the "teaser rig." To make one, simply tie in a feathered hook about 18" ahead of your lure. To the gamefish this combination will appear to be a small baitfish being chased by a larger fish. With this rig, double-headers are often registered.

If you continue east on the Belt Parkway you will parallel Rockaway Inlet. Turn right at Exit #11 S and head for Jacob Riis Park. You will pass through Floyd Bennett Field and come to the Marine Parkway Bridge. Crossing the bridge will bring you to Riis Park and Breezy Point, both of which are another unit of the *Gateway National Recreational Area*. Save for Fort Tildon, which is off limits, the recreation area offers surf and jetty fishing for the general public all the way from the tip of Breezy Point through to Jacob Riis Park.

If you intend to use the fishing jetty at Breezy Point, you must first acquire a parking permit from Building #1 in Fort Tildon. The permit is free and entitles you to park and fish. Breezy Point is a fine spot both for the surfcaster and the jetty jock, but some specialized gear is desirable. This would include boot cleats, gaffs, and a portable light source for night fishing.

There are other requirements and restrictions pertaining to fishing these Gateway Units. They include offroad regulations for the tip of Breezy Point, Private Property Rights, Fish and Game Laws, and general rules and regulations for the fisherman. This is a beautiful area and these easy to follow rules are merely intended to keep it that way. So, what can the rule-following fisherman catch?

During the spring, flounder, blackfish, weakfish, and striped bass are tackled with. During the summer, blues can be added to the list, while flounder and blackfish depart. In the fall, porgies, sea bass, and lafayettes

Sonny Adela with a 13-pound bluefish caught between Great Kills Park and the Reach.

(in some years) become available, and in the winter, whiting and ling can be caught near dusk along most beaches.

Another location you may want to investigate in this area is the seawall running along Rockaway inlet behind the Marine Parkway Bridge. On occasions, all the previously mentioned species traverse this inlet. Stripers can often be caught 12 months a year. Worms and clams are good bait choices, but unfortunately Bergalls and lafayettes can become pesky bait stealers. When they do, don't try to fight city hall. Switch to light tackle and fish for them!

Brooklyn's Jamaica Bay offers tremendous fishing potential for all species in season. The bay is composed of many flats, islands, and channels, most of which fall within the protection of the Jamaica Bay Unit of *Gateway.* Overall the channels seem to deliver the best results to bay fishermen. Also concentrate on deep water drop-offs, pilings, concrete piers, and muddy bottoms. Spring and fall flounder in particular favor a clean mud bottom. Porgies, blackfish, lafayettes, weakfish, bluefish, striped bass, blue claw crabs and eels galore can be caught in Jamaica Bay during their respective seasons.

The waterway that flushes Jamaica Bay, Rockaway Inlet, is a good spot to catch a mess of fluke in the summer. Fish the channel edges, as fluke like to wait in ambush at such locations. Drift along with the current and when the first fluke is caught, drop a marker to indicate the spot. Where you catch one, others are sure to follow. Blues can also be caught in the inlet with good consistency.

MANHATTAN

Manhattan is a collosal and intensely developed island, but there is still room for the prosaic pastime of angling. There is literally fishing all around Manhattan. All along the Westside Highway there are tons of old piers from which to fish (although if Westway goes, the situation will change) and along the East River there is a pedestrian path that hugs the river. A good word of advice here would be to never forget where you are fishing – Manhattan can be a rough town. Fish with friends, and always try to keep your car in sight.

Manhattan's lunch break opportunities include striped bass, tommy cod, eel, flounder, and an occasional bluefish or weakfish in season.

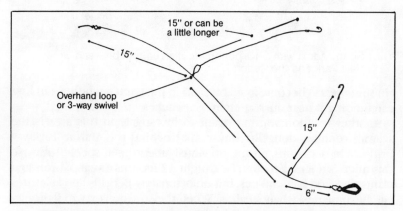

Figure 21-b. "High-Low" Rig. Many species, and combinations of species, i.e. Cod/Flounder, Weakfish/Porgy, etc. It is hand-tied, or sold, several different ways.

RICH GIESSUEBEL

Mike Kersey with a dandy striper taken "Between The Channels." Striped Bass is one of the primary gamefish of the New York Bight.

Several safe locations exist along the Westside Highway. For example at the end of the infamous 42nd Street, where many tour boats originate, there is an expanse of fishable water. Parking is readily accessible and all you have to do is get out of your car and fish. Worms are prime bait, while top lures include the flat metals and bucktails. Striped bass is the most cooperative species around the big island and can be caught around the clock and sometimes around the calendar. However if the winter proves too cold, the stripers will head far upstream to a big Hudson River wintering area near Ossining.

There are locations along the East River where one can try for these very same species. Besides the concrete pedestrian path, you can try under the Brooklyn Bridge, at the South Street Seaport at the end of Wall Street, or at Battery Park.

In Queens, access to the water is limited. However, a few shore spots are described in Chapter 22. Several access spots in the Bronx are named in Ch. 17.

FRESHWATER FISHING

Freshwater angling within the five boroughs is certainly not auspicious, but it is available. Sometimes literally in the shadow of behemoth buildings, little ponds are alive with the shadows of fish: Panfish, carp and in some cases even largemouth bass. Fig. 21-c lists some of the more noteworthy five borough ponds, along with fish present. This is not a complete list, though. There are quite a few others, and these can be located with a Hagstrom New York City atlas on sale all around the city in stationery and other stores.

Several of the city ponds have been stocked with bass in recent years. These include Wolfes Pond in Staten Island, Kissena Lake in Queens, Oakland Lake in Queens and Crotona Park in the Bronx. A few others have bass, too.

There is not a wide variety of panfish in these small waters. Generally it's sunfish, though yellow perch may be present here and there. Most city ponds have carp, and there are a number of people who chase after this often jumbo-sized fish. Carp are taken with natural baits only – doughballs, or cheese and dough or other strange combinations.

FRESH WATER PONDS WITHIN THE FIVE BOROUGHS
(See locator map, fig. 19-a, in Ch. 19)

Ponds	Borough	Acres	Under Authority Of	Large- mouth Bass	Carp	Panfish
NEW YORK CITY (No boats)						
1 Wolfe's Pond	Staten Island	15	N.Y.C.D.P.R.	X	X	X
2 Martling Lake	Staten Island	5	N.Y.C.D.P.R.			X
3 Central Park Ponds	Manhattan	23	N.Y.C.D.P.R.			X
4 Van Cortlandt Park	Bronx	30	N.Y.C.D.P.R.			X
5 Crotona Park Pond	Bronx	3	N.Y.C.D.P.R.	X		X
6 Prospect Park Lake	Brooklyn	57	N.Y.C.D.P.R.			X
7 Meadow Lake	Queens	100	N.Y.C.D.P.R.		X	X
8 Willow Lake	Queens	40	N.Y.C.D.P.R.	X	X	X
9 Kissena Lake	Queens	8	N.Y.C.D.P.R.	X	X	X
10 Oakland Lake	Queens	15	N.Y.C.D.P.R.	X		X
11 Baisley Park Pond	Queens	25	N.Y.C.D.P.R.	X		X

Figure 21-c.

22.
THE PLEASANT PECONICS, AND NORTH SHORE HIGHLIGHTS

It was three leftover meals past turkey day, and nothing but a break in the deer season, really. But it was something I'd always wanted to do: Fish for giant blacks off Long Island's north fork. On the farm pond outside Sag Harbor, a quintet of puddle ducks were perched funny. Ice! I was glad I'd left all my deer hunting clothes in the car.

A day before, a fierce north wind had blown across Shagwong, but this day broke fine and clear. Artie Lach aimed his party boat "Wilheric" east northeast just as a gorgeous orange orb pushed up over Gardiner's Bay.

Well, it turned out to be a grand tour of the east end. We passed Orient Point, Plum Gut and Plum Island, and finally made a drop off Little Gull Island. Nothing there we quickly jumped The Race to Fisher's Island, and eventually even tried over a wreck off Rhode Island.

It was, I gathered, typical late season fishing — not too many fish, but some real prizes, including a huge, 12-pound bulldog that bought the pool. All I could manage, though, were Bergalls. On the three-hour marathon back to port, I couldn't help thinking of a story Gene Hill had once written for *Field & Stream* titled "Low Rod."

Later, both the ice and the ducks were gone from the little pond outside Sag Harbor. But I knew at that very moment, a certain elusive buck was cautiously leaving his bed on a beechnut ridge in upstate New York.

THE NORTH SHORE of Long Island is synonymous with blackfishing. But the eastern islands, especially in late fall, are synonymous with *big* blackfish. Every year in November and often into December, party boats sail from Montauk, Greenport and Sag Harbor to try for jumbo tautog off the north fork. These are fish of a size seldom seen elsewhere. In contrast to the western sound and the south shore, where an 8-pounder is a big black, an east end fish of that size is a probable pool loser. Ten or twelve usually takes the money, and even bigger ones are boated.

First drop for many is the north side of Plum Island; some will also try in treacherous Plum Gut if it is near slack water (the last of the flood is best here). If that doesn't pan out, the skipper will likely head to Little or Great Gull Island, or even across The Race to Fisher's Island. The waters north and northwest of Fishers can produce top blackfishing. In recent years, east end boats have in general been extending their domain, and some will even make for wrecks off the coast of Rhode Island if closer spots don't pan out. Of course there are other game fish taken in quantity around these rich waters, and some of this semi-offshore fishing is touched on in the next chapter. However, in keeping with the approach of this book, we will discuss mainly the bay and shore fishing of the providing north shore. Then we will briefly touch on fishing in the Peconics.

THE NORTH SHORE
The waters washing the north shore of Long Island can be as peaceful as a beaver pond, or, when whipped to a froth by a fierce north wind, as treacherous as the north sea in mid-winter. How well the angler adjusts to these diverse weather and sea conditions often determines success or failure.

In its more tender moods, the shores of Long Island Sound are a favorite place for fly fishermen to whip wisps of feathers to a cautious school bass. At the opposite end of the spectrum, rubber clad surfmen force three-ounce wooden plugs into a maelstrom of wind-driven froth in an attempt to reach monster bluefish just off the beach. The majority of anglers, though, pursue methods somewhere in between, using a variety of techniques to catch fish ranging from humble flounder to trophy-sized striped bass.

It should be pointed out right away that access to much of the north shore, especially for non-residents, is difficult at best. Of course boatmen can sail their craft anywhere, but even boating anglers are hampered by the scarcity of good, public launches. There will be more on launches and launching as we go along.

Parking is the major obstacle when access to exclusive shoreline property is desired. The closer one approaches the sound, the more difficult parking becomes. A few anglers have overcome this difficulty by ringing doorbells, but receptions are not generally too warm unless you know somebody. Some enterprising piscators park their car in a legal area and use a bicycle for transportation to the shore. Another gambit is to go with a buddy, and have him drop you and the gear off near the shore. Then he drives back to the legal parking area and hooves it (or cycles it) back to the beach. It's understandable why fishermen who crack the north shore's armor are very, very quiet about their success.

One bright spot is that, in many instances, restrictions to town beaches and waterfront facilities are not strictly enforced outside of the Memorial Day to Labor Day summer season. In all cases, though, prior investigation should precede your fishing trip. Conditions change rapidly, open spots close, laws are amended, regulations become enforced more or less strictly. Generally the local beaches and ramps mentioned in this chapter should be considered regulated with varying degrees of enforcement. Even the few state parks on the north shore, which we'll mention, require a permit, especially for fishing after dark.

There are six important species caught from the north shore of Long Island: Blackfish, flounder, porgy, striped bass, bluefish, and weakfish. Of course other species are present, and of these lesser fish fluke is most noteworthy. Fluke are not as plentiful as on the island's south shore, but in a good year, they allow some good fishing. Smelt can make early season spawning runs in many north shore creeks, but there hasn't been a good smelt run in the sound in years. Then of course there are tomcod, eels, and some of the other occasional sound visitors discussed in Ch. 17.

We will here concentrate on the "big three": Stripers, blues and weaks. Flounder can be taken from shore almost anywhere there is a clean and preferably muddy bottom. Spring action is best, and it begins in the inner harbors and tidal ponds where the water warms first. As the spring sun gets hotter, flattie action gradually moves deeper and deeper until you really need a boat past about April. Blackfish, for shore fishermen, is also primarily a springtime affair, but the run is about a month later than the flounders. Blacks can be caught around most of the rocky jetties or reefs that extend outward from the north shore's many "headlands." Porgies are closest to shore from around mid-September to mid-October.

The numbered spots that follow are keyed to the maps, Figures 22-a and 22-b, and are discussed in a west to east direction. Although mainly the big three gamefish are discussed, blacks and flounders can be taken at many of these access points.

Little Neck Bay (1) has long been recognized as *the* place to land that first-of-the-year striped bass. Following a mild winter, that initial striper might be caught as early as the last few days of March, but as a general rule, early April is more like it. Worms – sand, blood or ribbon – are customarily used at the start, and these are fished either on the bottom by beach anglers or trailed behind a slow moving boat. Critical elements for success are threefold: Darkness, high water and little or

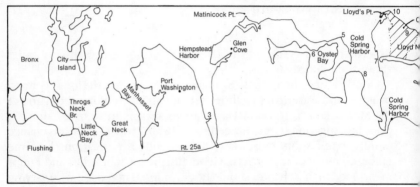

Figure 22-a. North shore Long Island, west.

no wind. The majority of this bay is shallow mud flats which are flooded to a fishable depth only two hours on either side of high tide.

As the season progresses, artificials begin to displace bait. Small, floating minnow-type swimming plugs and slowly worked whiptails are current favorites of plug casters working the shoreline. Such action continues well into May but as the water temperatures rise, anglers are more inclined to concentrate their efforts in the deeper waters at the north end of the bay, near Fort Totten. Throughout the season, persistent fishermen will continue to pick away at school bass during the off hours. On occasion, in late summer, teen-size bluefish will work their way into the western reaches of the sound, including Little Neck Bay, and these provide some thrills for the daytime angler in the right place at the right time.

While the eastern shore of the bay (also excellent for striped bass) is pretty much closed off except to locals, those bound to land will find easier access to the western shore adjacent to the Cross Island Parkway and the fringes of the fort. There is public property here.

The sole crack in the privately owned shoreline of Kings Point is a small Village Of Great Neck waterfront park (2) located a short distance northeast of the Merchant Marine Academy. As with most areas in the western sound, school bass predominate, but there is always the possibility of bluefish action from early summer through October. In fact, when hordes of rampaging blues are mauling schools of bunker, consistent action can occur deep within the harbors and bays of this irregular coast.

Bar Beach (3), a Town of North Hempstead park deep in Hempstead Harbor, is one of the more popular locations for area shore fishermen seeking monster blues. As its name implies, this is a spit of sand which narrowly constricts the waters of the harbor at a point directly opposite an electric generating plant. The warm discharge here attracts and

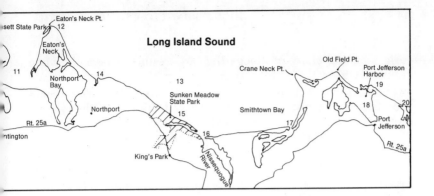

holds a wide variety of fish. Included within Bar Beach is a launching ramp which provides boaters the opportunity to chase bluefish throughout the bay.

Nestled between Matinicock Point and Peacock Point is a Town of Oyster Bay park (4) which provides for the beach fisherman. A bit further east, immediately west of Centre Island, is another town facility. Not as good as some other locations, these two parks nonetheless offer some opportunity. For instance, Centre Island Reef (5) has long been known as a choice spot for striped bass, and there is always the possibility of bluefish settling in for a prolonged stay. This reef is also well within the domain of north shore weakfish.

Deep inside Oyster Bay, the Bayville Bridge (6) is a well known early season spot for striped bass – not just any bass but *big* bass following the seasonal run of herring. A more consistent and extended run of large fish occurs within this bay later on in the season, when schools of bunker win the interest of cow bass and monster bluefish. Two ramps located within Oyster Bay provide local boatmen access to this fishing, and much more, within a short distance.

The eastern shore of adjacent Cold Spring Harbor features two prime fishing locations, suitable for boating and beach fishing alike. The stretch of shore commonly known as the Causeway (7) is an excellent place for striped bass or weakfish. A small swimming plug coupled with a teaser, or a hook baited generously with worms, is effective. The waters directly across the harbor, off Coopers Bluff (8) have produced many fine bass for boatmen trolling sandworms or quietly plugging the shoreline. Deep within the harbor, in the general vicinity of a launching ramp and an accessible bulkhead, the ebb and flow of the harbor's waters is restricted by a series of sandbars. It is here, frequently within reach of fishermen lining the shore, that bluefish corral terrified bunker schools. As with all such activity, early morning effort produces the best results, especially when coupled with a flood tide. Large plugs, poppers or metal-lipped swimmers often account for a fair share of fish but more consistent action can be had using bait. Freshly snagged bunker, usually available on the spot, can be either live-lined or presented in chunk form.

The point of land shielding the mouth of Cold Spring Harbor from the rising sun is known as Lloyd Neck or Diamond Point. Fortunately, located here is Caumsett State Park (9). Unfortunately, Caumsett is a restricted-use park which provides only a limited number of permits for shore fishing. Although the tidal rips forming off the point itself draw the most attention from surfmen and boatmen, gamefish can be found the entire length of this shoreline. Knowledgeable and often secretive anglers, working the winds and tides to best advantage, frequently discover fish of their own, far from the congestion encountered at the point. School bass open and close the season here but in the interim, herring, mackerel, fluke, bluefish and weakfish provide both sport and food.

After the early season flurry, action along much of the north shore settles down to the night-time pursuit of weakfish and bass with additional sporadic daylight bouts with ever-roaming schools of blues. Summer-long fishing of this sort can take place at any time and place, but certain locations are more likely to attract and hold fish than others. Lloyd's Point (10) is one such place. The most opportune time to seek these obliging gamefish is during the early morning hours, before the rising sun or unthinking boaters force the fish to deeper water. During the fall months, bottom fishermen using bunker or mackerel chunks are rewarded with line-stripping encounters with bluefish occasionally approaching the 20 pound mark. It is also at this time that brisk northerly winds often stir these larger fish into striking a plug.

Before the decline of striped bass, several areas within Huntington Bay (11) were the locale for knowing boatmen to seek out trophy-sized stripers. The moon in June would find these sharpies drifting live eels or bunker in the waters surrounding Target Rock or the Huntington Light. Nowadays, these inner harbor areas are more apt to find anglers drifting live bunker for large bluefish.

Eaton's Neck (12), and the well known "Eaton's Triangle," is truly one of the most consistent fishing areas on Long Island. On this sharply-rising shoal, just north of Eaton's Neck Lighthouse, methods used by boaters to take a variety of fish cover a broad spectrum of salt water fishing: Plug casting, trolling, jigging, bottom fishing, clam chumming, drifting sandworms. At one time or another they all will

produce fish. Like all productive fishing areas, crowding detracts from
the appeal of the Triangle, but you can beat the crowds somewhat by
fishing early morning or off-season.

Asharoken, Crabmeadow, Makamah, the Brickyards and Callahan's
line the western rim of Smithtown Bay (13). All are well known by
locals and knowledgeable outsiders as excellent places to fish through-

PER BRANDIN

The north shore of Long Island can be tempest-tossed in
the face of a north wind. More often, though, it's as gentle
as a lamb.

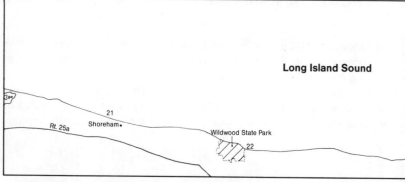

Figure 22-b. North shore east, and Peconics.

out the season. Stretches of sand and gravel interspersed by clusters of rock and mussel beds provide the habitat sought by a variety of prey and predatory fish. Early season encounters with school bass and mackerel, followed shortly by weaks and harbor blues, add up to usually good rewards for the visiting rod and reeler. Schools of various sized bluefish roam these waters from mid-May on, frequently foraging within casting range during the early morning and evening hours. These same fish offer less discriminate boat fishermen sport, into mid-autumn, through a variety of techniques. The exceptionally fine launching ramp, on the western shore of LILCO's inlet lagoon, affords the trailer boatman direct access to Smithtown Bay.

Freezing temperatures in late fall force many wild creatures to warmer climes. But the infusion of heated water from the power plant at Northport (14) provides an artificial environment which attracts and holds several species of fish throughout the winter. Striped bass, occasionally reaching weights of 30 pounds, perch, and sometimes bluefish lure anglers from considerable distances. For sure, this is one of the better spots on the island to rid oneself of cabin fever during the off months.

The center and eastern portions of Smithtown Bay present a similar scenario. While Short Beach, Long Beach and Westmeadow provide access to resident surfcasters, Sunken Meadow State Park (15) affords all anglers the opportunity to fish a prime section of shoreline . . . one where a sizeable stream and a series of drainages enter the bay. The intricate and ever shifting series of sand bars created at the mouths of these outlets provide beach fishermen an ideal, though often dangerous means to reach the fish.

Because its western shore lies within Sunken Meadow Park, the banks of the Nissequogue River (16) get the most attention, but the small jetties lying along the eastern outlet of Stony Brook Harbor

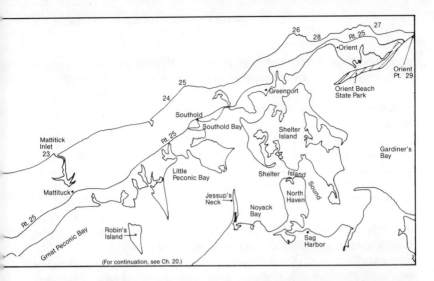

Mattitick Inlet 23
Mattituck
Rt. 25
Great Peconic Bay
Robin's Island
(For continuation, see Ch. 20.)
24
25
Rt. 25
Southold
Southold Bay
Little Peconic Bay
Jessup's Neck
Noyack Bay
26
28
Rt. 25
Greenport
Shelter Island
Shelter Island
North Haven
Sag Harbor
27
•Orient
Orient Pt. 29
Orient Beach State Park
Gardiner's Bay
Sound

(17) should not be overlooked. All species of predatory fish frequent these estuaries, their patterns a copy of the bay at large. It should be pointed out that with deeper water encountered within an easy cast of the river banks, sinking plugs and bucktail jigs are more likely to be used by those skilled in taking fish from these swift currents. The same shallows that prove so useful to beach fishermen are more of a headache to boatmen using any of the three launching ramps located a short distance inside these waterways.

Immediately east of Port Jefferson Harbor (18) lies the reknowned Mt. Misery Shoal (19). Possibly second only to the Eaton's Triangle, Mt. Misery is one of the north shore's premier fish producers. This is almost exclusively the domain of boat fishermen, since the properties adjoining these waters are controlled by exclusionary villages.

East of Mt. Sinai Inlet, beach access becomes somewhat more achievable. Unfortunately, Brookhaven Town regulations are in a state of change these past few years, thus shoreline access between the town beaches at Mt. Sinai and Shoreham are questionable. Past procedure here was for an angler to simply park his vehicle at the road ending nearest the current hotspot. Miller Place Landing, Hegerman's Landing and Hallock Landing are but a few of the local favorites, but signs severely restricting off road parking now present an obstacle which must be circumvented. This particular problem is repeated throughout Riverhead and Southold Townships, but thankfully these towns relax their enforcement during the off season.

The launching ramp located at Cedar Beach in Mt. Sinai Harbor (20)provides the small boat operator with his last hardtop ramp until he reaches Mattituck Inlet. The shoreline between these two major inlets remains unbroken for all practical purposes. Thus the inflow at the Shoreham nuclear plant and the tidal creek at Wading River are of little use to boatmen who would have to cruise a long way to get to them.

The beach at Shoreham (21) and the west jetty at the nuclear plant can be reached via the town parking lot, which is cut into the bluff at Shoreham. The shore east of the plant, with the exception of the state park at Wildwood, lies under the jurisdiction of the Town of Riverhead, It features the typical north shore mix of sand and gravel, plus rocks of varying sizes, routinely broken by bulging points of land. This entire area generally receives little attention, except from local anglers. The notable exception is Wildwood State Park (22).

An excellent north shore fishing spot is the twin jetties guarding the inlet at Mattituck (23). The west jetty is the more popular of the two, simply because access here is gained with less effort. Weakfish, small blues and school bass are the mainstays in the first half of the season.

RIGGING FOR BLACKFISH
By Ted Keatley

When blackfishing, hardware is best eliminated to minimize snagging on the rocky bottom where they are found. Double the line and tie an overhand knot to form a loop about six inches long. Insert both strands of the mono through the eye of the bank sinker. The doubled line reduces cut-offs due to abrasion. Attach the loop of a snelled hook to that doubled loop immediately above the sinker. A second hook can be tied into the middle of the first snell. The hook snells should be heavy, stiff monofilament to prevent tangles and also to reduce the chance of cutting the line on rough rocks or barnacles.

To bait with a fiddler or half of a green crab, insert the hook point through the claw socket and bring it out at a leg joint. Leave the point exposed to facilitate hook setting. Some remove the legs and back shell when using green crabs. However, this makes the bait more vulnerable to bergalls and other thieves. Any blackfish worth catching has no trouble taking an "unshucked" green crab half. If soft clams are used, run the hook through the black rubbery neck and into the body. Then, crack, but do not remove the shell.

Figure 22-c.

Occasional flurries of blues, around dawn and dusk, is the most obvious sport to be had until fall, but sharpies working the hours of darkness, at times using fresh bait, beach a hefty striper from time to time. Fall, here, is bluefish time – not the small fish but ones that make for Kodak pictures and wall trophies.

While the inlet at Mattituck and its accompanying jetties provide the beach fisherman a break in the routine, it also provides the boat angler with a place to launch. From here, seaworthy craft can make the run east to Horton Point, the east end's answer to the Mt. Misery Shoal. The fishing here often resembles the action of farther west, but in November some truly fabulous fishing for teen blues and school bass can materialize. Smaller boats, those which can be launched from less than a top notch ramp, have used the small ramp at Hashamomuck Beach, which lies a short run east of the Horton's Point Lighthouse. Boats working the outer rip at Horton's, on the ebb tide with umbrella rigs or bucktails, are often rewarded with enough memories and fish filets to last the winter.

Back on the beach, the waterfront parking areas at Kenny's (24) and Horton's (25) offer ideal access to very productive waters. Fishing here continues the pattern established farther west, but it is in the fall that this region takes on a character of its own. Autumn finds local anglers patiently dunking chunks of cut bait, while waiting for periodic opportunities to cast plugs or tins at various-sized blues. In November, when the north winds howl and the sound is whipped to a froth, the ebb tides at Hortons become the place to be for monster bluefish. Then as the ranks of these blues thin, school bass come to the fore. At this time, tins and teasers or tins and tubes prove to be the favorite lures for many.

The remainder of the North Fork shoreline receives little attention from visiting surf fishermen. This is not to say that the area is void of fish. On the contrary, local anglers keep the nearby beaches honest and enjoy some fine action when conditions come together. Two good spots between Hortons and the Orient Point are Rocky Point (26) and Mulford Point, (27) both frequented almost entirely by local anglers but both offering the classic habitat for gamefish seeking prey. Truman's Beach (28), lying alongside Rt. 25 between these points, should not be overlooked for at times excellent shore action can pop here.

The raging tides found off the tip of Orient Point (29) should be approached with extreme caution. The area, reached after a moderate walk from the ferry slip, lies within a stone's throw of Plum Gut, one of the most famous and violent sluiceways on the entire east coast.

THE PECONICS

The Peconics – Little and Great Peconic Bay and the maze of adjacent sounds, necks, channels and guts – play host to two important species of salt water fish. Fishing from shore for these is not generally good, so we will restrict ourselves here to boat fishing.

Synonymous with the name Peconic is Weakfish. Weaks winter to the south off the mid-Atlantic coast, but every year they migrate north and many mature fish move into the Peconics to spawn. Weaks are serial spawners, meaning that they do so over a long period of time and in many areas. In the Peconics, fishing is at its best when the Lilacs bloom. Unfortunately, weaks are now tapering following a 10-year period of abundance.

Weaks enter the Peconics both from the east end and through Shinnecock Inlet and Canal. The anglers who line the banks of the canal in March and early April for flounder return for an encore. But as always, fishing is subject to the opening and closing of the locks. The well established tackle shop, Altenkirch & Son, is located right on the canal and can give you information on the opening and closing times of the locks at any given time. If you'd like to compute these times yourself, the formula is simple. Just secure a south shore tide table and check when it is dead high at Shinnecock Inlet. The canal locks will open about two hours before. They will close again about six hours later.

Inside the Peconics, the big tiderunners gravitate to certain ledges and other bottom structure, and to the mouths of tidal creeks. Some traditional hotspots, besides the canal, include Jessup's Neck, the North and South Race at Robin's Island, the hole near buoy 16, the rip south of buoy 22, and the mouths of such streams as Deep Hole, East, Richmond, Wickham and Goose Creeks.

Though most of the big weaks have left the Peconics by mid-June, a second body of small weakfish move in sometime during the summer. As with Great South Bay, these late-run weaks average two to three pounds and provide a lot of sport on light tackle.

Porgies are the other important gamester in the Peconics; these fish, too, use the area for spawning. Generally, the action can be good all summer, but the biggest fish are the early ones of late May and early June. Some of these jumbo scup go 2½-3 pounds. During most of the summer, though, Peconic porgies average only about a half a pound.

Flounder are taken all around these east end waters, but it's mainly an early spring affair. Many flatfish afficianados also rent small boats from the several liveries in the area. Exceptionally early flounder action can commence in some of the protected bays and tidal ponds where the water warms first. One good example is Three Mile Harbor. It's important to note that east end flounder have a decided preference for shellfish as opposed to the worms that seem to work better farther west on the island. This makes sense. The bottom of these east end waters produces clams and other shellfish in astounding numbers.

Blues are found throughout these waters from July onward, although they tend to be small. They are, nonetheless, pursued by hundreds of anglers who revel in the fact that blues are the least picky of the local gamefish. Stripers are also caught in restricted areas, but not in any great numbers. Look for moving water and rocks. Fluke, too, are found in the Peconics and while they're not usually too abundant, they are of a quality size.

RICH GIESSUEBEL

Big tiderunner weaks, like these two held by Floyd Moore, invade the Peconics almost every spring.

23.
MONTAUK!

Montauk! The legend loomed large in our sleepy brains, and pulled us, like a beckoning wave, ever eastward on the Long Island Expressway.

Montauk! What would it be like? At 3:00 a.m. our Kodak fantasies of leg-long stripers were more like night dreams than daydreams. Still, it wasn't something we wanted to do — it was a pilgrimmage, a crusade, a baptism. It was, after all, Montauk.

Tumas, Salivars, the Viking! As we pulled into wakening Montauk Harbor, all the names came back to me from a thousand magazine articles I'd read when I should have been studying.

"There's no surf fishing here, boys" the grizzly old diner cook told us. Then he pointed east.

As you drive from Montauk Village out to the point, and the land narrows, you get the overwhelming feeling that you are, in fact, going somewhere. Still, we wondered if Long Island would ever really end.

North Bar, False Point, Scotts Hole! The fishermen in the parking lot barked out directions and place names that rang like old Yankee baseball greats. The lighthouse beacon swept the dawning fog as we walked a little sandy road down to the water.

Montauk! It was, simply, beautiful, from the piles of blue mussels, to the cottontail brush, to the small stripers that hit all day Long. In a salty town ginmill later that night, we drank beer and shot pool underneath behemoth sharks, marlin and striped bass.

"You know," I said to Roger. "It's a shame you can only get to see Montauk for the first time once."

MONTAUK IS THE tip of a piece of land that juts into the Atlantic Ocean. It is also a good place to fish.

Either of these assertions could rival the proverbial understatement of the century.

Off West Lake Drive there is a sign that says. "Welcome To Montauk,

Fishing Capital Of The World." It may well *be* the world's most important sportfishing center. It may also be the best, if not in terms of potential then at least in terms of productivity. In fact, more International Game Fish Association records belong to Montauk than any other port anywhere. Let it be clear: The quality and variety of inshore and offshore saltwater fishing at Montauk is among the best in the world. There is also a little bit of surf fishing, as you may have heard.

Where is Montauk? In the narrowest sense, it is the very eastern tip of Long Island, Montauk Point, where there is a lighthouse and a state park. In the broadest sense, it is the point plus all the shoreline back a dozen odd miles on either side, Montauk Harbor and Village, and all the waters inshore and offshore to Block Island and the Gulf Stream. Offshore fishing is not within the scope of this book, but a rough offshore timetable is included (Fig. 23-c). Here, we will cover access for surf fishermen in detail, and then talk a little about the nearshore boating.

While Montauk is still relatively close to New York City, it is the farthest spot of those covered in this book. Thus a little bit of destination information would be in order. At the same time, we can give an overview of what's available to the visiting fisherman.

Getting to Montauk is really academic. Just head east on Long Island until you can't go any farther. This means, for most, the Long Island Expressway to Rt. 27 before Riverhead, then Rt. 27 the rest of the way out. It's about 2½-3 hours from the city line. If you don't have a car, the Long Island Railroad runs to Montauk Village, its terminus. From the station you can easily walk to a motel, but you'd have to take a cab or otherwise hop a ride out to the party boats. For surf fishing at the point, the railroad won't help. You must have a vehicle.

Montauk Village is located about five miles west of the point (for all references in this chapter, see Fig. 23-a). Here is where you will find many motels and other accomodations as well as restaurants and bait & tackle shops. Montauk Village has an active Chamber Of Commerce and they will be glad to help you. Call or write them at Box CC, Montauk, NY 11954. Tell them you're interested in fishing and they will send you brochures that will include lists of motels, charter boats, etc. Or, stop by their office in person. They are right on Rt. 27 in the middle of town and are open seven days a week in summer.

A few miles north of Montauk Village is Montauk Harbor, also called Lake Montauk. This beautifully sheltered harbor was once a fresh water lake until a storm opened it to the sea. Now, the boats that ply the Montauk waters dock here. For visiting boaters, docking facilities are available, and these are also listed in the brochures distributed by the C.O.C.

The harbor is where you can hop on a party boat almost any day of the year from early spring to late fall. Even in winter some boats sail, primarily for cod, albeit with cut-back schedules. Besides the ten or so party boats, there are scores of charter boats, not to mention many more private boats of every size and description.

By the way, there really is very little bay-type shore fishing (as opposed to surf fishing) in the Montauk area though Lake Montauk does offer a little action on flounder.

Surf fishermen heading to Montauk Point should keep in mind that there are no services out there, other than restrooms and a snack bar (in season) in the park. Food, bait, tackle and supplies should be gotten ahead of time in Montauk.

Why are the waters surrounding Montauk so good? It's a combination of factors, really, and there is only room to touch on them here.

The tides at Montauk are at once a panacea and a waterloo for anglers. These complex, varied and often fierce racing tides and currents provide excellent feeding areas for gamefish. However, to fish them properly and at the right stage, and to maneuver a boat in them takes experience. Part and parcel with tides, as a factor in Montauk's productivity, is the bottom topography. The many rising reefs and rocks create riptides and disorient baitfish, and they also foster the growth of shellfish. Tons of blue mussels and other shellfish are naturally cultured in the waters around Montauk, and this provides food for many different species.

Perhaps the most obvious attribute of Montauk is its geographical position. Long Island provides a natural block for migrating fish, and Montauk – being the extreme tip of that island – is a key crossroads for gamefish heading north to south or vice versa. Montauk also sits in a transition zone between the relatively smooth, even-sloped sandy coastal zone to the south and the rockier littoral zone of New England. Since both types of habitat occur around Montauk, the sheer variety of species is unmatched along the Atlantic Coast.

The conditions for a fine offshore fishery are also ideal. For one thing, Block Island Canyon is very near, and the Gulf Stream passes relatively close to the point. Further, the range of water temperatures around Montauk is extremely varied, ranging from warm surface currents south of the point, to cold, deep water east and northeast of the point. Thus you have pelagic southern species like tunas, sharks and marlin, as well as cold-water fish like cod and pollack. The fact is, one never really knows what one is likely to hook into around Montauk.

ANGLER'S GUIDE TO MONTAUK POINT

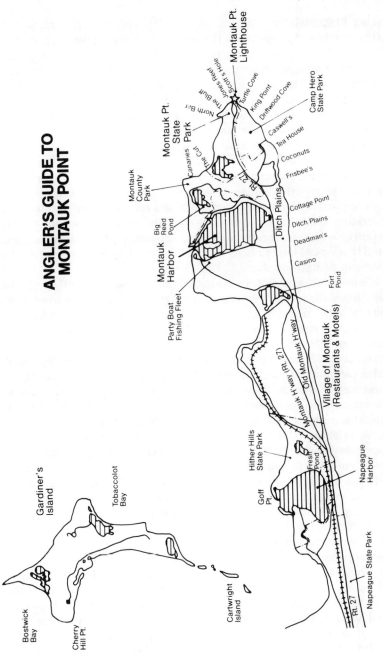

Montauk Pt. Lighthouse

Montauk Pt. State Park

Scott's Hole
North Bar
The Bluff
Turtle Cove
King Point
Driftwood Cove
Caswell's
Tea House
Coconuts
Frisbee's
Camp Hero State Park

Canares Cut
Rt. 27
Montauk County Park

Big Reed Pond
Montauk Harbor

Ditch Plains
Cottage Point
Ditch Plains
Deadman's
Casino
Fort Pond

Party Boat Fishing Fleet

Montauk H'way (Rt. 27)
Old Montauk H'way
Village of Montauk (Restaurants & Motels)

Hither Hills State Park
Goff Pt.
Fresh Pond
Napeague Harbor

Rt. 27
Napeague State Park

Gardiner's Island
Bostwick Bay
Cherry Hill Pt.
Tobaccolot Bay
Cartwright Island

Figure 23-a.

SURF FISHING

Although boat fishing is superlative, Montauk is probably best known for its surf fishing. In truth, surf fishing has never been easy here, what with the rocks, strong currents and surf, changing conditions and crowds of people. Further, the surf fishing is probably not as good as in years past, thanks in large part to the decline of the striper. Nonetheless, for the expert who has paid his dues and learned Montauk's fancies, it can proffer the just rewards and more.

Striped bass is king, and even though stripers have declined, bluefish – amazingly abundant in the early 80s – have not risen much in esteem with the hardcore, hardfishing Montauk surfmen. Still, between sneers, these guys will patrol the shoreline by day looking for schools of choppers that hit the beaches on and off. In higher regard is the weakfish, the third member of Long Island's surf triumvirate. Highly cyclical, weakfish are now tapering after a period of strong abundance, and that would look to make the bluefish even more dominant on the local surf fishing scene.

Fluke are also sometimes pursued off the east end, both with bait and lures. Bottom fishing in the surf is really quite common out here, in fact, and sinker slingers will not only prop up their rods for blackfish, flounder, porgy and even occasionally cod and pollack, but for the big three gamefish as well.

Most surf fishermen stick to the immediate environs of the point. That means under the light, west along the north shore to "north bar", and just south and west of the light. When surf casters speak of Montauk, this is often the specific piece of geography they are referring to. This entire area is within Montauk State Park (Fig. 23-a), so you have a right to be there. There are a couple of big parking lots and by day, you can simply get out and walk down to the water. There is no park entrance fee and no permit is needed for this. However as all serious surf fishermen know, night is usually the best time. Here is where things get stickier. First, you need a special permit for after-dark parking. Details of this permit are summarized in Fig. 23-b. This permit excludes cars. Only *self-contained* camping vehicles are allowed to park overnight for fishing purposes and most Montauk regulars have pick-up campers or motor homes.

The other necessary permit would be for off-roaders who wish to drive and/or park on the beach. Currently costing $25 annually, this permit is of course something serious surfmen with beach buggies will want to have. Details of this permit are also gone over in Fig. 23-b.

Good surf fishing is not restricted to the immediate area of the point. The north shore west from the lighthouse to Montauk Harbor

PER BRANDIN

Montauk Point! It's where land meets the sea, and where only the most persevering surf fisherman tastes success. Hopkins lure (right) is a time-tested fish catcher in these waters.

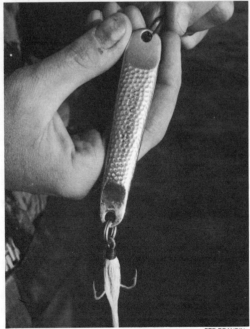

PER BRANDIN

can provide some fine action. As discussed, you can fish the entire beach within Montauk State Park. But the state property ends a ways east of Shagwong Point, a well-known and productive surf fishing location. From the state park boundary west to Montauk Harbor inlet, the beach falls within Montauk County Park, and to fish here you must be a Suffolk resident or a guest of one. Bona fide county residents can park and walk in to fish, or buy a $25 beach vehicle permit to run this entire piece of excellent shoreline. Camping is also allowed for residents.

In spite of the county restrictions, non-residents are usually not bothered if they walk in to fish the beach. The problem, besides a potentially long walk, is parking. One place is the town parking lot by the east jetty at Montauk Harbor. If you're not a town of Easthampton resident, you can still obtain a guest pass to use this lot if you are staying in a local motel. On a recent trip out here, I also saw private landowners "selling" daily parking space on East Lake Drive.

Yes, access to Long Island's ocean can be as complicated as airline tickets. Best advice is for all fishermen to write to the various municipalities that control so much of the access. The address for state parks is given in Fig. 23-b. You can also obtain some good literature from the Suffolk County Park Office in West Sayville. Suffolk has a great many parks where fishing is permitted, and in certain cases non-county residents can get in on the action.

The turf immediately below the lighthouse – "up front" in Montauk jargon – is very important for the surf caster. Experienced jetty jockies who know the ropes score well, and in fact, the light has been one of the better Montauk surf spots in recent years. There is a strong rip right below the light, but the deep water keeps most anglers on "The Balcony" of rocks that lie beneath the cliff. In the hot autumn periods, it's smart to arrive early before a good night tide to stake out your own rock. It can get very crowded here. In all cases, bring a long-handled gaff and felt-soled or cleated waders, and check the area out by daylight ahead of time.

If you're like me and you refuse to fish among a crowd, the south shore may be for you. South and west of the lighthouse is the majestic rocky area known as "The Bluffs" or "The Fort." Very rocky all the way west to Ditch Plains, this segment is difficult to walk, difficult to wade and usually hit by a strong surf. But for all these reasons – and also because a long walk may be entailed – it is much more lightly fished. When stripers are plentiful, this rocky area is choice. In recent years, it has been very productive for weakfish, and of course blues will

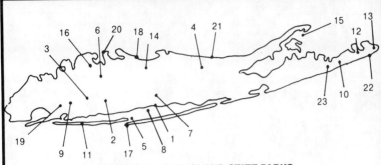

FISHING IN LONG ISLAND STATE PARKS

	Bayard Arboretum - 1	(FW)	Belmont Lake - 2
	Bethpage - 3		Brookhaven - 4
(SW)	Captree - 5	(SW)	Caumsett - 6
(FW)	Connetquot River - 7	(SW)	Heckscher - 8
(FW)	Hempstead Lake - 9	(FW, SW)	Hither Hills - 10
(SW)	Jones Beach - 11		Montauk Downs - 12
(SW)	Montauk Point - 13	(FW)	Caleb Smith - 14
(SW)	Orient Beach - 15		Planting Fields - 16
(SW)	Robert Moses - 17	(SW)	Sunken Meadow - 18
	Valley Stream - 19		Walt Whitman House - 20
(SW)	Wildwood - 21		Camp Hero - 22
	(SW) Napeague - 23		

There are 23 state parks on Long Island, as shown and listed above. Those prefaced with a (FW) offer fresh water fishing. Those prefaced with a (SW) offer salt water fishing. Many of these parks are also discussed in other chapters.

All these parks are open to the public though seasons, activities, fees and regulations will vary. Excellent maps and brochures are available free from the Long Island State Park and Recreation Commission, P.O. Box 247, Babylon, NY 11702. This is your central source of information. They will also give you the number of the individual park you are interested in.

For fishermen, there are two important permits, both pertaining to salt water angling only. First is the *Sport Fishing Permit.* Essentially this is the permit that allows you to park during the night hours for surf fishing (most if not all parks are closed, *except* to fishermen, after sunset). The current fee is $10 annually, and this permit may be obtained in person only at the Babylon headquarters *or* at the parks where the permit applies: Captree, Hither Hills, Jones Beach, Montauk Point, Robert Moses, Sunken Meadow and Wildwood. As of 1985, permits will be issued *only* between January 2 and April 30 and then again between September 3 and December 31. Note that there are special limited permits, some drawn on a lottery basis, for Caumsett State Park. Call Caumsett or the Babylon office.

The second permit is the *Beach Vehicle Permit,* which allows access to designated areas at the following parks only: Robert Moses (Democrat Point), Hither Hills, Napeague and Montauk Point. Currently costing $25 annually, these too must be obtained in person, but they are available *only* at Hither Hills or Robert Moses. In 1985, this permit will be issued only between January 1 and April 30. The following items must be in your beach buggy at the time you apply for a permit *and* at all times while you are on the beach: Pail, tow rope or chain, shovel, vehicle registration, fishing rod and portable toilet.

Figure 23-b.

Thick, snowshoe flounder is a hallmark of these rich, east-end
waters. Three-pound fish, like this one, are relatively common.

come and go with the steadiest action in September and October (in
recent years, surf action has held right through November).

Right now, the only real access to The Fort is from the light or from
Ditch Plains. That is because the intervening stretch is mostly private
property. However, recently the state has acquired the old Camp Hero
military base (Fig. 23-a). At present, this property is completely closed
to the public pending utilization planning, but it is possible that at
some time this new addition to Long Island's state parks could mean
better access to The Fort. Surf fishermen should keep their eye on this
situation.

Nor does good surf fishing stop at Ditch Plains. Moving westward
from this hamlet, the rocks eventually give way to sand, and the fishing,
especially in the fall, can be good. As always, access here will be much
more achievable before Memorial Day or after Labor Day. But access is
guaranteed, year-round, in two state parks: Hither Hills and Napeague.
Both of these parks stretch from one shore to another, as shown on the
map. On the ocean side, they are mostly sand as opposed to the rocks
at the point. Best action is on migrating bluefish, but weaks and
stripers will also be beached, especially at night. If you're a camper,
Hither Hills is a magnificent base of operations. Call the park though
– it fills up very quickly.

The least publicized shore fishing at Montauk is the north shore
from Montauk Harbor west to the western boundary of Napeague

Park. Fortunately, you have here public access from both parks. Even the private sections can be accessed at certain times, though; all it takes is a little sleuthing. These are gentle waters and conditions can be bay-like.

NEARSHORE BOATING

The Pollack Rip, Gardiner's Island, Cartwright, Shagwong Reef – the place names of the inshore waters at Montauk read like a who's who in great fishing spots of the Atlantic Ocean. One could certainly write a volume or two just about Montauk, but even if there were such a book it would not guarantee success. As mentioned earlier in this chapter, many of the factors that make Montauk waters so productive are the same ones that make fishing here so challenging. You simply have to put in your time . . . but Montuak is more worthy of that time than just about any other spot you might think of.

All the inshore species found in Long Island waters, and summarized in Fig. 17-b, are present around Montauk. These include fluke, flounder, blackfish, porgy, seabass, striped bass, bluefish and weakfish. Cod and pollack, semi-offshore fish, are taken very close to Montauk, sometimes even right from the beach.

Some species have a knack for being bigger at Montauk than anywhere else. The east end angling for jumbo blackfish is very good, and is discussed in Ch. 22. Porgy also run large near Montauk as do fluke, flounder and seabass. The true "snowshoe flounder" of 4-7 pounds aren't seen too much any more, but anglers commonly catch fish of 2½-3½ pounds (true weight, not eyeball weight!).

Gardiner's Island is included on Fig. 23-a for good reason: The waters surrounding it are an intricate part of the inshore boating scene at Montauk. These waters are semi-protected and relatively calm, especially on the west side of the island. Thus even beamy 14-foot boats will run out to them from Montauk and Napeague Harbor, though such small boats should be acutely aware of the weather.

Flounder and fluke are the primary targets directly around Gardiners, with seabass, porgy, blackfish and blues also present in season. The founder action starts in April, but the steadiest pick, especially on the bigger fish, is usually during the last three weeks of May. It can continue on into June, but usually starts to taper quickly after the first of that month. While the flatties do run large, the quantities are not as impressive as in Moriches Bay and other locales.

North of Gardiner's Island is a shoal that extends to "The Ruins", the remains of an old fort. Both sides of this shoal produce stripers as well as bluefish. Fluke and flounder are taken here, too.

A super area for gamefish, especially stripers, is Shagwong Reef, which extends about three miles off Shagwong Pt. Night action on bass can be excellent here, while by day, blues, blacks, porgies and seabass are often available. Shagwong Reef is also a top area for weakfish when that species is abundant.

The Cartwright Grounds have been a dynamic spot for gorilla bluefish in recent years. Located about five miles south of Montauk, this spot is still within reach of relatively small craft. Cod, pollack and other species are also taken here.

While inshore angling is fine both south and north of the point, there is also excellent action to be had just east of Montauk. Stripers are usually cooperative in an area known as The Elbow, while in the Montauk Triangle, stripers are joined by bluefish and weaks.

Shagwong is not the only significant fish-holding reef off Montauk. Great Eastern Rock, Endeavor Shoals and other bottom formations are all within reasonable boating distance of Montauk Harbor. Saltwater fishing is far from static, but these bottom structures will usually provide some action season after season.

It is hard not to at least mention the offshore opportunities available near Montauk. Some of the mammoth blue-water battlers, listed in Fig. 23-c, are coaxed close to the point by the Gulf Stream current, which in some years swings quite near to the east end of Long Island. Marlin,

APPROXIMATE TIMETABLE FOR FISHING IN LONG ISLAND'S OFFSHORE WATERS

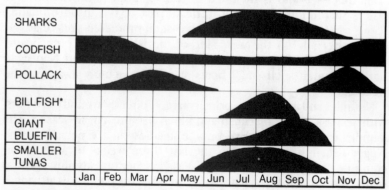

*There are three billfish in New York offshore waters. Two of these — Blue Marlin and Swordfish — are very rarely taken. Fishing for the third, White Marlin, has improved in recent years.

Figure 23-c.

PROPOSING A BLUEFISH STANDARD

There couldn't possibly be another fish with as many nicknames as the bluefish. Actually these monickers are not really nicknames but definitions of different size bluefish. Unfortunately, there seems to be no written standard to de-confuse this situation. Perhaps this will help:

Snappers	— Up to 12 inches long
Harbors	— 12 to 18 inches
Cocktails	— 1½ to 3 pounds
Taylors	— 3 to 5 pounds
Choppers	— 5 pounds to 10 pounds
Alligators	— 11 pounds to 15 pounds
Monsters	— 16 pounds to 20 pounds
Gorillas	— Over 20 pounds

Any suggestions for changes or additions? Send them along to us for the next printing.

---

both white and blue, and swordfish are the most highly prized targets, and are all the more savored because of their relative scarcity. Tuna, on the other hand, are taken in much greater numbers. There are several species taken near Montauk, including bigeye, yellowfin, longfin, bluefin and blackfin. They vary greatly in size, from footballs of under 50 pounds to monstrous bluefins of over (occasionally) 1000 pounds.

Sharks are abundant, and many are taken by relatively small boats quite close to shore. The blue shark is the most abundant, while the white shark of Hollywood fame is rare. Other sharks taken with some regularity near Montauk include mako (prized for its delicious flesh), hammerhead, sand, porbeagle, tiger, lemon and thresher. Many charter captains out of Montauk now specialize in shark trips. Late spring to early fall is the best time.

While Montauk is the end of this book, this discussion is really only the beginning for the serious salt water fisherman. Due to space limitations, only a few highlights have been touched on. To learn more, spend some time on the Montauk party and charter boats, and poke around in the tackle shops, diners and ginmills out that way. All the tackle shops and many of the stores have free, hand-out maps that depict both the famous surf fishing spots and the inshore and offshore grounds near the point. The Chamber of Commerce, mentioned earlier, also offers helpful maps.

REFERENCE

SYNOPSIS OF THE CROTON WATERSHED

The Croton River is born in the Great Swamp of Dutchess County. Here, little native brookies dart beneath an undercut bank when a foot-heavy pheasant hunter trods a bit too close. At its terminus, the Croton melts with the half-salt of the Hudson, becoming a mini tidal estuary for its last mile; there is good fishing here, too. In between, the range of angling opportunities is extraordinary.

New York City has constructed 15 reservoirs upon this river system, though one – Boyds Corners – is currently drained. These lakes, and the spider-web of connecting rivers, are clean, fish-filled and open to everyone.

In the reservoirs there are Rainbow, Brown and Lake Trout, both Largemouth and Smallmouth Bass, a plethora of good-eating panfish, and several "rough fish" that many people nonetheless find appetizing. Detailed charts of these reservoirs are found in the main text and also following this synopsis. The rivers contain stocked rainbows, brookies and browns, but some native (naturally reproducing) browns and brookies as well.

Again, all these waters are open to the public, residents and non-residents alike. However there are certain permits you must have. First, a current New York State fishing license is required. Mandatory, too, is a free, good-until-or-unless revoked watershed permit. This permit is obtained by appearing in person with two passport-size (1½"x1¼") full-face b&w photos and valid fishing license at one of the following places:

> NYC Watershed Office by the
> Kensico Reservoir Aerators
> West Lake Drive, Valhalla, N.Y.

> NYC Municipal Building
> 24th Floor
> 1 Center Street, New York City

Generally, these Dept. of Water Resources offices are open Monday to Friday, 9:00 a.m.-4:00 p.m.

Last, you'll need a boating permit for each lake upon which you plan to keep a craft. Also free, this permit may be obtained by writing to the Center Street address listed above. Only rowboats are allowed, and no motors of any kind are permitted. No boat rental facilities exist on any of the reservoirs. Boats must be inspected each year and they must be left chained at a specific reservoir. Day-to-day cartopping is not allowed. Be sure to ask for a copy of the complete rules and regulations when you apply for your watershed permit.

All the reservoirs may be fished year-round, and there is at least some good sport to be had in every month. All but Kensico are open to ice-fishing, and trout fishing is permitted year-round on eight of the reservoirs. Shore fishing can be excellent, so a boat isn't strictly necessary. But it does help a lot, especially in summer.

IMPORTANT STATISTICS OF THE CROTON WATERSHED RESERVOIRS

RESERVOIR	Date Put Into Service	Size (Acres)	Maximum Depth	Yr. Round Trout Fishing	Ice Fishing Permitted	Has Restricted Areas	Relative Degree of Use	Most Recent DEC Survey
Kensico	1915	2218	160	•		•	Moderate	1974
New Croton	1905	2259	151		•	•	Extremely Light	1981
Muscoot	1905	1166	30+	•	•	•	Light to Moderate	1981
Amawalk	1897	606	78	•	•	•	Moderate	1980
Cross River	1908	769	120	•	•	•	Moderate	1983
Titicus	1893	669	90	•	•	•	Light to Moderate	1982
Croton Falls	1911	1062	100	•	•	•	Light to Moderate	1980
West Branch	1895	1083	50	•	•	•	Light to Moderate	1983
Gilead	1870	122	120	•	•		Moderate	1983
Glenida	1870	161	108	•	•		Moderate	1983
Bog Brook	1892	399	63		•	•	Extremely Light	1953
East Branch	1891	557	70		•	•	Light	1982
Middle Branch	1878	428	50		•	•	Light	1980
Diverting	1911	154	39		•	•	Extremely Light	1981
Boyd's Corners	1873	297	45		•	•		Currently Drained

COMPLETE FRESHWATER STOCKING REPORTS FOR SOUTHERN NEW YORK AND LONG ISLAND

This is a summary of fish stocked by the New York State Department of Environmental Conservation in 1983. Stocking Quotas tend to remain very similar for years . . . in some cases 10 years or even more or until a particular body of water can be re-surveyed.

State stocking is a matter of public record, and copies of the annual stocking report can be obtained from the regional offices of DEC.

LEGEND: ST — Brook Trout; BT — Brown Trout; RT - Rainbow Trout;
WBxSB — White Bass/Striped Bass Hybrid

WESTCHESTER COUNTY

WATER & LOCATION (Township)	NUMBER	SPECIES	SIZE (Inches)
Amawalk Inlet (Somers)	343	ST	9.00
	365	BT	8.75
Amawalk Outlet (Somers)	2,500	BT	6.75
Bergholz Lake (New Rochelle)	172	ST	9.00
Bronx River (N. Greenburg)	343	ST	9.00
	457	BT	10.50
Byram River (N. Castle)	257	ST	9.00
Cross River Outlet (Bedford)	172	ST	9.00
	183	BT	10.25
Cross River Reservoir (Bedford)	3,490	BT	10.25
	6,000	BT	9.00
Croton River (Cortlandt)	343	ST	9.00
	365	BT	8.75
Croton River, E. Br. (No. Salem, Somers)	257	ST	9.00
	365	BT	8.75
Hunter Brook (Yorktown, Cortlandt)	257	ST	10.25
	257	ST	9.00
Kensico Reservoir			
(Mt. Pleasant, No. Castle, Harrison)	2,500	BT	9.00
	4,565	BT	8.75
	63,418	LT	3.25
	3,815	RT	11.00
Mamaroneck River (White Plains)	365	BT	10.50
Mianus River (No. Castle, Bedford, Poundridge)	257	ST	9.00
	274	BT	8.25
New Rochelle Reservoir (New Rochelle)	457	BT	8.25
	382	RT	10.00
Peekskill Hollow Brook (Cortlandt)	548	BT	8.75
	457	RT	10.00
Sawmill River (Mt. Pleasant, Greenburg)	900	ST	9.00
	939	BT	10.50
	848	BT	8.75
	300	RT	11.00
	300	RT	10.50
	300	RT	10.00
Stonehill River or Beaver Dam Brook (Bedford)	257	ST	9.00
	274	BT	10.25
Titicus Reservoir (No. Salem)	1,000	BT	9.00
	6,575	BT	8.75
Titicus River (No. Salem)	172	ST	9.00
Waccabuc River (Lewisboro, Poundridge)	274	BT	10.25
	183	BT	8.25

PUTNAM COUNTY

Canopus Creek (Putnam Valley)	686	ST	8.75
Croton Falls Reservoir (Carmel, Southeast)	2,282	BT	8.50
Croton River, E. Br. (Southeast)	1,702	ST	9.00
	2,400	BT	9.25
	2,278	BT	8.50
	500	BT	8.25
	1,800	BT	6.75
	1,800	RT	7.50

PUTNAM COUNTY (continued)

WATER & LOCATION (Township)	NUMBER	SPECIES	SIZE (Inches)
Croton River W. Br. (Kent, Carmel)	800	BT	9.00
	639	BT	8.25
Foundry Brook (Phillipstown)	274	ST	8.25
	230	ST	10.00
Lake Gilead (Carmel)	3,052	RT	10.25
Lake Glenida (Carmel)	3,660	RT	10.25
Peekskill Hollow Brook (Putnam Valley)	800	BT	9.00
	730	BT	8.25
	610	RT	10.00
Peekskill Hollow Brook, Tr. 12 (Putnam Valley)	274	BT	8.25
Quaker Brook (Patterson)	172	ST	9.00
Stillwater Pond (Kent)	343	ST	8.75
	2,000	ST	7.00
	4,000	RT	7.50
West Branch Reservoir (Carmel)	2,000	BT	9.25
Wiccopee Brook (Putnam Valley)	172	ST	8.75

ROCKLAND COUNTY

Hessian Lake (Woodbury)	686	ST	9.00
Mahwah River (Ramapo)	514	ST	8.75
	548	BT	8.50
Minnisceonga Creek (Haverstraw)	274	BT	8.75
	274	BT	8.50
Minnisceonga Creek, No. Br. (Haverstraw)	365	BT	8.50
	365	BT	8.25
Ramapo River (Ramapo)	772	ST	8.75
	822	BT	8.75
	822	BT	8.50
Sparkhill Creek (Orangetown)	365	BT	8.75
	365	BT	8.50
Stony Brook (Ramapo)	343	ST	8.75
	365	BT	8.50
Tiorati Brook (Stony Brook)	343	ST	8.75
	365	BT	8.50

ORANGE COUNTY
(Only those waters covered within the radius of this book.)

Askoti Lake (Tuxedo)	1,643	BT	8.75
Cold Brook (Port Jervis, Deer Park)	86	ST	9.00
Cold Brook, Tr. 1 (Port Jervis, Deer Park)	257	ST	9.00
Double Kill (Warwick)	86	ST	8.75
Greenwood Lake (Warwick)	5,480	BT	8.50
Island Pond, Bear Mt. Park (Tuxedo)	1,115	ST	9.00
Moodna Creek (Cornwall)	400	ST	9.00
	700	BT	8.75
	700	BT	8.50
	400	BT	8.25
Queensboro Brook (Highland, Woodbury)	257	ST	9.00
Ramapo River (Tuxedo)	1,272	ST	9.00
	2,644	BT	8.75
	500	RT	10.25
	500	RT	9.75
Round Pond (Monroe)	913	BT	14.00
Rutgers Creek (Minisink, Wawayanda)	610	RT	11.00
	610	RT	10.00
	610	RT	9.75
Skannatati Lake (Tuxedo)	429	ST	9.00
Walton Lake (Monroe)	3,650	BT	9.75
Washington Lake (Newburg, Windsor)	913	BT	14.00
	383	RT	10.00
Wawayanda Creek (Warwick)	730	BT	8.25
Woodbury Creek (Cornwall, Woodbury)	686	ST	9.00
	730	BT	8.75
	730	BT	8.50

NASSAU COUNTY

Osyter Bay Mill Pond (Oyster Bay)	229	RT	10.25

SUFFOLK COUNTY

Avon Manor Pond (Babylon)	230	RT	9.75
Beaverdam Creek (Brookhaven)	3,000	BT	6.75
Canaan Lake (Brookhaven)	900	RT	11.00
Carlls River (Babylon)	342	ST	9.25
	343	ST	9.00
	300	BT	9.00
	365	BT	8.75
	365	BT	8.25
Carlls River, Tr. #3 (Babylon)	172	ST	10.75
	172	ST	9.50
Carmans River (Brookhaven)	274	BT	10.50
	1,500	BT	9.00
	457	BT	8.75
	275	BT	8.25
	384	RT	11.00
	230	RT	10.50
	534	RT	10.25
	998	RT	9.75
Champlain Creek (Islip)	172	ST	9.50
Connetquot River (Islip)	10,000	BT	7.00
East Lake (Brookhaven)	365	BT	10.50
	200	BT	9.00
	382	RT	10.25
East Pond	7,000	BT	7.00
Fort Pond (Montauk)	1,800	WBxSB	3.50
	5,000	WBxSB	1.50
Hard's Lake (Brookhaven)	1,735	RT	8.75
	763	RT	10.50
	1,068	RT	9.75
Kahler's Pond (Brookhaven)	457	RT	9.75
Laurel Lake (Southold)	548	BT	10.50
	500	BT	9.00
Lower Lake (Brookhaven)	687	RT	10.25
	916	RT	9.75
Mill Pond (Islip)	382	RT	9.75
Nissequoque River (Smithtown)	457	BT	8.75
	10,000	BT	7.00
	382	RT	10.25
	10,233	ST	3.75
Orowoc Creek & Tr. 1 (Islip)	257	ST	10.75
	200	BT	9.00
Randall Pond	300	RT	11.00
Rattlesnake Creek	6,000	BT	7.00
Southards Pond	400	RT	11.00
Swan Lake (Brookhaven)	300	BT	9.00
	183	BT	8.75
	182	BT	8.25
	10,000	BT	6.75
Upper Mill Pond	305	RT	9.75
West Lake (Brookhaven)	730	BT	10.50
	610	RT	10.25

PORTS OF CALL

SHEEPSHEAD BAY
Nestled behind Brooklyn's Coney Island is Sheepshead Bay, a fishing port that has long catered to metropolitan area anglers. There are more than 20 head boats sailing out of Sheepshead, as well as several charters. Boats leave early in the morning daily from 6:00-8:00 a.m. Afternoon trips depart from 1:00-2:00 p.m. and night boats leave between 7:00-8:00 p.m. in season. During spring, summer and fall, boats sail for all species in season. Many run special offshore, wreck and tuna trips. In winter, a few head boats still get out for cod, whiting and ling weather permitting.
There are several bait & tackle shops on the street as well as restaurants catering to fishermen. Many of these sandwich factories open very early. This is a year-round port with year-round activity.

FREEPORT
This important port is situated in Nassau County, just south of the village of Freeport. About a dozen party boats and twice that many charters tie up here. Besides your choice of boats, there are several bait & tackle shops as well as an early a.m. diner or two. Most of the boats work around the mosaic of islands, creeks, channels, cuts, drains, and bridges that characterize this part of the south shore. Flounder, fluke and blacks are sought in these calmer backwaters, while blues, stripers, weaks and doormat fluke are pursued just inside and outside Jones Inlet. CAUTION! Small boats should avoid the inlet, which can be extremely turbulent and dangerous.

CAPTREE
Part of Captree State Park, this clean and fairly new port is situated on an island just inside Fire Island Inlet. It is reached by taking the Robert Moses Causeway south. Approximately 25 party boats and nearly that many charters sail from here. Captree is a "no-hassle" port: No hawkers or traffic jams, but plenty of parking, a nice little cafeteria, bait & tackle and generally short runs to the fishing grounds. While most if not all skippers here do sail outside the inlet, they also concentrate on the gentle waters of Great South Bay. Persons prone to seasickness can do these bay trips with little fear of symptoms arising. In spring and fall, flounder get most of the effort, while fluke fishing can be excellent in summer. An adaptable lot, the Captree captains seek whatever's available, including sea bass, blackfish, weakfish, mackerel, blues and even frost fish.

MONTAUK
Montauk is such an important port that it has received its own chapter in this book. Thus it is not covered here.

GREENPORT
Greenport is kind of the north fork's answer to Montauk, but it is not nearly as busy. Located just a few miles from the tip of the north fork, Orient Point, it is a charming village that any true fisherman will love to soak in. At present there are a few party boats and perhaps ten charters operating regularly. For the early arriving angler, there is plenty in the way of parking, bait & tackle and early morning chow. This community opens early. Boats here work the productive and varied east end waters for such species as flounder, blackfish, bluefish, striped bass and others. Of course these boats also hit the Peconics for weaks and porgies in season.

PORT JEFFERSON
Within easy reach of the famous Mt. Misery shoal, Port Jefferson has become increasingly important as a sportfishing center. Now, about three or four party boats operate alongside several charters. Blackfish, which the north shore has plenty of, are very much favored by these boats, but they will also zero in on all the important gamefish species on Mt. Misery shoal and certain other nearshore spots.

HUNTINGTON
As Port Jefferson keys in on Mt. Misery shoal, Huntington boats frequently aim for the well-known Eaton's Triangle just north of the Eaton's Neck lighthouse. There are three or four party boats, and several other charters, and these boats fish off Eaton's Neck and Lloyd Neck for blues, stripers, weaks and mackerel. They also hit the waters inside Huntington Bay, chiefly for flounder and blackfish.

MISCELLANEOUS LONG ISLAND PORTS
There are quite a few coastal points on Long Island where only a few party and/or charter boats tie up. A good example is Shinnecock. Although a great many private boats still moor at this once bustling port, there is now only one party boat and a few charters. Similarly, in Sag Harbor there is one party boat and perhaps a charter or two. On Moriches Bay, where the flatfishing is par excellence, there is a party boat or two and there must be a few charters though I'm not aware of them. Other Long Island ports where boats-for-hire operate include Bay Shore, Mattituck, Glen Cove and Pt. Lookout.

CITY ISLAND
This island, just offshore of and actually part of the Bronx, is one of the few places in the Western Sound (north shore) where you can jump aboard an open boat. At present, there are four party boats, and dozens of private boats that will hire out to anglers. These boats ply the fertile waters of Western Long Island for bluefish, mackerel in season, blacks, porgies and other species such as stripers and weaks. Many work a good ways east in the sound, all the way to Mt. Sinai on the Long Island side and up to about Stamford on the West-Conn side.

MISCELLANEOUS WESTCHESTER-CONNECTICUT PORTS
Besides City Island, there are not too many places with operational party boats along this side of the western sound. There is one in New Rochelle, one or two in the Stamford area, and a few in the Bridgeport area. Charter boats are scattered here and there.

To locate all these open and charter boats, refer to the ads in *The Fisherman* magazine: Long Island edition or New England edition (the latter of which covers West-Conn locales).

OTHER RESOURCES

I. **NEW YORK STATE DEPARTMENT OF ENVIRONMENTAL CONSERVATION**

    Region 1 (New York City)
    2 World Trade Center, 61st Floor
    New York, NY 10047

    Region 2 (Nassau, Suffolk –
            handles *most* fisheries affairs for Region 1)
    Building 40, SUNY
    Stony Brook, NY 11790

Region 3 (Westchester, Putnam, Rockland, Orange, Dutchess,
            Sullivan, Ulster)
21 So. Putt Corners Road
New Paltz, NY

II. **SOURCES OF MAPS**

U.S. Geological Survey
Washington, D.C.
Distribute very detailed topographical maps

Hagstrom Map Co.
46-35 54th Road
Maspeth, NY 11378

Publish a wide range of maps, including their extremely detailed
street atlases. These show every street and virtually every drop of
water. There is an edition for each county within the scope of this
book, and one for the five boroughs.

International Map Co.
595 Broad Avenue
Ridgefield, NJ

Publish a wide range of maps of use to the fisherman, including
their "Angler's Aid" series of lake and reservoir contour maps.

Nautical Charts
U.S. Department Of Commerce
National Oceanic And Atmospheric Administration
Washington, D.C.

Detailed charts of coastal waters, including depths, channels, obstructions, etc. Available from larger marine suppliers.

III. **HELPFUL MAGAZINES**

The Fisherman (Long Island Edition)
P.O. Box 1993, Bridge St.
Sag Harbor, NY 11963

Published weekly. Excellent source of up-to-the-minute info on the
LI fishing scene; predominantly salt-water.

Field & Stream
1515 Broadway
New York, NY 10036

Publish an "east edition" with periodic stories on fishing in the
metropolitan area.

Outdoor Life
380 Madison Avenue
New York, NY 10017

Publish a "northeast edition" with a good number of stories dealing
with fishing in our region.

Fins & Feathers — New York
318 West Franklin Avenue
Minneapolis, MN 55404

This New York edition of a nationally-run magazine is focussed completely on fishing and hunting in our state. Stories on fishing in the metro area will appear.

New York Fish Finder
P.O. Box 2411
Syracuse, N.Y. 13220

Monthly magazine, distributed free at many local tackle shops. You can also buy a subscription by writing to the above address.

OTHER TITLES AVAILABLE

HOW TO CATCH CRABS BY THE BUSHEL!
THE MANUAL OF SPORT CRABBING
Jim Capossela

How, when and where to catch blue claws along the Atlantic Coast. Includes a 16-page anthology of 40 excellent crab recipes, plus cleaning and storing tips. 72 pp. (softcover only) $3.95 | .75 postage.

PART-TIME CASH FOR THE SPORTSMAN
25 WAYS FOR THE FISHERMAN AND HUNTER TO EARN EXTRA MONEY
Jim Capossela

One of-a-kind booklet describes 25 ways for the sportsman to earn extra cash while enjoying his or her hobbies! 72 pp. (softcover only) $3.95 + .75 postage.

HOW TO WRITE FOR THE OUTDOOR MAGAZINES
A CONCISE GUIDE TO WRITING FISHING, HUNTING AND OTHER OUTDOOR ARTICLES
Jim Capossela

Unique booklet shows how any sportsman can help pay for his sporting goods by writing about his experiences. Describes every step in the article writing process. 72 pp. (softcover only) $3.95 + .75 postage.

ABOUT THE AUTHOR

JIM CAPOSSELA has been a professional writer for 12 years and a fisherman for 30 years. The founder and president of Northeast Sportsman's Press, he is the author of four outdoor books, including *How To Catch Crabs By The Bushel!* which is already in its fifth printing.

Jim sold the very first magazine article he ever wrote, to *Field & Stream* back in 1975. Not so surprisingly, it was a piece about the New York City Watershed. Since then, he has contributed to most of the prominent outdoor magazines, including other articles for *Field & Stream, Outdoor Life, Sports Afield, Fins & Feathers, The Fisherman* (all three editions) and other publications. Many of these articles have focussed on fishing in the metropolitan region, and have thus put him into close touch with every aspect of rod & reel sport in our area.

Recently, one of his *Sports Afield* articles was reprinted in *The Orvis Anthology,* a compilation of the best contributions to the Orvis Writing Contest 1980-1982.

Jim was in the best possible position to write a book such as this – not only because of his background but because he is a true "generalist." He fishes in fresh water and in salt, in bay and in surf, with flies and with bait. He is also an avid ice fisherman, and there really is no month when he is not out actively pursuing fish and game, photographing and writing.